DISCORD

AND

COLLABORATION

Essays on International Politics

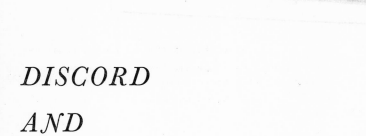

DISCORD
AND
COLLABORATION

Essays on
International
Politics

By Arnold Wolfers

Baltimore   THE JOHNS HOPKINS PRESS   1962

Distributed in Great Britain by Oxford University Press, London

Printed in the United States of America by J. H. Furst Co., Baltimore

Library of Congress Catalog Card Number 62-14363

This book was brought to publication with the
assistance of a grant from the Ford Foundation.

FOREWORD

by

Reinhold Niebuhr

In recent years the power of the United States has come to exceed the power of any state known to history. In exercising the global responsibilities concomitant with its vast power while maintaining its traditional commitment to ideal principles, the United States has had to deal with international problems of great political and moral complexity. Accordingly, the systematic study of international relations has assumed the greatest vitality and importance, and to that study these essays by Arnold Wolfers represent a most welcome contribution.

Dr. Wolfers, Director of the Washington Center of Foreign Policy Research, has long been a respected pioneer and leader in this field of political philosophy. His leadership has been achieved by the wisdom and circumspection of his judgments, by his capacity for discriminating analysis of the complex factors and forces that operate in the international field, and by his disposition to weigh the arguments of contrasting schools of thought thoroughly and without prejudice.

These essays, many of them published here for the first time, are perfect examples of the distinction of mind and temper that have given Arnold Wolfers his unique eminence in this exacting discipline. Whether analyzing the actors or agents that shape the relations of nations; whether discussing "the people," the nation, or the leaders of nations; whether weighing the relative importance of the external and internal factors—geographic, historical, economic or psychological—that determine national policy, or the moral content of political decisions, he is always coolly fair and circumspect. The qualities which have given Walter Lippmann his eminence in the journalistic analysis of complex problems are analogous to those that account for Dr. Wolfers' achievements in the field of political theory.

The issues discussed by Dr. Wolfers are by no means "academic." They go to the heart of many of the burning problems of contemporary foreign relations. Whether the "national interest" is the final norm, or only the most pervasive force, in foreign policy, or in what sense the "realists"—or "Machiavellians"—or the "idealists" are right are questions that underlie many debates. Similarly, the issue of the temper of nations toward other nations with its wide spectrum from "amity" to "enmity," or the question of various degrees of cooperation and collaboration, all bear directly on pressing current problems. Some of the historical essays, as for instance those dealing with the unique compound of national initiative and international cooperation that went into the Korean war, or those that throw light on the factors and forces which promoted the alliances of many European nations between the two world wars, are valuable efforts to draw from the experience of the past in order to guide policy in the present.

Insofar as the distinction within the discipline of politics between "Political Philosophy" and "Political Science" is valid, Dr. Wolfers is a "political philosopher" rather than a "political scientist." He is a philosopher in that he scrutinizes and weighs the validity of various theories, concepts and presuppositions, and discusses the larger patterns of international relations. But as any good philosopher, he is also a scientist in the sense that empirically ascertained facts serve him as the final criteria for the adequacy of general concepts or for the validity of general suppositions.

As this nation, through the extension of its power, has assumed new responsibility for the fate of many other nations, so the scholars within it have a new responsibility to illumine the complexities of international politics and to raise the level of reflection on which American policy decisions are based. Arnold Wolfers well performs that task, and it is to be hoped that his wise and learned book will have the widest possible reading.

REINHOLD NIEBUHR

ACKNOWLEDGMENTS

It is customary for an author who wishes to express his gratitude to name the individuals who have made significant contributions to the studies he is presenting to his readers. I shall deviate from this practice because I find it impossible to identify the many colleagues, assistants, students and fellow-authors who in one way or another enriched and influenced my thinking during the long period in which these essays were conceived and, in part, published. Instead I shall address my thanks to two great universities: to Yale, at which I spent almost a quarter of a century, chiefly for exposing me to the constant stimulation and criticism of remarkably gifted graduate students in international relations; and to Johns Hopkins, for allowing me to organize and direct the Washington Center of Foreign Policy Research, an affiliate of its School of Advanced International Studies, in such a fashion as to subject me, since 1957, to the thoughts and arguments, the advice and criticism, of highly sophisticated associates with broad experience in scholarship and in the practice of foreign policy.

At both institutions I enjoyed the further privilege of having able and dedicated research assistants who patiently improved the style and substance of the present essays, as well as skilled and industrious secretaries who relieved me of innumerable chores, and even permitted me to meet deadlines.

Washington, D.C.   Arnold Wolfers
March, 1962

CONTENTS

ON THEORY
AND PRACTICE

Unless forewarned, the reader may not advance beyond the first few pages of the essays presented here before laying them aside with disappointment. Even if he enjoys theoretical analysis and speculation as a rule, he may question the usefulness of discussing international affairs on a high level of abstraction at a time when the burning concrete events of the day are his overriding concern. It may also seem doubtful to him whether policy-makers can gain much from generalizations about "actors," "goals of policy," "peace strategies," and the like which tell them nothing about how to deal with such matters as the menacing demands of an opponent or the conflicting views of members of a coalition on which the security of the nation depends. Yet only on a few occasions—and then only as illustrations of general propositions—will concrete events or real persons be mentioned in the following chapters.

The relationship between theory and practice has been a topic of much debate not only in international relations but in all fields of human activity—in medicine, adjudication, military strategy, and athletics. Wherever choices have to be made and decisions taken, the gulf between generalizations, even of a low order of abstraction, and the unique case that calls for action is deep and cannot be bridged by any theorizing operation. Nothing can substitute here for that inscrutable composite of experience, common sense and intuition on which the practitioner must ultimately rely. No matter how far theory succeeds in elaborating the rules and principles of military deterrence, for instance, it does not provide the statesman with propositions from which the proper policy for coping with a specific would-be aggressor can be deduced; yet the fate of mankind may hinge on his choice of policy in the particular instance.

The inherent shortcomings of all generalized knowledge have led many practitioners of statecraft to conclude, whether with resignation or with glee, that the only sensible way to deal with their problems is to "play it by ear" and to rely on their hunches. However, though it would be foolish to underestimate the role of the intuitive touch—what the Germans call *Fingerspitzengefühl*—it is self-delusion on the part of the decision-maker to believe that he can get along without theoretical propositions. If one looks more closely, one discovers that rather than emerging out of an intellectual vacuum, his hunches rest, in fact, on generalizations of some sort. A statesman who decides in favor of a punitive peace treaty may act on the general notion that aggression will be repeated unless it is punished; another statesman who opposes such a treaty and pleads instead for a peace of reconciliation may be guided by the general notion that peace can be made enduring only if the enmities of yesterday are surmounted in a spirit of generosity. Both sides conceive of the issue at stake not as unique but as one of a category of analogous cases.

Often the underlying propositions and principles are only dimly perceived by the actor; they are part of his intellectual heritage and environment. As a result, a host of naive, oversimplified or patently false hypotheses become reflected in support of acts of intuition. The choice, then, is not between theory and no theory, but between relatively informed, sophisticated, and objective theoretical propositions carefully formulated in the course of disciplined and dispassionate professional analysis, and crude hit-and-miss "theories" against which the statesman, even if aware of the pitfalls, may not be able to immunize himself. The role of systematic theorizing, then, is to inject into the intellectual climate, in which hunches are made and have to be made, an element of considered thought, as advanced as the existing conditions of the discipline permit.

The theorist can gain both encouragement and humility by comparing the place of theory in medicine and in international politics. Nobody would question the value of the medical sciences to the practice of medicine: their development and application has transformed the medicine man of earlier days into the modern physician. However, these sciences have not rendered the intuition of the practicing physician superfluous—as anyone should realize who has relied on a doctor possessing profound scientific knowledge but devoid of the gift of empathy and comprehension for the individual patient.

Unfortunately those who theorize about the causes and cures of diseases in the international arena suffer from serious handicaps— to say the least—compared to their counterparts in the medical field. In the first place, they are unable to subject their "patients" to direct laboratory tests or controlled experiments, which have contributed more than any other single factor to scientific progress. Tests on animals, children, or adults carried out by zoologists or psychologists may not be entirely barren of results if transferred by analogy to the international field; anything that can be learned about human or analogous animal behavior—behavior induced, for instance, by fear, provocation, and rewards, or attitudes attributable to amity and enmity—throws some light on events occurring on the stage of world affairs. Human behavior is human behavior, after all, on whatever level of social intercourse and under whatever circumstances it occurs. Yet, the impact of the particular circumstances of international politics, in which the actors act for corporate bodies in a milieu of multi-state conditions and power struggles, can hardly be exaggerated. It is one thing to learn from experiments that children are more likely to clean their teeth if promised rewards than if threatened with the painful consequences of neglecting their teeth, quite another to generalize about the respective chances of influencing dictators by threats of deprivation or promises of gratification.

There is a second reason, which has been frequently stressed, why the level of generalized knowledge in international relations compares unfavorably with that attained in the natural sciences and some of the social sciences. The attention of scholars, practitioners, and the public is centered here on such large and complex phenomena as military coalitions, dominant powers, empires in liquidation, or autocratic regimes. But the number of cases belonging to any of these categories, even if one goes back to the beginning of recorded history, is infinitesimal compared with the number of comparable units on which other theorists base their generalizations. However, the history of the natural sciences suggests that scarcity of relevant cases on certain levels of observation and conceptualization need not be a permanent liability to the theorist. The "fire and water" stage in physics, as Kurt Lewin has so aptly called it, came to an end to make room for modern physics once the analysts had learned to penetrate to relatively simple and abundant components such as atoms, ions, and velocities. Similarly, the analyst of world events is not condemned to move exclusively on the "fire and water" level of his discipline. He, too, has come to realize that what he is exploring when employing such symbols as "major powers," the "national interest," or "allied solidarity" can be conceived as a bundle of simple elements and forces that abound in the relationships both among men and between man and his environment. The elements that go into processes of power distribution, of conflict and conflict resolution, of alignment and de-alignment, are not peculiar to a multi-state system but can be observed in the relationships and activities of juvenile gangs, university faculties, trade unions, and a host of other groups of men. Even such factors as propinquity and spatial distance, a major subject of geopolitics, operate in many places creating opportunities for friendship or friction among groups and institutions of various kinds.

Thus, the "laboratory" that can provide the theorist of international relations with insight and experience transcends the records of diplomatic history and of his personal observation of contemporary history, indispensable and rewarding as these are to him. It includes analogous events in other social fields and—accessible to him by way of introspection—comparable events within his own person, whether actual or imagined. If he has any capacity for dispassionate self-analysis he can find out a great deal about what under given conditions would be likely to induce a man to collaborate or to withdraw into isolation, to make concessions or to resort to force, to seek to gain more power or to be complacent about the position he holds. Therefore if he fails to reach worthwhile general conclusions he cannot blame his failure entirely on the paucity of cases capable of being compared for their similarities or differences. The data should be sufficient to permit at least the refinement of crude common sense propositions and, as a consequence, an improvement of the intellectual climate in which policy is formulated.

After what has been said to persuade the reader that, normally at least, it is no waste of his time and effort to subject himself to exacting abstract exercises, it still remains to be asked whether in a revolutionary age such as ours the existing general concepts and propositions pertaining to international politics may not, as some have suggested, be rapidly becoming obsolete. Most of the thinking in international politics has been predicated after all on the continuing primary role of nation-states within a multi-state system, and on the persistence of modes of behavior within the system conforming to a Western tradition of many centuries. Yet, are not national territorial units outdated today and on the way out, now that the age of nuclear weapons, long-range missiles, and earth satellites is upon us, and is not the rise to influence of scores of peoples of non-Western culture disclosing the parochial character of many principles and patterns of behavior formerly regarded as universal and perennial?

It would be foolish to close one's eyes to the extent of change—political, technological, and psychological—that is transforming many striking features of the world of the nineteenth and early twentieth centuries. One need only compare with the methods of traditional diplomacy the "parliamentary diplomacy" of crowds of delegates at the United Nations or the crudeness of the language recently introduced into the verbal exchanges between unfriendly governments to appreciate the extent of the change that has occurred in diplomatic procedures, at least, to concede a measure of plausibility to the obsolescence hypothesis. And, obviously, general propositions that had ceased to refer to the real world could have no claim to the attention of policy-makers or be of much interest to the public.

However the situation of theory is not as precarious or dismal as the hypothesis suggests. In the first place it is an open question which is the most striking feature of the international order—the extent and rapidity of change or the astonishing persistence of tradition. One need only focus attention on the way the people of the post-colonial world are striving to constitute themselves as nations and states on the Western model, observe the similarities between the balancing-of-power process in the nuclear and pre-nuclear age, or note how neutrality survives in an era of opposing coalitions, to be tempted to use the French phrase *"plus ça change, plus c'est la même chose."*

In the second place, worthwhile general concepts and propositions emerge not from a static or dogmatic type of theory but from a live theorizing process, directed at modifying, qualifying, and enriching earlier formulations in the light of new facts and new experiences. As a matter of fact, if one can criticize some recent studies it is not because they fail to take account of change but because they exaggerate its impact to the point of loosing sight of the aspects of continuity and of successful resistance to change that are equally conspicuous in our day.

The reader is referred to some of the chapters below for a more detailed attempt to evaluate the contributions to knowledge of different schools of thought, and to Chapter 15 for a discussion of theory as it refers not to the way nations actually do behave but, normatively, to the way they should behave.

DISCORD

AND

COLLABORATION

Essays on International Politics

I.

Action and Interaction Among Nations

Chapter One   THE ACTORS IN
                  INTERNATIONAL
                  POLITICS

THEORIZING ABOUT almost any feature of international politics soon becomes entangled in a web of controversy.[1] Even the identity of the "actors"—those who properly can be said to perform on the international stage—is a matter of dispute which raises not unimportant problems for the analyst, for the practitioner of foreign policy, and for the public. If the nation-states are seen as the sole actors, moving or moved like a set of chess figures in a highly abstract game, one may lose sight of the human beings for whom and by whom the game is supposed to be played. If, on the other hand, one sees only the mass of individual human beings of whom mankind is composed, the power game of states tends to appear as an inhuman interference with the lives of ordinary people. Or, take the diplomat who sees himself as accredited to an entity called Indonesia or France: he may behave quite differently from the diplomat who considers his mission addressed to specific individuals or to ruling groups or to a people. A statesman accustomed to analyzing international politics in terms alone of state behavior will treat the United Nations differently from one who believes in the rise of international organizations to a place of independent control over world events similar to that control exerted by states.

Until quite recently, the states-as-the-sole-actors approach to international politics was so firmly entrenched that it may be called the traditional approach. After the Napoleonic wars, nation-states, particularly the European "great powers," as they were called, re-

[1] This chapter is reprinted, with minor changes, from *Theoretical Aspects of International Relations*, ed. William T.R. Fox (University of Notre Dame Press, 1959), by permission of the publisher.

placed the image of the princes or kings of former centuries as the sovereign, independent, single-minded actors, the movers of world events. To nation-states were ascribed the acts that accounted for changes in the distribution of power, for alignments and counter-alignments, for expansion and colonial conquest, for war and peace —the chief events in international affairs whenever a multitude of sovereigns have been in contact with one another. The concept of a multistate system composed of entities of strikingly similar character and behavior appeared realistic to observers and analysts.

Starting in the period between the two world wars and gaining momentum after World War II, a reaction set in against the traditional states-as-actors approach. This reaction has taken two distinct forms: one new theory has placed individual human beings in the center of the scene that had been reserved previously to the nation-states; the second theory emphasized the existence, side by side with the state, of other corporate actors, especially international organizations. Both reactions have led to valuable new insights and deeper understanding of the dynamics of world politics, but they are in fact supplements to the traditional theory rather than substitutes for it.

I

THE INDIVIDUALS-AS-ACTORS approach first appeared in the minds-of-men theory of international politics. It was soon to be followed by the decision-making approach which was a reaction against tradition from another angle. Both demanded that attention be focused on individual human beings as actors. Together, the new schools of thought represent a swing of the pendulum from an extreme "state" emphasis to an equally extreme emphasis on the men who act for states. These new approaches must be credited with humanizing international politics by attracting attention to the human element minimized in the traditional approach. It was the aim of the new theories to replace the abstract notion of the state with the living realities of human minds, wills, and hearts. But the result, on the whole, was to substitute one set of abstractions for another because, in politics, it is also an abstraction to examine the individual apart from the corporate bodies by means of which he acts politically.

The minds-of-men approach received its emotional stimulus from two sources: the realization that, in the age of mass communication, propaganda, and ideological movements, there were growing opportunities for the masses to play a significant role in international affairs, and a general desire to see the masses take advantage of these opportunities. To stress men rather than states and thus to focus attention on the common man—traditionally more the victim than the beneficiary of international politics—seemed to offer a way out of conflict, war, and power politics generally. It is not surprising that UNESCO should have become an exponent of the theory, since it was established, as Frederick Dunn points out,[2] with a view to constructing peace in the minds of men. The utopian undertones of many early pronouncements by those who espoused the new approach were unmistakable, but should not detract from the contribution which the new approach can make to realistic understanding of world affairs.

The new approach's criticism of the states-as-actors theory turns mainly on the distinction between genuine human needs and what appear to be the a-human interests of the state. There are those who claim that too great an emphasis on the role of states and their interests in power, prestige, territory, and the like, will divert political action from the satisfaction of the common man's real needs and desires to the service of the few who can parade their interests as those of the nation. Is it credible, they ask, that Egyptian fellaheen and Pakistani peasants, desperately in need of food, shelter, and improved conditions of health, should, as their governments contend, yearn for the satisfaction of such "state interests" as the liquidation of Israel or the unification of Kashmir under Pakistani rule, when the pursuit of such interests requires great sacrifices of the masses? Does the state not take on the character of an a-human monster to whom dignity is given gratuitously, if it is regarded as an actor in its own right, at liberty to place its interests above those of the human beings who compose it?

Still, one may question whether the quest for national security and power, for national independence, aggrandizement, or unification is any less "human"—and therefore necessarily less appealing to the masses—than the quest for food, shelter, comfort, and happiness. Actually, the minds-of-men theory and its humanization of international politics must be carried several steps further than its exponents have gone. Any analysis of the dynamics of international politics must take into account the fact that man is more than a

[2] *War and the Minds of Men* (Harper & Bros., New York, 1950), pp. xi-xiv.

private individual concerned only with his personal welfare or with the welfare of his family. Often enough he is ready to compromise his own well-being for the benefit of the groups and organizations with which he identifies himself. Psychologically, nothing is more striking today than the way in which men in almost every part of the globe have come to value those possessions upon which independent national statehood depends, with the result that men, in their public capacity as citizens of a state, are willing to make the most sweeping sacrifices of their own well-being as private individuals in the interest of their nation. Therefore, state interests are indeed human interests—in fact, the chief source of political motivation today.

One can argue that a nationalistic age has distorted men's pattern of values or that the manipulators of public opinion are chiefly responsible for this distortion. Nevertheless, the fact remains that a sufficient number of men identify themselves with their state or nation to justify and render possible governmental action in the name of state interests. To say that something is in the interest of the state is like saying that a good roof is in the interest of the house, when what one really means is that a good roof is considered vital by the house's inhabitants who value the safety, completeness, and reputation of their residence.

There is, however, nothing absolute or unchanging about the value men attach to state interests. The position of the value of national unification in the hierarchy of values, for instance, especially its position relative to particular private needs and desires, is subject to change and differs from group to group and from individual to individual. Therefore, it is proper to be aware of individuals as the actors behind the scene, so to speak, whenever needs and interests, private or public, come into play in international affairs. Whether a state has a "vital interest"—in access to the sea or in the return of a lost province, for example—depends on the relative values attached by its citizens to these national objectives, on the one hand, and to private interests which would be sacrificed in the pursuit of the national objectives, on the other. In losing sight of the individuals who comprise a state, exponents of the states-as-actors theory may come up with a relatively accurate analysis of national behavior in a period when value patterns remain static, but they are more likely to be mistaken in a period of upheaval when elites and values undergo rapid and radical change.

One wonders today, for instance, whether the bulk of the population in countries facing the risks of nuclear war will long continue to regard as vital, and thus worthy of defense in war, all the state interests they were once ready to place in this category. Signs point to the likelihood that the masses, who have gained greater influence as behind-the-scenes actors, will push for greater restraints upon the pursuit of those state interests—such as national security or prestige —that are seen to conflict with private welfare needs. Such a development will indicate not that individuals are suddenly taking over the function formerly performed by states, but rather that larger bodies of individuals are sharing the role once reserved to the members of small elites who formerly decided what the "national interest" demanded or justified. It always would have been possible to interpret international politics through an examination of the individuals responsible for state action: the "humanizing" approach. But it must be recognized that in the course of the present century the number of these individuals has been greatly enlarged.

The failure to see man in his double capacity, as a private individual and as a political being, accounts for an illusion common among the more idealistic exponents of the minds-of-men approach. They assume that better understanding between peoples opens the safest path to peace, while Dunn has pointed out that peoples who know and understand each other perfectly may nevertheless become involved in war.[3] The explanation for this apparent paradox is not hard to find, provided one thinks in terms of the whole man rather than in terms solely of his private aims and desires. If one were in contact with the people of the Soviet Union today, one probably would find them preoccupied with the tasks of furthering their personal welfare, happiness, and social advancement in much the same way as any similar group of people in the United States. The discovery of such similarities of interest and aspiration tends to arouse a sense of sympathetic understanding; it certainly does not provoke fear or serve to justify policies based on the expectation of international conflict. As a result, people who think exclusively in terms of private individuals and who experience harmonious relationships with citizens of "hostile" countries are inclined to see nothing but unhappy misunderstanding, if not evil, in the way governments act toward one another.

Yet, the fact that Americans and Russians, in much the same fashion, pursue the same goals when acting as private individuals,

[3] *Op. cit.*, p. 7.

gives no indication of their aims as citizens who are concerned with
the national interests of their respective countries. Here there is far
less chance that their aims will be found to be in harmony. Better
understanding may in fact reveal the incompatibility of their respective objectives. Thus, it may be revealed that Russians, if good
Marxists, want their government to drive capitalism toward its inescapable doom, or, if good nationalists, to secure safe access to
warm water ports. At the same time, Russians may find that their
American counterparts demand the containment, if not elimination, of Communist tyranny, and a halt to Russian expansion before
it reaches the Mediterranean or Persian Gulf and endangers American security. It appears, then, that to humanize the image of world
politics by penetrating to the minds and hearts of actors does not
necessarily give us a more peaceful picture of the world. As long as
men identify themselves with their nation and cling to such
national possessions as sovereign independence, territorial integrity,
and national security, the establishment of harmonious private
relations across national borders will have little impact on the
course of international political events and encounters.

It is therefore clear that an exclusive minds-of-men approach with
its concentration on the motives and activities of individual actors
is inadequate and misleading. It is undeniable that men alone, and
not states, are capable of desires and intentions, preferences and
feelings of friendship or hatred; men, not states, can be tempted or
provoked, can overestimate or underestimate their own country's
power relative to the power of other states, and can establish the
goals of national policy and sacrifices consistent with national
security. However, although nothing can happen in the world
arena unless something happens inside the minds and hearts of
scores of men, psychological events are not the whole stuff out of
which international politics is formed. If they were, the political
scientist would have to leave the field to the psychologist.

The minds-of-men approach, while able to render important and
indispensable services to a comprehensive theory of international
politics, cannot do justice to all the essential events that fill the
international arena. There can be no "state behavior" except as the
term is used to describe the combined behavior of individual
human beings organized into a state. Not only do men act differently when engaged in pursuing what they consider the goals of
their "national selves," but they are able to act as they do only
because of the power and influence generated by their nations

organized as corporate bodies. Therefore, only when attention is focused on states, rather than on individuals, can light be thrown on the goals pursued and means employed in the name of nations and on the relationships of conflict or co-operation, of power competition or alignment that characterize international politics. To abstract from these aspects of reality is as unrealistic as it is to abstract from the events occurring in the minds and hearts of the men who act in the name of the state. But because theory cannot proceed except by means of abstraction, it becomes necessary here to supplement one set of abstractions with another and thus keep in mind the double aspect of events that must be conceived of as emanating simultaneously from individuals and from corporate bodies.

A comprehensive theory does not call for a division of international politics into two compartments, one comprising the realm of the state as the actor in power politics, the other the realm of the human actors, the masses of common men with their psychological traits and their pursuit of human purposes. Instead, all events occurring in the international arena must be conceived of and understood from two angles simultaneously: one calling for concentration on the behavior of states as organized bodies of men, the other calling for concentration on human beings upon whose psychological reactions the behavior credited to states ultimately rests.

One need only look closely at a feature as significant in high politics and as strongly stressed in the states-as-actors approach as the balancing of power process. Often it has been assumed that a process involving state power and its distribution among nations has a place in the states-as-actors approach alone and can be treated adequately by means of this approach. But if one wishes to answer the question, for instance, whether the United States is in a position today to deter the Soviet Union by balancing the Soviet power, one cannot escape an examination of the psychology of individuals—in this case, of the leaders in the Kremlin. Deterrence can only work in the minds of the men in charge of Soviet policy by convincing them that acts they might otherwise wish to undertake would prove too costly in light of the punishment the United States would, in their opinion, be able and prepared to inflict. It would be foolish, however, to go to the other extreme and try to comprehend the struggle for power between the two countries in purely psychological terms. The Soviet estimate of American resistance to acts of the U.S.S.R. cannot be understood or predicted except as the objective facts concerning the respective power of the two states are taken into account. Moreover, the whole balancing process between the two antagonists, with its tremendous impact on world events, would drop from sight if attention were devoted exclusively to individuals or groups of individuals and to their psychological reactions.

As mentioned earlier, the once firmly established states-as-actors theory has been reacted to in a second way which also implies a shift of attention to individuals and groups of individuals as the true actors. This second form is properly called the decision-making approach, since it is concerned with decisions, the way they are made, and the men who make them. What interests us here is the role this approach assigns to identifiable human beings and their predispositions. Although the emphasis on the decision-makers, like the emphasis on the minds of men, developed in protest against the states-as-actors theory, it was not also a reaction born of humanitarian or social considerations; it was provoked, instead, by the sweeping, seemingly oversimplified psychological and anthropological presuppositions on which the traditional theory rests.

If nation-states are conceived of as the sole actors, it is inevitable that they be treated as if endowed, like human beings, with wills and minds of their own that permit them to reach decisions and to carry them out. Moreover, if state behavior is to be intelligible and to any degree predictable, states must be assumed to possess psychological traits of the kind known to the observer through introspection and through acquaintance with other human beings. States must be thought capable, for example, of desires and preferences, of satisfaction and dissatisfaction, of the choice of goals and means.

Actually, the states-as-actors theory postulates a limited number of such traits which, moreover, all states are assumed to have in common. States are presumed to possess a will to survive and a will to power; they live in fear of losing their possessions to others and are tempted by opportunities of acquiring new possessions. Because these basic traits are shared by *all* states, the exponents of the traditional approach can afford to treat these psychological presuppositions in a cavalier fashion. Little attention need be given to traits that, because they are constants or invariants, are incapable of helping to explain any differences in state behavior.

If, as Hobbes assumed, all states were equally and constantly driven by fear that their survival, the most cherished of their state possessions, might be threatened, then the multistate system would of necessity become an all-round struggle for security. If, instead, all states worthy of the name were as eager for expansion as Kjellén maintained, the ensuing struggle would turn on efforts at territorial acquisition and on counterefforts at territorial preservation.

The decision-making approach questions the possibility of reaching realistic conclusions from any such crude and generally applicable psychological presuppositions. Its exponents insist that decisions and actions taken in the name of the state cannot be understood unless one penetrates to the individuals from whom they emanate. In contrast to what is implicit in the views of the opposing school, the basic hypothesis here is that all acts of states, as we are used to calling them, are vitally affected or determined by the particular predispositions of particular decision-makers or of particular groups of participants in the decision-making process. Thus, differences in such individual psychological traits as motivation, value preferences, temperament, and rationality are considered essential variables, and so are differences arising from affiliation of individuals with particular parties, agencies within the state, or with peoples of different culture.

One can illustrate the contrast between the two hypotheses by means of important past decisions in international politics. According to the states-as-actors theory, American employment of the A-bomb over Hiroshima, or American intervention in the war in Korea, could have been foreseen—to the extent that foresight is possible at all—on the basis of the supposed common psychological disposition of states, coupled with an analysis of the existing circumstances which were external to the actors. Those who hold to the decision-making approach, on the contrary, consider it necessary to probe into the personal events that took place within the psyches of men like Stimson, Truman, and Acheson—perhaps also of their advisors, backers, and opponents—and led them to choose one particular course of action rather than some alternative course.[4]

The decision-making approach naturally appeals to the historian who is interested in identifying the unique aspects of past events, which necessitates consideration of all conceivable variables, including the personal traits of particular human actors. But it poses a serious problem for the theorist whose task is not to establish the

[4] See Richard C. Snyder and Glenn D. Paige, "The United States' Decision to Resist Aggression in Korea: The Application of an Analytical Scheme," *Administrative Science Quarterly*, Vol. 3, No. 3 (December, 1958), especially pp. 348, 374.

be absent. The reactions of different inhabitants might range all the way from hurried window-opening and loud complaints to complete indifference. To formulate expectations concerning behavior in an overheated house, one would need intimate knowledge of the varying individual predispositions and of the symptoms by which they could be recognized. Here, then, the decision-making approach would become necessary to supplement vague generalizations about reactions to discomfort that might be deduced from human nature in general, and such supplementation would become the more necessary the less overheated the house.

A second illustration should serve to show what is meant by compulsive action arising not from external danger but from an opportunity for gain. Here, the corresponding internal pressure for action comes from appetite or temptation rather than from fear. Let us assume that several individuals were attending a horse race, where they found themselves unable to see the race clearly because of the crowds who had arrived before them. Suddenly an opening occurs in front of them, offering an opportunity to move up close to the track. Under these circumstances, it would be reasonable to expect and predict that a rush to fill the gap would ensue. Here again, even with no knowledge about the individuals in question, behavior could be explained or predicted by reference to a general trait of human nature (the desire for benefit or enjoyment) coupled with an external circumstance (the opening of the ranks). Here, also, a decision-making analysis would be useful only in regard to individuals who decided to remain where they were rather than join the general and expected rush.

Much of what happens in international politics shows a striking resemblance to these cases from ordinary life just described. To take the case of the house on fire, it is easy to envisage an international situation in which both the external and internal factors— a dire and unmistakable threat to national survival, plus the fear it engendered among those responsible for state action—would place statesmen under the influence of almost irresistible compulsion. Instead of running for the exits, they would rush to enhance or maximize national power. When, for example, Mr. Acheson was advised not to favor the production of the first thermonuclear bomb, he is reported to have declared that its production was a matter of necessity and not of choice: in other words, that he was experiencing "compulsion," as the term is used here.

Appropriate examples can also be found to illustrate situations in the international arena that correspond to the race track analogy. The most obvious example would be the powerful nation that finds itself bordering on a power vacuum. Since nations, like nature, are said to abhor a vacuum, one could predict that the powerful nation would feel compelled to fill the vacuum with its own power.

Yet, if one considers the conditions of danger and opportunity, of fear and appetite that have to exist in order to produce anything approaching inexorable compulsion, one will see that the highly abstract model used by exponents of the states-as-actors theory cannot offer more than a first approximation to reality. Certainly the employment of the states-as-actors theory in predicting the outcome of a crisis in which less than extreme compulsions were operative would prove dangerously unreliable and would need to be strictly qualified.

In international politics, the house is not always, nor everywhere, on fire although the temperature may not be comfortable, even under the best of circumstances! This means that danger as well as opportunity for gain, and fear as well as appetite, are not constants but important variables. The external threat to any South American republic today is incomparably less than the threats with which Israel or Iran have to cope. It may be a threat to national independence in one instance, while merely the loss of an increment of security or of economic advantage in another.

Where less than national survival is at stake, there is far less compulsion and therefore a less uniform reaction. It is hard to predict the course that Nehru will follow as a consequence of the rather remote threats of the cold war to India. On the other hand, any serious threat to India's control of eastern Kashmir can be expected to result in Indian military action, despite Nehru's alleged pacifist inclinations.

The differences in behavior arising from variations in the internal pressures are no less great. While a propensity for fear and an appetite for gain may be universal, men's reactions to danger and opportunity are far from identical and vary among those who are responsible for the fate of their nation. Complacency no less than hysteria, and willingness to demand sacrifices no less than desire for popularity, affect the interpretation men give to what the "necessity of state" requires. Moreover, the "exits" are not clearly marked, with the result that some statesmen seek safety in military preparedness while others expect to find it in appeasement. Although statesmen who are entirely indifferent or blind to serious national danger and opportunity are the exception that proves the rule, it is hard to conceive of situations that leave no room at all for choice and thus for the expression of differences. While Eden believed Nasser's nationalization of the Suez Canal Company endangered Britain's economic lifeline and required military action, most other British statesmen would have reacted differently—and no one could have said with certainty at the time what course of action would be the most rational under the circumstances. If Nasser had attacked the British homeland, thereby really "setting the house on fire," the reaction of any British government, whatever the personal traits of its members, could have been predicted.

From what has been said, it seems proper to conclude that the closer nations are drawn to the pole of complete compulsion, the more they can be expected to conform in their behavior and to act in a way that corresponds to the deductions made from the states-as-actors model.

It is worth noting that a similar degree of conformity may be found where danger and compulsion are at a minimum. When not more than minor values are threatened by international discord, governments usually find it expedient to act according to established rules, since their interest in seeing others do likewise exceeds their interest in winning an occasional and minor advantage. Under these circumstances, they may forfeit an immediate national gain for the sake of sustaining the rule of law with its long-run benefits.

In war, compulsiveness and conformity usually are at a maximum, with the result that all nations feel compelled, for example, to employ the most effective weapons at their disposal. Hiroshima, as we said earlier, requires little if any decision-making analysis to explain the American action. Such an analysis might prove useful as a means of throwing light on varying attitudes of men or groups within the American government, some of whom opposed use of the bomb on the grounds that victory already was assured and that there existed, therefore, no external compulsion requiring application of the strongest weapon.

The American decision in the Korean War not to use atomic bombs against tempting military targets north of the Yalu River is a far more promising area for decision-making analysis, because it represents a deviation from the practices generally associated with warfare. Explanation for the decision may lie in a particularly high degree of foresightedness, or, as others believe, in an unusual degree of compliance with the wishes of friends and allies. In any case, General MacArthur, whose inclinations differed from those of the men charged with the final decision, might well have felt "compelled" to pursue the opposite course.

While there may be leeway for choice, and thus for the impact of psychological factors which distinguish individuals rather than abstract states, it is by no means useless or misleading to take the relatively simple and very abstract states-as-actors model as an initial working hypothesis. Thus, in formulating expectations, it is possible and helpful to assume that no state will voluntarily make unilateral concessions to an opponent if these would seriously affect the existing distribution of power. When an exception to this general proposition is encountered, it calls for special analysis: for example, as a "deviationist" move, France's initiation of discussions on the Saar in 1949, pointing toward French withdrawal before West Germany itself had raised any such demand. Various explanations are possible—that France's fear of Germany was exceptionally strong or that French statesmen were exhibiting a unique degree of foresight in realizing that the French position would in time become untenable. The entry of the United States into the war in Korea represents another case of deviation, here from the usual disinclination of nations to take up arms unless "compelled" by an attack on vital national interests which, prior to the attack, South Korea was not considered to represent.

These illustrations particularize the services that the two theories on the "actors" are able to render. By establishing the "normal" actions and reactions of states in various international situations, the states-as-actors model sets a standard on which to base our expectations of state behavior and deviations. At the same time, a far more complex model is required if our expectations are to become sufficiently refined and realistic to take into account at least the predispositions of typical categories of decision-makers.

There is no reason why intensive and comparative study of actual decisions should not, in time, provide much needed insight into the behavior peculiarities of such types of countries as those with dictatorial or democratic governments, with Asian or Western, Bolshevik or bourgeois elites, with predominantly military or civilian regimes, with a fanatical or a complacent public.[5] While it may be impractical to aim at knowledge about the decision-making of individual

---

[5] Morton A. Kaplan in *System and Process in International Politics* (John Wiley & Sons, New York, 1957, pp. 54 ff.) calls for a typology of national actors.

actors—if only because it is hard to foresee who will be the future decision-makers—it may prove useful to analyze the approach and behavior of certain "subnational" actors such as the business community, the trade union leaders, the Christian Democrats, or the American political parties. Only if it becomes possible to understand and predict typical kinds of nonconformist behavior can theory hope to approach reality. Moreover, because different degrees of compulsion will be operating at different times, it is not enough to know how states tend to act in situations of extreme danger or extreme temptation; one must also know what action to expect when the actors are relatively free to choose among alternative courses.

One example will serve to show what insight may be gained by applying the states-as-actors and the individuals-as-actors approaches simultaneously. Almost all analysts of international politics distinguish between nations that are satisfied with the *status quo* and others that are eager to change it. The controversial question is whether states fall into one category or the other primarily because of differences in the psychology of their leaders and peoples or because of differences in the objective conditions in which they find themselves. According to the states-as-actors theory which ignores the factor of possible psychological differences, objective or environmental factors alone can account for either a *status quo* or a revisionist attitude and behavior. This theory expects a nation to be revisionist if denied the enjoyment of any of its national core values, provided it has or hopes to obtain enough power to enable it to seek satisfaction of its objectives. On the other side, any analyst who focuses on individual actors and their varying predispositions will look for an explanation of revisionist behavior primarily in such traits of statesmen as their peculiar aggressive and acquisitive appetites, their rebellious temperaments, or their subjective dissatisfactions.

In my opinion, empirical study would validate the hypothesis of the states-as-actors theory that almost any nation which has suffered a loss of territory or has been subjected to discrimination will, when its power permits, take some action to redress its grievances—and thus fall into the "revisionist" category, regardless of the personal characteristics of its leaders or the peculiarities of its national culture. Victors who fail to foresee this reaction on the part of the vanquished are in for a rude awakening.

Yet it would be a mistake to ignore the impact of individual or national differences on the behavior of states that express dissatisfaction with the *status quo*. One must expect deviations from any general pattern discovered by means of deduction. The case of German "revisionism" after World War I offers a good illustration. Before Hitler came into power, Germany, under democratic leaders, already was demanding redress of certain grievances. Yet had the democratic leaders remained in power, they might well have refused to satisfy their demands by means of war, even if Germany had become as powerful as it did under Hitler (or as powerful as Hitler, in his megalomania, believed it to be). Theory, therefore, must descend below the high level of abstraction at which only states are seen as the actors; consideration need be given to such significant factors as the inclination of dictators to overestimate their nation's power, the ability of demagogues to arouse and make use of popular dissatisfactions, or the reluctance of democratic leaders to initiate war.

II

UP TO THIS POINT, the discussion has been devoted to criticizing the states-as-actors theory for its neglect of the individuals as actors. Another kind of objection to the theory has been raised on the ground that it fails to allow for the possibility of corporate actors other than the nation-states. It is asked whether a realistic image of the contemporary international scene should not include such non-state corporate actors as the United Nations or the Communist International. If it should, the term "multistate system" no longer would be fully adequate to describe the environment in which statesmen and other actors operate in the world today.

The "billiard ball" model of the multistate system which forms the basis for the states-as-actors theory leaves room for no corporate actors other than the nation-state. By definition, the stage is pre-empted by a set of states, each in full control of all territory, men, and resources within its boundaries. Every state represents a closed, impermeable, and sovereign unit, completely separated from all other states. Since this obviously is not an accurate portrait of the real world of international politics, one can say that reality "deviates" in various ways from the model, because corporate bodies other than nation-states play a role on the international stage as coactors with the nation-states. To the extent that these corporate bodies exert influence on the course of international politics, knowledge about them and about the deviations that permit them to operate becomes indispensable to the development of a well-rounded theory.

More even than in the case of the individual actors, one is justified here in using the term "deviation" to indicate that any important impact of nonstate corporate actors constitutes the exception rather than the rule. As things stand today—and are likely to remain for an indefinite period—there can be no serious doubt about the paramount position of the nation-state or about the superiority of its influence and power. Even enthusiastic supporters of the UN realize that there can be no UN action of any consequence if a single great power refuses to permit it. To date, no nonstate corporate actor has been able to rob a nation-state of the primary loyalty of more than a small fraction of its people. If this should ever occur—if, for example, a Communist International could persuade a state's soldiers and workers to refuse obedience to their own national government—the nation-state in question would prove an empty shell when put to the test of war. Occurrences of this kind were well-known in medieval times, before the age of nation-state predominance, when excommunication by the pope, a supranational actor, could deprive a king of control over his people.

There is no lack of a suitable vocabulary to identify a set of nonstate corporate actors, but it is not without significance that all the terms refer to something called "national" which is the characteristic feature of the nation-state. One distinguishes between international, supranational, transnational, and subnational corporate bodies as potential coactors on the international stage. Some have criticized this terminology on the very ground that it creates a prejudice in favor of the nation-state as the center of things; they suggest that the term "international politics" be replaced by the term "world politics." One is hard put, however, to define where world politics begins and domestic politics ends, unless world politics comprises acts that transcend national boundaries—which brings one back to the nation-state with its territorial borders.

It is not hard to see what kinds of deviations from the billiard ball model of a multistate system are possible, or to see that certain types of deviations facilitate the operations and increase the influence of nonstate corporate actors.

If the states of today are not monolithic blocs—and none but the totalitarian states are—groups, parties, factions, and all sorts of other politically organized groups within such states can take a hand in matters transcending national boundaries. They may do so directly, in negotiating and dealing with similar groups abroad or even with the governments of other states, or they may exert their influence as domestic pressure groups so effectively that foreign statesmen would be ill-advised to ignore them. Some democratic states have exhibited such pluralistic tendencies that they offer to the world a picture of near-anarchy. They seem to speak to the world with many and conflicting voices and to act as if one hand—one agency or faction—does not know what the other hand is doing. There also are states, some of them new states in the process of consolidation, where integration is so poor that other states must deal with parts, rather than with a fictitious whole, if diplomacy is to be effective.

Another deviation bears on the degree of separateness or, if one prefers, of cohesion between nations. Here, too, one can visualize a wide gamut of gradations. Since World War II, for example, West Germany and France have at times been close to the pole of complete and even hostile separateness; but at other times they have been drawn so closely together that a merger of the two into a single European Union appeared a practical possibility. While such a union might have become a new superstate, it might instead have remained a more loosely knit international organization, like the British Commonwealth, which can exert considerable influence on the behavior of its members.

Then, again, there are deviations from the complete impermeability of the nation-states envisaged in the billiard ball model.[6] Some peoples today are shut off from contact with the rest of the world by an Iron Curtain, but the boundaries of most states are permeable, leaving the inhabitants relatively free to organize into groups transcending national boundaries. If they desire, they can do so even for the purpose of exerting international influence. One need only think of the international Communist movement, of international Socialist groups, or of international cartels which have, at times, been able to perform as transnational actors.

[6] In *International Politics in the Atomic Age* (Columbia University Press, New York, 1959, p. 104) John H. Herz uses the term "impermeability" to indicate the protection that the classical nation-state was able to provide until, with the advent of the air and missile age, "the roof blew off the territorial state."

Finally, sovereignty, in the political sense of the term, is not everywhere and always as undivided and total as the legal concept would indicate. The behavior within the Soviet orbit of the satellite states, legally recognized as sovereign, can be understood only if the role of the Soviet Union is taken into account, either as a coactor in the background or as the master actor. Another case of divided sovereignty is presented by the European Coal and Steel Community which can act with considerable independence within the field of its competence.

Whether the United Nations has become a center of decision and action in its own right is a *quaestio facti,* as it is in the case of all the competitors of the nation-state. Theoretically, there is no reason why the real world should not "deviate" from the condition of complete nation-state sovereignty to the point of permitting an international organization, such as the UN, to become a relevant actor. It would have to be recognized as a relevant actor if resolutions, recommendations, or orders emanating from its organs should, for all practical purposes, compel some or all member governments to act differently from the way in which they would otherwise act.

A theoretical discussion of the actors is not the place to answer the question whether nonstate corporate actors are presently gaining or losing ground in their competition with the nation-state. But because there has been much speculation about an alleged trend away from the state system and toward an ever-increasing role of international bodies, if not of a single supranational world government, it is worth noting that two sharply conflicting tendencies can be detected in the world today: one toward the enhancement, the other toward the diminution, of the paramount position of the nation-state. Which of the two tendencies will gain the upper hand depends in the end on so many factors that a reliable prediction seems impossible.[7]

In recent times, the nation-state has been gaining much ground geographically. There is hardly a region left in the world where nation-states are not either already functioning or in the process of being established. There also has been a marked increase in the power over men that can be exercised in the name of the state. Never before has the state achieved so complete a monopoly of control within large areas as is enjoyed today by the totalitarian Soviet Union with its Iron Curtain and its ability to radiate

---

[7] Herz (*op. cit.*) sees two "blocs" replacing the now obsolete nation-state.

ideologically far beyond its own borders. Satellitism and international Communism represent more of a triumph of the Russian state than a break with the traditional multistate system.[8]

But there are other developments which point in the opposite direction. It is not enough, obviously, to point to the impressive array of international and other nonnational organizations that have mushroomed in recent years; these organizations may constitute or develop into mere instruments of national policy. Nor is it enough to prove on rational grounds that the nation-state is becoming increasingly less fit to satisfy the needs for security and economic development. However, there is ample evidence to show that the United Nations and its agencies, the European Coal and Steel Community, the Afro-Asian bloc, the Arab League, the Vatican, the Arabian-American Oil Company, and a host of other nonstate entities are able on occasion to affect the course of international events. When this happens, these entities become actors in the international arena and competitors of the nation-state. Their ability to operate as international or transnational actors may be traced to the fact that men identify themselves and their interests with corporate bodies other than the nation-state.

Here, then, there appears a connection between the phenomenon of nonstate corporate actors and the individuals-as-actors approach. No deviations from the states-as-actors or billiard ball model are conceivable *unless* it is unrealistic to assume that men identify themselves completely and exclusively with their respective nation-states, an assumption that excludes the possibility of nonstate corporate actors' exerting any influence of international significance. But in order to discover how men in the contemporary world do in fact identify themselves—or what they refer to, as Paul Nitze puts it,[9] when they speak of the "we" in international affairs—attention must be focused on the individual human beings for whom identification is a psychological event.[10] If their loyalties are divided between the nation and other political organizations, such sub-

[8] George Liska in *International Equilibrium* (Harvard University Press, Cambridge, Mass., 1957, p. 132) points out that "the trend to horizontally expanding functionalism has been at least equalled by the drive to enlarge the vertical power structures of major states by the addition of dependable allies and dependent satellites."

[9] See his essay, "Necessary and Sufficient Elements of a General Theory of International Relations," in *Theoretical Aspects of International Relations*.

[10] In Kaplan's words, "Individuals, after all, have no biological ties to the nation" (*op. cit.*, p. 157).

national bodies as the UN and such transnational bodies as a Communist International can, in principle, become significant factors in the shaping of world events. Tito's actions often are unintelligible if it is forgotten that he identifies himself not only with Yugoslavia but with some loose grouping he calls the Socialist camp. What Arab leaders mean when they speak from the point of view of their primary corporate interest may be a purely national interest or instead a changing composite of national, Pan-Arab, and Pan-Islamic interest. Whether the pope merits recognition as an actor in world affairs cannot be determined merely by reference to the fact that he lacks the military power states are able to muster. If nations and statesmen do, in fact, act differently when under the impact of orders or admonitions from the Vatican, to disregard the pope as an actor would mean overlooking a significant aspect of international politics. Similarly, the actor capacity of the United Nations depends on whether the policies of national statesmen are affected by resolutions of the General Assembly, by reprovals of the UN Secretary-General, and by orders of the Security Council.

One may conclude, then, that only an empirical analysis, penetrating to the minds of men and to their manner of choosing one course of action over another, can throw light on the role of non-state corporate actors and thus supplement a possibly oversimplified and unrealistic concentration on the nation-states as sole corporate actors. While it would be dangerous for theorists to divert their primary attention from the nation-state and multistate systems which continue to occupy most of the stage of contemporary world politics, theory remains inadequate if it is unable to include such phenomena as overlapping authorities, split loyalties, and divided sovereignty, which were pre-eminent characteristics of medieval actors. These phenomena, which indicate serious deviations from the billiard ball model, also deserve attention from the analyst today. Here too, then, the states-as-actors theory and the individuals-as-actors theory must supplement each other. If they can be made to do so, they will contribute to the development of a theory that rightly can claim to be "realistic" since it will throw light on all chief aspects of the realities in contemporary international politics.

Chapter Two

AMITY AND
ENMITY
AMONG NATIONS

IN THE THEATER and in movies the actors attract attention
as individuals; yet, both actors and audience realize that the drama
arises from the interrelations among the actors. Similarly, although
individual nations and statesmen have a great and sometimes spectacular impact on the course of events, international "relations" in
the literal sense require foremost attention. In the political arena,
conflict as well as co-operation is part of the interaction among the
actors; an actor's goals take shape in the form of demands on others;
the means each employs can be measured only in relation to the
means of others. Even in assessing the importance of a mountain
range or a stretch of ocean, the relationship between the nations
on both sides of the mountains or the sea determines whether they
constitute a protective shield or an undesirable barrier. The
Atlantic Ocean, for example, which once helped this country avoid
entanglements, has today become an obstacle to American protection of Western Europe. Not geography, but the relationship
between the United States and Western Europe has changed.

Terms like "amity" and "enmity"—even more, terms like "friendship" and "hostility"—must be used with caution in discussing
interstate relationships. These terms are taken from the universe
of interpersonal relations and they convey a sense of emotional
involvement. In contrast, diplomatic postures of amity and enmity
do not depend on emotional conditions and may in fact contradict
them. Thus, some Americans may feel enmity for the colored races,
but this does not prevent "cordial" or "friendly" diplomatic relations between the United States and many African and Asian
nations. Again, while public opinion polls might indicate that the

American people harbor little enmity toward the Chinese, relations between Communist China and the United States are thoroughly inimical. A government which represents a nation-state as corporate actor is expected to be guided not by sentiment—the sentiment either of the policy-makers themselves or of the people—but by a dispassionate assessment of the national interest. However, this dissociation between the cold-blooded pursuit of the national interest and human feelings is never complete. Only as a first step in the analysis of the problem does it make sense to treat interstate relations as if they were immune to human sentiment.

Relations among states can vary in a wide spectrum from the extreme of total enmity of two belligerents in a fight to the finish to the extreme of amity when two states let down their guards completely, as have the United States and Canada.[1] Public attention and most writers focus on the pole of inimical relations because world affairs naturally arouse little interest when the going is as smooth, for instance, as it has been in recent times between the United States and Great Britain. Yet, even in an age of strife, nations do not continuously remain, as Hobbes pictured them, "in the state and posture of gladiators."

There is a type of relationship that at first does not seem to fit into the amity-enmity spectrum. It could be described as a state of "minimal relations." Nations deciding to "go it alone" in order to avoid entanglement in the disputes of others, as illustrated by the United States prior to World War II and by Switzerland to this day, seek to minimize political contacts with other nations. They work to convince others of their impartial friendliness, expecting that abstention from making demands on and interfering with others will evoke a response of at least diplomatic amity. They may not succeed, however, in eliciting such a response if one or more of these other nations is hostile to the very idea of nonalignment or neutrality. John Foster Dulles' denunciation of neutrality as immoral, barring exceptional circumstances, will be remembered in this connection;[2] his attitude—which threatened to disrupt cordial relations between the United States and many nonaligned

---

[1] Kenneth Boulding suggests classifying the "reciprocal relations of nations along some scale of friendliness-hostility" and calls the extremes "stable friendliness" and "stable hostility." "National Images and International Systems," *International Politics and Foreign Policy*, ed. James Rosenau (The Free Press of Glencoe, Inc., New York, 1961), p. 374.

[2] Secretary Dulles' remarks about neutrality occurred in a commencement address, "The Cost of Peace," at Iowa State College on June 9, 1956, and were

countries—was later revised, when the potential alternative to neutrality became alignment with the Soviet bloc.

Nonaligned countries seek to avoid not only conflict but also commitments for common and co-operative action. Their positive efforts in foreign policy are limited to proving the absence of inimical intentions. One novelty of our age, however, deserves mention. No longer do all nonaligned countries shun political ties altogether; most of them, in fact, co-operate within the framework of the United Nations. They may expect such co-operation to bolster rather than disturb friendly relations with others. Yet, this does not necessarily follow, because nations lining up in the UN voting process risk being counted on the side of one or the other disputant.

The cool, nonentangling relations of the kind sought by the nonaligned countries can be pictured in our amity-enmity spectrum as relations of minimal amity. Moving out toward the extremity one approaches the more intense types of amity which can be described as active co-operation or as a relationship of "going it with others." Allies may even work toward merger or federal union. Co-operation means sacrificing some degree of national independence with a view to co-ordinating, synchronizing, and rendering mutually profitable some of the political, military, or economic policies the co-operating nations intend to pursue. Such co-operation can spring from two incentives which are distinct in motivation and effects. Co-operation may arise from a desire to improve relations within the co-operating group, in which case the interest is turned inward and is independent of threats from outside the group. The second incentive—which, to the disappointment of idealists, proves much more potent—is the desire to meet a common external threat by co-operative effort; here co-operation is predicated on the continuance of the threat.

The "inward-directed" co-operative relationship usually binds together nations of a region and is treated, therefore, in the United Nations Charter under the heading of "regional arrangements." In principle, however, there is no reason why geographically separate nations should not be interested in organizational devices to further

---

reprinted in the Department of State *Bulletin,* Vol. 34 (1956), pp. 999-1004. The relevant section is as follows: "These treaties (mutual security treaties between the U.S. and other countries) abolish, as between the parties, the principle of neutrality, which pretends that a nation can best gain safety for itself by being indifferent to the fate of others. This has increasingly become an obsolete conception and, except under very exceptional circumstances, it is an immoral and shortsighted conception."

their common welfare by collective measures. The British Commonwealth falls into the category of an arrangement among nations that
has no regional base. As of today, there is no regional inward-
directed arrangement that does not also pursue outward-directed
defensive purposes or is not strongly influenced by an external
threat. The Organization of American States is regarded as the
model of regional co-operation yet, since under the Rio Pact it
commits its members to take common action against outsiders as
well as against members who commit acts of aggression, it partakes
of the character of both types of co-operative arrangement. In the
case of Western European integration the inward-directed purpose
of promoting the peace and welfare of the area has been dominant;
yet the Soviet threat acts as a potent spur and it might, as some
feared, have changed the character of the process of integration if
the European Defense Community, clearly outward-directed, had
come into being.

Inward-oriented co-operation does not come easily to sovereign
governments. Only in exceptional cases, as in Western Europe,
have nations gone far in committing themselves to such co-operation
even in the economic field where the opportunity and the advantages are most apparent. Usually sentiments of nationalism, as well
as vested interests, are blamed for the failure of "regionalism," but
the chief obstacle lies elsewhere. In the absence of an external
threat requiring collaboration with others for defense, sovereign
governments aware of their prime responsibilities toward their own
people usually do not dare to relinquish their freedom of action;
on their continuing freedom in policy-making rests their ability to
safeguard the national interest. Only in the case of genuine federation in which sovereignties are merged does this obstacle disappear;
then the national interest becomes the federal interest, and the
responsibility is shifted to the supranational or federal government.
It is an open question whether an intermediary stage—referred to
as confederacy, union, or political community—lying somewhere
between national sovereignty and federal or supranational sovereignty can provide a stable basis for close co-operation and effective
common action. Such an arrangement might become a source of
friction by impairing the freedom of action of national governments
without substituting a reliable new source of authority and responsibility. Some form of regular and institutionalized political co-
operation among nations retaining their power of ultimate decision
—perhaps after the model of the British Commonwealth—may be

able under certain circumstances to assure a high degree of amity among the participants without interfering in the proper functioning of the national governments.

The second type of co-operative arrangement, which lines up nations for mutual assistance against a common external foe, faces fewer obstacles than the inward-directed type. All alliances or collective defense agreements fall into this second category. As mentioned earlier in connection with inward-directed arrangements, the distinction between the two categories is not rigid: allies frequently supplement their co-operation for collective defense with some inward-directed activities, as NATO has been seeking to do in the political, economic, and cultural fields. Moreover, allies sometimes play down their external purpose by not specifying an external foe in their formal treaties in order not to provoke him. Governments deceive themselves and their people, however, if they fail to appreciate the difference between the two types of co-operation. Where external defense rather than economic co-operation or the pacific settlement of disputes among members of the group is the essential aim as in an alliance, any diminution of the external threat or of the will to meet it will tend to undermine cohesion and render futile any attempts to save the alliance by inward-directed "diversions." Also, because the external threat is essential, it is erroneous to see multilateral agreements for collective defense as a step in the direction of universal collective security or world government. Such agreements are predicated on the existence of at least "two worlds" or two antagonistic camps and, like national armaments, are a symptom of international conflict rather than of growing world unity.

While amity among allies, particularly among wartime allies, may be as intimate as relations between independent nations can ever become, it would be a mistake to underestimate the strains that almost any alliance in war or peace places on such amity. More will be said about these strains in a later chapter.[3] It is enough to say here that most dangerous to the amity between peacetime allies are suspicions concerning the reliability of allied pledges of future assistance; most disruptive in wartime alliances are suspicions that one ally may be contemplating a separate peace with the enemy. Because coercion—as a substitute for diplomatic persuasion—has little place among allies, "amical diplomacy" directed at the prevention or resolution of interallied conflict becomes particularly important here.

[3] See Chapter 13, "Stresses and Strains in 'Going it with Others.'"

Enmity reflects the existence of a conflict of interests. Peace is threatened at that stage of the conflict when physical coercion, by one side or both, becomes a practical possibility. Relations between inimical but nonwarring nations are often described as competition or rivalry and are compared with the competition of athletes on the race track or of businessmen on the market. But these analogies are misleading. Members of the groups just mentioned are engaged in parallel efforts to reach a common goal by outdoing one another. Among nations in conflict competition usually exists too, but it pertains only to their struggle to equip themselves with arms and alliances as the means of attaining their objectives. When it comes to the objectives, the conflict resembles a head-on collision of parties pursuing different, opposing, and incompatible goals. The clashes between football teams or between capital and labor during a strike offer better analogies for relations between inimical but non-warring states. It would be ironic to characterize the relationship between Israel and its Arab neighbors as a competition for territory when the latter desire to wipe the former off the map while the former is seeking to hold on to or possibly enlarge its territory.

If it is true that competition, even the competition for arma-ments, is not what lies at the heart of conflict and enmity, then certain conclusions follow with respect to disarmament. As long as the incompatibility of the goals has not been resolved by com-promise or by renunciation on the part of one of the opponents, it is hard to conceive of any side intentionally giving up an advantage in the competition for means. The only restraints on competitive efforts that have a chance of gaining favor are those that assure equal advantage or equal disadvantage to both sides. In view of the extraordinary difficulties in devising such symmetrical accords on armaments—and in convincing both sides that the effects will indeed continue to prove symmetrical throughout the duration of an accord—it is not surprising that agreed measures of disarmament or arms control have materialized only in exceptional cases so far. Agreement to restrain the competitive quest for allies to my knowl-edge has not ever been attempted.

The reasons for enmity in any multistate system are so plentiful and various that stable friendship between all the members of the system can hardly be more than a rare exception. As long as there are conflicting aims, there will be instances of enmity. But enmity need not lead, and has not regularly led, to a resort to coercive power. If it did, there would be war permanently. Since it takes two to make a war, two parties must decide that war is preferable to its alternative. The alternative, in the case of a country seeking to change the *status quo* by force, consists in foregoing such change as is attainable only by coercion; in the case of a country that can preserve the *status quo* only by resisting attack, the alternative to war consists in acceptance of those changes that only the use of counterforce could prevent.

In the absence of war, enmity may continue indefinitely and may be expressed in several ways, from a mere cessation of friendly intercourse to exchanges of any of the many types of inimical acts that fall short of war in the technical sense of hostilities involving the use of regular military forces. On whatever level the inimical confrontation takes place, it is bound to have far-reaching consequences both for the nations directly involved and for the other members of the multistate system. As a case in point, governments will experience a strong compulsion to expect the worst from their enemy, if only to be properly prepared. Yet excessive expectations concerning enemy action can have serious drawbacks; instead of deterring an opponent from taking action for which he has the capability, it may lead to preparations so massive that hostile action by the opponent is provoked rather than prevented. As another consequence, enmity between two nations generates pressure on others to take sides.

In this context of interenemy action and reaction, the problem of escalation deserves the very serious attention it has attracted in the nuclear age. Inimical confrontation on any level involves potential escalation to higher levels, and ultimately to the level of general war. If in a conflict between nuclear powers, the leaders on both sides are convinced that a nuclear war would be intolerably destructive to their own countries, the fear of escalation tends to restrain their conduct. The degree of restraint will vary widely among the parties; it will be much greater for a nuclear power that expects to suffer intolerable self-destruction even if it should strike first. If both parties operate on the assumption of a reliable "nuclear stalemate," escalation to any level short of general war might be sought rather than feared. Thus, to a country that believed itself inferior on the level of guerilla warfare but superior on a conventional level, escalation to the conventional level would be tempting. In fact, such escalation would be a condition of success because mere counterguerilla activities cannot restore peace and order to a territory torn by guerilla warfare.

The dividing line between amity and enmity is not always clear cut. There is a twilight zone in which governments have trouble deciding whether a tenuous relationship of amity has given way to enmity or vice versa. Even among the friendliest of countries, there usually is a dormant conflict that may suddenly come alive. Although the Suez crisis did not create enmity between the United States and its major European allies sufficient to justify any expectation of violence between them, it nevertheless seriously disrupted their previous friendly relations. The United States, to give another example, has no assurance that a Yugoslav desire to restore solidarity with the Communist bloc might not at any moment gain the upper hand over the wish to maintain cordial relations with the United States. It is in situations like these that diplomacy, as a means of keeping bonds of friendship from snapping, faces the gravest test of its effectiveness. Unfortunately, governments as a rule are too preoccupied with open conflicts and enmities to be able to deal preventively with those that are still latent; they may often fail to anticipate trouble.

One of the striking features of diplomatic amity and enmity is the suddenness and ease with which one may change into the other. Abrupt switches from amity to enmity cause little astonishment because they correspond to everyday experience in personal relations. A good friend of yesterday who betrays or offends may be the bitterest of enemies tomorrow; and, similarly, two allies seeming to be intimately linked by common interest may become foes if one suspects the other of collusion with the enemy. Rapid switches from enmity to amity among states, however, may arouse passionate criticism because the public's hatreds usually die slowly. Yet the ability to turn an enemy of yesterday into an ally of today is not only traditional in diplomacy but an indispensable condition for any successful balance of power policy. There could be no better validation of our opening proposition that amity and enmity between states must be distinguished from their emotional setting than to point to the way Germany and Japan, the two major wartime enemies of the West, became important pillars of the West's system of collective defense long before hatreds generated by the war had had time to subside. Here, the change of alignment did not depend on any prior change of public sentiment but did much to hasten such change.

Turning now to the emotional setting, it almost goes without saying that friendly personal feelings and sympathies either between the statesmen or between the peoples of two nations facilitate the conduct of amical interstate relations and also tend to be developed as a result of such conduct. The men who act for their respective states are likely to find the going easier if they have sympathy and understanding for their opposite numbers and for their peoples. Moreover, any government exposed to the pressures of public opinion is embarrassed if the amical relations it is seeking to maintain with another country are contradicted by public expressions of hostility. Some of the neutralist countries may learn in time that vociferous attacks on "imperialist America" are not conducive to cordial relations with the United States! In democracies, where public attitudes have a powerful impact on the conduct of public policy, popular revulsion against despotic regimes may create serious obstacles to policies of co-operation with them even though the government considers such policies to be in the interest of national security. While traditionally neutral democratic countries like Sweden or Switzerland may uphold the principle that the public is free to express its private sentiments and need not, like the government, abstain from partisanship, they nevertheless are often led to counsel moderation in public expressions of opinions and feelings that might interfere with a policy of amity.

Close and effective interstate amity as among allies should tend to promote emotional friendship. The mere experience of successful common effort can make for mutual confidence and sympathy although it does not necessarily do so; old grudges, suspicions, resentments, and jealousies may prevail at least in some parts of the population. But then, even democratic governments need not wait passively for the spontaneous development of public sentiments of friendship to complement their policies. There are many ways in which a favorable image of another nation can be sold to the public, even though anything as radical as the way totalitarian governments manipulate public opinion is incompatible with democracy.

There is an inclination, particularly in the United States, to exaggerate the importance of feelings of friendship or gratitude for the maintenance of amical relations. While it may not be agreeable to witness outbursts of anti-Americanism in countries with which the United States seeks to maintain friendly or allied relations, co-operation between the governments and mutual respect for one another's interests are not at the mercy of these outbursts. Most states most of the time—the new states as well as those with long diplomatic experience—maintain amical or inimical relations with others on the basis of calculations of interest rather than in response to popular sentiments whether of gratitude or resentment. People-to-people diplomacy and cultural exchanges can be useful, however, if they help to bolster popular feelings of friendship where and when amical interstate relations or a relaxation of interstate tension is in the national interest.

The relationship between diplomatic enmity and hostile feelings is not less complex than that between diplomatic amity and friendly feelings. There is one difference, however: in war it is almost inevitable that the two types of enmity, private and diplomatic, should coincide, particularly since wars have come to be fought between entire nations rather than between professional military forces. When sentiments of hatred for the enemy are absent prior to hostilities, governments usually see to it that they do not remain absent long. Hate-provoking caricatures of the enemy and atrocity stories, supposedly conducive to a high state of morale among fighting men and the population generally, are widely used although it remains controversial whether feelings of hatred for the enemy are indispensable in war. In any case, the tendency for hostile feelings to linger on after the war is over may lead some governments to regret the skill with which they instilled hatred in the hearts of their people while fighting morale was at a premium.

The emphasis so far has been on popular emotions which, when hostile, may reach a point of mass hysteria that leaves the government little room for moderation. Much more important are the emotions of sympathy or antipathy, love or hatred, of the policy-makers themselves. There is the well-known case of the diplomat who becomes so enamored with the country to which he is accredited that he cannot conceive of its conducting policies detrimental to the interests of his own country. Leading statesmen, too, may become blinded by their personal grudges against a particular nation or against a particular foreign statesman. If they are thereby rendered incapable of a dispassionate view of the situation, they may fail, for instance, to seek amical solutions to conflicts that actually would be capable of peaceful resolution.

In our age of revolutionary and ideological conflict another point needs to be emphasized. Of many of today's revolutionary leaders it may be assumed that their hatreds are directed less against people or foreign statesmen than against social systems, institutions, or conditions symbolized by terms such as imperialism, capitalism,

Wall Street or Bolshevism. Where these hatreds are dominant, it is hard to say whether the interpretation of the national interest is perverted by emotional attachment to ideology and dogma, or whether subjective emotions merely accompany the pursuit of ideological goals to which the nations or regimes in question are dedicated anyway, thereby simply adding more drive and forcefulness to the ideological pursuit. In any case, it would be a mistake to assume that the ideological cleavages between East and West, or between some of the neutralists and the West, accompanied though they are at times by violent explosions of emotion, necessarily preclude cordial interstate relations. Long periods of mere nonbelligerency, a tenuous form of amity, may go hand in hand with unabridged latent conflict, as relations between the Soviet Union and the bourgeois national regimes of neutralist states demonstrate.

Many men of sensitive conscience are disturbed to see their country either entertaining cordial relations with nations, regimes, and individual rulers whom they condemn for unethical behavior or engaging in war with a people for whom they feel no hatred. Yet, if the nation's interests dispassionately perceived shall guide statesmen, it is necessary that they be able to disassociate themselves from their own private feelings and from those of the public when as statesmen they shape the relationships of their country with other nations. It would be disastrous if they sought instead to build on the quicksands of emotion, especially today when emotions are at the mercy of mass media of communication and of high-powered propaganda.

Chapter Three

THE DETERMINANTS
OF FOREIGN POLICY

IF ATTENTION IS focused exclusively on the goals and means of policy with no consideration of the forces that determine or influence the actors in choosing among these goals and means, one is left without any guide to anticipate future choices and without any way of affecting policy. Statesmen as well as scholars are forever engaged, therefore, in probing the decisions by which others set their course. As in all other fields of human activity, decisions and actions in the international arena can be understood, predicted, and manipulated only in so far as the factors influencing the decision can be identified and isolated. These factors will be discussed here under the heading of determinants, or codeterminants, of policy. The actors can be pictured in a matrix of internal and external forces that affect their behavior through pulls and pressures. Decisions can be altered either by relieving these pulls and pressures or by setting up counterpulls and counterpressures. Thus, if the chief determinant of a particular government's militant attitude were identified as the resentment of an influential minority about some specific aspect of the *status quo,* a policy directed toward satisfying this minority through a change in the existing order might reduce the attitude of militancy; in another case, where aggressive behavior derived primarily from the temptations of unopposed power, the balancing of that power might prove an effective remedy.

One hesitates to speak of determinants because the term might suggest a deterministic philosophy excluding any freedom of choice in the formulation and execution of foreign policy. Nothing of the kind is intended here. Looking with hindsight at any past policy, assuming all of its antecedents are known, it is possible to see every

act as fully determined by the totality of its antecedents. Every decision or choice of policy is the necessary result of all of its antecedents. But this proposition in no way implies that the decision-
makers were not "free" to act as they did. The elements internal
to the actor that went into the process of "making up his mind"—
his preferences and prejudices, his will power and determination,
his assessment of risks and opportunities—are included among the
factors. As a result the actor's choice among alternative courses of
action, experienced by him as a matter of personal responsibility,
becomes merged with the determinants external to him. Subconscious or neurotic psychological compulsions over which the actor
actually has no control would fall into the category of external
determinants.

The extensive debate about the chief determinants of foreign
policy covers all that has been written over the ages about the causes
of war and conflict, about aggression and imperialism, as well as
about the causes of relatively long periods of peace and international harmony. I do not intend to review this debate, but shall
discuss the views of the more influential schools of thought about
the determinants in foreign affairs.

One question which led to heated controversy in the past can be
disposed of here quickly. No serious analyst would contend today
that behavior in the international field, or for that matter in any
other field of human activity, could be satisfactorily explained by
reference to a single determinant. Undeniably, "single factor theories" have proved excellent instruments of propaganda. Marxists,
as well as their opponents in the German school of Geopolitik, were
aware of the advantage to be gained from accounting for all major
moves in international politics in terms of the economic system or
the geographic situation, respectively. But such theories can at
best be rated as simplifying abstractions that may serve to bring
into relief one particularly powerful codetermining factor. The
living world does not fit into any such simple mold. Napoleon
could say that geography dictates the course of foreign policy, but
presumably even he knew that it took his special characteristics as
well as the geography of Russia to lure him to Moscow. Were one
to believe that geography dictated Napoleon's and later Hitler's invasion of Russia, one would have to ascribe to geography a vicious
design to fool and defeat ambitious conquerors! Similarly, no serious historian would blame World War II exclusively on Hitler's
pathological predisposition, although psychologists can point with

reason to the extraordinarily potent determining effect that his personal traits were able to exert on the course of world events.

While the single versus multiple factor approach is not a serious issue of debate today, the controversy concerning the respective role of environmental and predispositional determinants has not come to rest and may never do so. Some see an expansionist policy as the result chiefly of a power vacuum and they call for a more balanced distribution of power among nations; others ascribe the same policy to the acquisitiveness of particular nations and ask that these nations be kept weak or under the control of others. Acts of aggression are explained in one case by the provocative nature of the environmental conditions under which a nation is made to live, for instance by having been partitioned or subjected to discriminatory treatment; they are accounted for in another case by the psychoneurotic traits of particular leaders. In the first case, a strategy of peace directed at changing the environment would be appropriate; in the second case, psychotherapy applied to the leaders or their removal from positions of authority logically would offer the best hope for future peace.

The direction of foreign policy may be affected by the official view concerning the decisive determinant or determinants. If Hitler had believed the tenets of German Geopolitik, he can be assumed to have discounted factors other than geography in his calculation of German expansionist opportunities in the east. Similarly, the exaggeration of the determining effect of personal predisposition may have caused statesmen to err, as did Franklin D. Roosevelt when at Teheran and Yalta he placed great importance on gaining Stalin's personal confidence and little on preventing a shift in the future European balance of power in favor of the Soviet Union.

One obviously environmentalist theory is that of Karl Marx to which the Soviet leaders profess to adhere even today. According to his well-known hypothesis, capitalist foreign policy is determined by the inner contradictions of the capitalist economy. The actors are puppets in the hands of inescapable pressures exerted by the economic system. Any differences of behavior within the capitalist camp—such as the difference that permits the Soviets to place the chief blame for world tension on the United States today—are explained by differences among Western countries in the degree of their capitalist maturity.

The German school of Geopolitik was consciously developed on the model of Marxism and as a response and antidote to it. Geopolitik shifted the emphasis from the economic system and its effects on social classes to geography and its impact on national interests and behavior. But here, too, the decisive determinant is seen in a situational factor,[1] with the decision-makers now appearing as puppets of the geographical milieu.

A third theory which has gained adherents in recent times may be called environmentalist, too, if one focuses on the behavior of the individuals who act for nations rather than on the nations themselves as corporate actors. Anthropologists have contended that the way governments behave in foreign affairs can be explained by reference to the culture of their people. Presumably, this implies that decision-makers tend to conform to the demands of this culture, of its values and taboos, whether or not they have internalized them and made them part of their own individual predispositions. Sometimes this cultural determinant is called the national character, to which, it will be remembered, German and Japanese aggression has been attributed.

A fourth school of predominantly environmentalist character deserves particular attention, both for its influence and for the valuable insights it has provided. It is customary to call this the realist school. In the extreme formulation—which may be meant merely as an abstract and initial working hypothesis, misrepresented if taken as a description of the real world—exponents of this school make the nation-states appear as the puppets of forces emanating from the anarchical international system of multiple sovereignty. The system is said to hold nations in the iron grip of state necessity and compulsion. As in the Marxist view, behavior in foreign affairs is seen as determined by external conditions; the political multistate system in this theory takes the place held by the economic capitalist system in Marxist theory.[2]

In recent years the predominant interest of scholars has shifted from environmental to predispositional determinants. Geopolitics, so fashionable in the thirties and during the war, has few spokesmen today. In many instances the pendulum has swung from extreme

---

[1] David Easton introduces the term *situational determinants* in contrast to psychological determinants to indicate "those determinants which shape activity in spite of the kind of personalities and motivations in the participants." *The Political System: An Inquiry into the State of Political Science* (Alfred A. Knopf, New York, 1953), p. 194.

[2] Concerning the power-political model, see Chapter 1, "The Actors in International Politics," and Chapter 6, "The Pole of Power and the Pole of Indifference."

environmentalism to the opposite extreme at which little is seen except traits internal to the actors. The change is hardly surprising since the environmentalist approach was suggesting that the psychology of particular decision-makers or of particular nations was of little consequence—at a time when the world was confronted with an array of leaders from Churchill and Roosevelt to Hitler, Stalin, and lesser dictators whose imprint on the policy of their countries could not well be ignored or minimized and when the arena of world politics was beginning to include more and more nations that differed greatly in national character from Western countries.[3]

As mentioned in the first essay, the reaction against environmentalism has been fruitful despite its one-sidedness. It has brought out the fact that human behavior, in the international as in any other social field, cannot be dissociated from the psychological traits, the personality, or the predisposition of the actors. No matter how powerful the onslaught of external forces, men are not transformed into mere automatons. The danger, as David Easton puts it, lies

---

[3] Harold Lasswell, a pioneer among political scientists in stressing the psychological determinants—which he calls predispositional—does not go to extremes. In the introduction to the book by him and Abraham Kaplan, *Power and Society: A Framework for Political Inquiry* (Yale University Press, New Haven, 1950), predisposition and environment are placed side by side as covariants. But then in the rest of the book nothing more is said about the environment or about the pulls and pressures it exerts on policy-makers. Similarly, R.C. Snyder, H.W. Brooks, and B. Sapin in *Decision-making as an Approach to the Study of International Politics* (Princeton, Foreign Policy Analysis Project Series, 1954) set out by saying that their inquiry will include a discussion of the international situation and its impact on decision-making, but then neglect it during the rest of their study.

The most radical psychopolitical approach is taken by the psychologists, psychiatrists, and sociologists whose views are contained in the two volumes of the "Tensions Project" of UNESCO, *Tensions that Cause Wars* (ed. H. Cantril, University of Illinois Press, Urbana, 1950), and *Tensions Affecting International Understanding* (by Otto Klineberg, Social Science Research Council, New York, 1950), as well as in *Psychological Factors of Peace and War* (ed. T.H. Pear, on behalf of the United Nations Association of Great Britain and Northern Ireland, Hutchinson & Co., London, 1950). Here tension and war are ascribed exclusively to the psychoneurotic traits of the leaders and elites of countries that initiate war, traits that in turn are seen as the result of unhappy childhood experiences of the individuals in question or of social conditions within the countries in which they lived. The international milieu, the clash of interests and demands among nation-states, or the injustices suffered by nations are not given any attention. While some of the social scientists who subscribe to the psychological approach to international affairs may agree with the extreme environmentalists that statesmen are puppets of forces beyond their control, they look into the subconscious self or the neurotic complexes of the actors for the invisible hands pulling the wires.

in an "inordinate commitment to psychology" that "can lead to the concealment of the situational aspect." [4]

There is no doubt that the predisposition of the actors enters into the stream of antecedents to any policy decision; the question is whether predisposition is the predominant factor accounting for the particular mode of behavior of some actors or merely one of the variables. After all, factors external to the actor can become determinants only as they affect the mind, heart, and will of the decision-maker. A human decision to act in a specific way, an event that occurs in the psyche of man, necessarily represents the last link in the chain of antecedents of any act of policy. A geographical set of conditions, for instance, can affect the behavior of a nation only as specific persons perceive and interpret these conditions. To say that insularity leads countries to neglect their military defenses can mean only that decision-makers are more likely to consider their country safe if it enjoys an insular position and that they will tend, as a result, to become complacent in matters of military preparedness. One can speak of geographical "determination," therefore, only in the sense that the actor responds to what he believes are the effects or "dictates" of a geographical condition.[5] Similarly, the capitalist system *per se* would produce an imperialist foreign policy only if it could be shown—a contention the Marxists have not even tried to prove—that capitalists as a matter of predisposition would rather push their countries into imperial conquest than see the margin of profit drop below zero.

Environmental factors, then, operate through a prism, represented by the personal traits of the actor, that may deflect or distort, transform or reflect, these environmental factors in a variety of ways, depending on the internal structure of the prism. Certainly there are striking examples in which an environmental factor, such as the lack of access to the sea, has provoked very similar responses from actors differing as widely in predisposition as the Bolshevik and the Czarist leaders of Russia. But there are other cases that

[4] *Op. cit.,* p. 208.
[5] In their brief and penetrating discussion of the relationship between geography and international politics, "Geography and international politics in an era of revolutionary change" (*Journal of Conflict Resolution,* Vol. IV, No. 1 [March, 1960], p. 147), Harold and Margaret Sprout stress that "what matters in the explanation of decisions and policies is how the actor *imagined* his environment to be, not how it actually was, whereas what matters in the explanation of accomplishments is how the environment actually was, not how the actor imagined it to be."

illustrate the important consequences of differing predispositions. For example, few would maintain that the fate of Czechoslovakia in 1938 would have been the same if the conditions of Europe at the time had been reflected in the mind of a Churchill instead of a Chamberlain or that the United States would have reacted to the North Korean invasion in the fashion it did if Robert Taft had been president of the United States instead of Harry Truman.

It takes a psychologist to identify the many individual traits and internal forces that may come into play whenever events reach that last link in the chain of determinants where choice and decision take place. Emotions and subconscious impulses are involved no less than rational calculations, theories about the outside world no less than images of other actors, stereotypes and myths and obsessions no less than reasoned expectations and creative hypotheses. In extreme cases what an actor may consciously perceive may bear little resemblance to what an objective observer would describe as the environment. But whether distorting or accurate, whether identical for all actors or widely different, there is no denying the role of the "prisms" that comprise the predispositional or psychological elements entering into the process of individual choice and action.

Despite the inevitable presence and under some circumstances predominant impact of psychological factors, their role nevertheless can be exaggerated. Nations as a rule are not governed by mad men who decide and act on the basis of inner impulses in response to a purely imaginary world.[6] Policy-making can, as a rule, be

---

[6] It is often asserted that the initiators of war are men of unbalanced minds, yet no empirical proof has been offered to sustain the thesis. Perhaps such proof is considered unnecessary on the ground that sane men would not start a war with all its horrors. But why then are leaders of social or anticolonial revolutions, frequently as horrible as international wars, not assumed to be neurotics too? In fact, the suspicion of mental imbalance in cases of revolution is more likely to fall on those who stubbornly defend the *status quo* and thereby provoke revolutionary violence. There would seem to be only one plausible explanation for this apparent inconsistency: the exponents of the neurosis hypothesis of war base their views implicitly on a moral judgment about the causes for which men resort to violence. They judge that there can be no injustice in international affairs serious enough to justify a resort to violence and thus to lead sane men to initiate it, while social and ethical injustice, on the contrary, can induce men of balanced minds to prefer the horrors of revolution to the continued perpetration of such injustice. If this explanation is correct, the neurosis hypothesis, though presented as a scientific proposition, turns out to be but another version of the aggression theory of war which, on moral grounds, clearly condemns as evil any initiators of war irrespective of the particular character of the international *status quo* they seek to change by force.

assumed to constitute a relatively rational response to existing and fairly correctly perceived external conditions. A statesman's decision to take action with a view to reunifying his partitioned country may reflect his personal ambitions or may be tainted by a personal inclination to fool himself about the chances of success; the fact remains that he is acting for a partitioned country, an external circumstance, and that efforts to remedy the situation are likely to be forthcoming eventually, whatever the particular psychology of the future leaders of the country. French governments composed of men with widely differing personal traits all sought security for France from what they considered the German threat through a policy of alliances during the period from the 1890's to World War II. Some of these men may have been swayed by false interpretations of existing conditions or by exaggerated fears; nevertheless, the real or potential superiority of the neighbor across the Rhine who demonstrated unsatisfied ambitions constituted an external factor that was bound to guide French reactions whatever the traits of the leading French policy-makers or the mood of the French public.

The psychology of the actors in the international arena, instead of operating in limitless space, is confined in its impact on policy by the limitations that external conditions—the distribution of power, geographical location, demography, and economic conditions—place on the choices open to governments in the conduct of foreign relations. Moreover, the international position of the country goes far in defining its interests and in determining, thereby, the outcome of the rational calculus of interest by which statesmen may generally be assumed to be guided.

Since every act has an infinite number of antecedents which can combine in an infinite number of ways, one must conclude that no two results can ever be identical. Never will two decision-makers find themselves exposed to exactly the same environment or possess exactly the same combination of personal traits; never will the same decision-maker be in an identical situation and with identical moods or ideas on two successive occasions. It is hardly surprising, therefore, that historians whose task it is to investigate specific historical decisions should be struck by the uniqueness of every case, often to the point that they question the possibility of valid generalizations and thus of any theory of behavior in the international arena. Here a nation arms feverishly while there another refuses to be burdened with military expenditure; here a government aggressively pushes its demands on a neighbor while its successor, though no less powerful, makes every effort to conciliate differences with its opponents; here again a strong country bullies its little neighbors while there another goes out of its way to show respect for the rights of weak countries. On first sight there is little to suggest uniformity.

Yet some degree of uniformity of behavior among actors belonging to any specific category is so persistently present that even the historian takes account of it at least by implication. It would make no sense for him to use terms like "great power," "landlocked country," or "have-not nation" in dealing with historical actors if it were not proper to assume that those who belong to one of these generic groups share one or more common traits of behavior, while differing in regard to these same traits from nations belonging to other groups. While few would challenge this assertion, disagreement is rife when it comes to deciding how prevalent and far-reaching such uniformities are, how widely they embrace the nation-states in space and time, and what are the particular combinations of determinants that account for existing similarities and dissimilarities of behavior. Answers can come from theoretical analysis only.

Chapter Four   STATESMANSHIP AND
MORAL CHOICE

THROUGHOUT THE AGES moralists have expressed horror
at the way princes and sovereign states behave toward one another.[1]
Behavior that would be considered immoral by any standard can
obviously be detected in all realms of life; but nowhere does the
contradiction between professed ethical principles and actual behavior appear so patent and universal as in the conduct of foreign
relations. Governments spy on one another and lie to one another;
they violate pledges and conduct wars, often at the cost of millions
of lives and untold misery. No wonder, then, that in Western
democracies if not elsewhere indignation over such practices should
be voiced with vehemence. In our day this frequently expresses
itself in wholesale denunciations of the multistate system on the
ground that sovereign states cannot deal with one another except
by the use of immoral means, derogatorily called "power politics."
Some draw the cynical conclusion that morality has no place in
international politics, while others would have men fulfill their
moral duty by substituting world government for the present immoral political system.

This sweeping moral condemnation of foreign policy as pursued
by all nations points to a striking and disturbing contradiction in
our public life. Most of our statesmen claim to be pursuing policies
of peace and they enunciate high moral principles upon which their
policy is supposed to be based; they and many publicists praise the
democracies for the moral superiority of their conduct of foreign
affairs over that of aggressive and ruthless dictators. Yet at the
same time many respected students in the field of international rela-

[1] This chapter is reprinted, with minor changes, from *World Politics*, Vol. I,
No. 2 (January, 1949), by permission of the publisher.

47

tions insist that all sovereign states alike are compelled by the "system" to play the evil game of power politics. The two positions would seem to be incompatible. Either our statesmen and their supporters are deceiving themselves and others, or those who without discrimination condemn all power politics as immoral are overstating their case. In a country like the United States where moral passion tends to run high and where the question of morality in politics is a matter of genuine and wide concern, it is important to try to resolve this contradiction.

The idea that power politics are beyond the pale of morality is not new. Down through the centuries Machiavelli and Machiavellianism have stood for a doctrine that places princes and sovereign states under the rule not of ordinary morality but of the "reason of state," considered an amoral principle peculiar to the realm of politics.[2] German writers have been particularly insistent that ethical standards that apply to private individuals cannot measure the behavior of states which are said to be guided by necessity if not by a *höhere Sittlichkeit*.[3]

The English-speaking world, not seldom accused of comfortably ignoring or hypocritically denying the contradictions between ethics and international politics, has usually been unwilling to admit of any peculiar ethics of state behavior. Because states are abstractions, or at best fictitious personalities, it is not the state that decides and acts but always individuals, though they be statesmen. Should their behavior be judged differently from that of individuals merely because they act for the state? To answer in the affirmative would mean accepting the hardly more palatable idea of a double standard of morality, according to which individuals when acting for them-

---

[2] One might question whether Machiavelli meant to draw a sharp distinction between the ethics of state behavior (the behavior of "princes") which was his main concern, and the ethics of individual behavior. In the same Chapter 15 of *The Prince,* in which he advises the sovereign to learn "how not to be good," he also speaks generally of the condition of man, saying that "whoever abandons what is done for what ought to be done will rather learn to bring about his own ruin than his preservation." He goes on to say that such a man "must necessarily come to grief among so many who are not good."

[3] Friedrich Meinecke's *Die Idee der Staatsräson* (Munich and Berlin, 1925) is a classic study of the relations between ethics and power politics as seen by Machiavelli and his continental disciples down to Treitschke. No similar study has been written on the views of their Anglo-Saxon contemporaries, although Gerhard Ritter in *Machtstaat und Utopie* (Munich and Berlin, 1914) makes a suggestive beginning to such a study. He contrasts Machiavelli, "pioneer of the continental power state," with Thomas More, "ideological father of the English insular welfare state," the former setting power above morality (p. 31), the latter seeking the "Ethisierung und Entdämonisierung der Macht" (p. 89).

selves shall follow one set of moral principles while the same individuals when conducting their nation's foreign policy shall be
bound by another and presumably less stringent code of behavior.[4]

At first sight the facts seem to bear this out. Do we not condemn
and punish citizens for committing the very acts of violence, treaty
violation, or untruthfulness that we condone in international
politics? Are we not constantly struck by the gulf that separates the
relatively peaceful and humane life within the national borders of
states from the events occurring on the international scene? This
contrast—more apparent than true as we shall see—has led some to
demand that statesmen be made to give up their sinful ways and
conform to the rules of behavior expected from individuals in an
orderly community. Unfortunately, advice of this kind often proves
so patently impractical that instead of inducing statesmen to mend
their ways it provokes in them a sense of moral cynicism. What is
the use of listening to moral advice, they ask, if statesmanship, to be
capable of mastering the problems that present themselves in practice, is apparently incompatible with morality?

The fundamental discrepancy which seems to exist between the
morality of state and private behavior would disappear only if it
could be shown that politics conducted in a multistate system is not
necessarily any more immoral than average private behavior, or
that the chief difference pertains not to the degree of immorality
prevailing in the two spheres of human action but to the circumstances under which men are required to act. Much of what strikes
people as the immoral practices of governments may prove to be
morally justified by the peculiar and unhappy circumstances that
the statesman has to face and, as a rule, cannot hope to change.

Any ethical perfectionist will be shocked at such a suggestion.
He will deny that an action which is evil under one set of conditions could be morally justified under another. If men are held to
be morally bound to act in accordance with an absolute ethic of
love such as the ethic of the Sermon on the Mount, obviously no

[4] While Hans J. Morgenthau (*Scientific Man vs. Power Politics,* University
of Chicago Press, Chicago, 1946, p. 179) declares that "no civilization can be
satisfied with . . . a dual morality," William Ernest Hocking (*The Spirit of
World Politics,* Macmillan Co., New York, 1932) writes that statesmen distrust
public opinion in international affairs because the public "takes for granted
that the codes (for individuals and for states) are the same." E. H. Carr (*The
Twenty Years' Crisis,* 1st ed., Macmillan Co., London, 1940, p. 199) in contrast to these authors asserts that most people, while believing that states
ought to act morally, do not expect of them the same kind of moral behavior
that they expect of themselves and of one another.

set of circumstances, even circumstances in which the survival of a
nation were at stake, could justify a resort to violence, untruthfulness, or treaty violations. The concern for self-preservation and
power in itself would have to be condemned as evil. This being the
case, the ethical perfectionist can offer no advice to statesmen other
than to give up public office and turn their backs on politics. As
some have pointed out, the perfectionist to be consistent must in
fact give the same advice to private citizens, requiring of them that
they abandon their concern for their own welfare, family, or business. If, as Hans Morgenthau holds, "the very act of acting destroys
our moral integrity," only a life of saintliness could come close to
satisfying perfectionist moral commands.[5]

We must address ourselves exclusively then to the nonperfectionist who demands of man not that he follow a code of absolutist
ethical rules—what Max Weber calls the "natural law of absolute
imperatives"—but that he make the best moral choice that circumstances permit.[6]

But surely, it will be objected, no moralist, at least in our culture,
could deviate so far from perfectionist standards as to condone inhuman practices such as the torture of enemy soldiers or the shoot-
ing of hostages even in wartime. One would wish this objection to
be valid always, but the nonperfectionist cannot escape the conclusion that circumstances may justify what superficially appear to be
the most despicable kinds of human conduct. Or would he without
careful prior investigation condemn all members of the French
Resistance movement who, in the face of brutal Nazi tactics, are
said to have answered their enemy in kind? What if they were unable to discover any other alternatives but either to stop the horrors
committed by the Nazis in this repulsive fashion or else to leave
their friends and their cause unprotected? This does not imply that
circumstances morally justify every act of power politics from the
violation of the pledged word to aggression and concentration
camps; in most instances they will not, whether because the cause is
unworthy of such extreme sacrifices or because other means are
available to assure morally preferable results. Nor does it mean
that even where circumstances do justify such acts men may not be
guilty of having brought about these circumstances or of having
failed to remove them.

[5] *Op. cit.*, p. 189.
[6] See Max Weber's "Politics as a Vocation," in *From Max Weber: Essays in
Sociology* (Oxford University Press, New York, 1946) , pp. 120 ff.

There is nothing peculiar to international politics in this impact of circumstance. Our conscience revolts at the idea of men's putting other men to death. Yet nonperfectionist moralists throughout the Western world agree in condoning the acts of those who kill either in self-defense, or in obedience to an order to execute a criminal, or in war, or possibly in the case of tyrannicide. In other cultures it has been considered morally proper, if not a moral duty, to put to death first-born children, aging parents, or widows. One and the same act, then, will be judged differently depending also, of course, on the ethical standards by which behavior is judged generally.

This is not the place to enter upon the age-old discussion of what the standards of a nonperfectionist ethic should be, nor is such a discussion necessary for our purpose. However much nonperfectionists may disagree on ethical standards and thus on the nature and hierarchy of values, they hold in common the process by which they reach their moral judgments. They start with the conviction that there can be no escape from sacrifices of value whether, as theologians maintain, because of man's original sin and essential corruption, or because of the dilemmas of a world in which man is faced with incompatible moral claims. With this as a basis they hold that men, statesmen and private individuals alike, are morally required to choose among the roads open to them the one which under the circumstances promises to produce the least destruction of value or, positively speaking, points toward the maximization of value.[7]

Moral condemnation, according to nonperfectionist ethics, rests not on the destruction of values *per se,* however deplorable such destruction may be judged to be. Instead it is based on the conviction either that the action in question rested on false standards of

[7] Max Weber's "ethic of responsibility" (*op. cit.,* pp. 118 ff.) comes closer to what is here described as a nonperfectionist ethic of maximization of value than it might appear from some of his statements. Weber declares, it is true, that "from no ethics in the world can it be concluded when and to what extent the ethically good purpose 'justifies' the ethically dangerous means and ramifications" (p. 121). He is here taking issue with the revolutionary fanatic who from the point of view of an "ethic of ultimate ends" considers every act of violence justified as long as it serves his ultimate end. But when Weber goes on to demand of men that they hold themselves responsible for the consequences of their acts, especially their acts of violence, he does not refute their moral right to "contract with the diabolic powers of violence" which as political men they must do, but implicitly calls on them to choose the road that will minimize the evil consequences for which they bear responsibility.

value or that in terms of agreed ethical standards a less destructive choice could and should have been made.[8]

Thus a private citizen who breaks family ties in order to serve what he considers a higher cause may find himself condemned because his cause is not considered worth the sacrifice or because there were other less costly ways of attaining his end. Similarly a statesman who decides to break off diplomatic negotiations rather than to accept the terms of the opposing side may be judged wrong because he placed undue value on an increment of national prestige which was at stake or because he failed to appreciate the dangers involved in his choice of action. There is no difference either in the method of evaluation or in the ethical standards, whether the case be one of political or private behavior. In that sense the ethic of politics is but a part of general ethics. The question that remains to be answered, however, is why the sacrifices of value in international politics should be as widespread, continuous, and shocking in extent as they so obviously are. Is it because the circumstances under which foreign policy is conducted are so different, and so unalterably different, from those under which private citizens make their choices?

German writers on international politics have emphasized what they consider a unique and all-pervasive circumstance characteristic of interstate relations. Writing in the heyday of German *Realpolitik,* Gustav Ratzenhofer declared categorically that the relations between sovereign states are unalterably relations of enmity.[9] His assertion reminds one of the no less dogmatic Marxist proposition according to which the relations between capital and labor in a capitalist economy are relations of enemies engaged in a class war.[10]

If one looks at history and the contemporary world, one cannot subscribe to this German view. As discussed earlier in more detail,

[8] Morgenthau (*op. cit.,* pp. 202, 203), following in the footsteps of Max Weber, also emphasizes the "ethical paradoxes" of politics. "Political ethics," he says, "is indeed the ethics of doing evil." Yet he too concludes that "it is moral judgment," meaning presumably the best a man can do, morally, "to choose among several expedient actions the least evil one."

[9] See *Wesen und Zweck der Politik* (Leipzig, 1893).

[10] Carl Schmitt in *Der Begriff des Politischen* (Munich, 1932) modifies Ratzenhofer's thesis by declaring that interstate and, in fact, all truly political relations are in the nature of "friend-foe" relations. While he does not claim that relations between all states at all times are inevitably hostile, he maintains that nations always group themselves as friends and foes and that there could be no such thing as statehood or politics if it were not for the existence of potential enmity, by which he means the possibility of deadly physical combat.

the relations between sovereign states no less than the relations between other groups or individuals run the whole gamut from almost
complete amity—take Canadian-American or Anglo-Canadian relations—to almost unmitigated enmity, as in war. Amity and enmity
appear as the two extremes of a wide scale of human relationships.
It remains true, however, and a matter of great political and moral
consequence, that the multistate system, for reasons which cannot
be analyzed here, has a tendency to push relations between at least
some states in the direction of enmity—and more so in our century
than in the last. The Nazis certainly saw to it that this would be so.
As faithful disciples of Ratzenhofer, Carl Schmitt, and others, they
not only believed in the inevitability of international enmity but
true to their theoretical assumption conducted German policy in
such a way as to arouse the fiercest kind of enmity in most parts of
the world.

The concepts of amity and enmity can usefully shed light on the
context within which statesmen are forced to make their choices.
Amity and enmity stand for the two opposite extremes of human
relationships. Behavior changes as the relationship approximates
one or the other of these extremes. The causes of enmity in interstate relations are significant to the moral problem only to the
extent to which statesmen may be responsible for bringing about or
not eliminating enmity, thereby to become responsible for its
consequences.

One can imagine a condition of complete enmity between states.
There would be no trace of community between them, no sense of
commonly held values or of common interest. Each individual state
would have to be looked upon as an entirely separate entity operating in the social vacuum of absolute anarchy. There would exist a
state of latent if not actual war all the time, turning diplomacy into
warfare with other means. With good reason nations could consider
themselves in a constant state of emergency gravely endangering all
the things to which they attach value. It would be a situation, as
we know from the experience of total war, in which the sheer quest
for survival would justify almost any course of action. "Out-group
morality" of the most extreme type would prevail.

Take the other extreme, that of amity or the friend-to-friend relationship. While there would not be complete identification, a
sense of community would exist sufficient to eliminate mutual fear
and suspicion. There would be no expectation of violence and
therefore no need for preparations with which to meet the dangers

of conflict. Despite the sovereignty of each state, such friendly nations could behave toward one another according to the code of "in-group morality" and live in peace with one another.

The more relations between states degenerate toward enmity the more nations become justified in fearing for the things they cherish and the more reason they have to make and require sacrifices by which inimical claims can be defeated. Greater enmity therefore increases the likelihood that Machiavellian practices will become necessary and morally justified. The degree of amity or enmity thus appears as a morally portentous circumstance. While in a state of amity, statesmen are likely to be able to choose between different avenues toward co-operation, compromise, and conciliation. Enmity may preclude such choices and place before the statesman a different set of alternatives. He may be able to take steps that promise to mitigate if not to eliminate existing enmity. Often, however, he will have to choose between efforts to deter his opponent, with a view toward neutralizing the effects of enmity, and efforts to defeat him.

This cannot be said to be a peculiarity of international politics or of the multistate system. The same phenomenon can be found in relationships between father and son, employer and employee, white man and colored man. There may be complete amity between them with no trace of distrust, no shadow of fear, no concern for self-protection, no awareness of conflicting demands or expectations. Instead, relations may degenerate into fierce hostility for reasons too numerous to detail. Behavior then may change beyond recognition. Two friends have lived in almost perfect harmony. But let suspicion arise that one is seeking to exploit their hitherto harmonious relationship in a treacherous fashion. Immediately, the other may feel justified in spying on his onetime friend; he may start laying traps; the case may end with one's killing the other. What is important to remember is that the killer may be judged to have been neither legally nor morally guilty, provided the treachery was sufficiently flagrant. Not only the courts but public opinion recognizes the excuses of self-defense and unbearable provocation.

Similarly, strife between industrialists and workers may lead to property damage or open violence. Here, again, moral judgment will take the circumstances into account. Public opinion has been aroused at times by the employment of industrial police in labor disputes and by acts of violence on the part of striking workers. In each such case, however, condemnation on the part of fair-minded judges of human behavior is based not so much on the use of tactics of power politics by the group in question as on the insufficiency in a given instance of the provocation or grievances to justify the acts of coercion or violence.

It will be objected, and rightly so, that intrastate relations are less likely than interstate relations to reach a degree of hostility that would call for the use of violence and other Machiavellian devices.[11] The state can also prohibit the use of means to which society is opposed and can enforce its prohibition—although only by those very means the members of the society have renounced for themselves. But only well-organized states can marshal sufficient authority and police power to prevent family feuds and social or racial conflicts from breaking into the open and degenerating into violence and the use of other Machiavellian means. While the pacifying influence of such states and their influence on human behavior should not be minimized, exponents of world government tend to exaggerate the case for statehood as a guarantor of peace. The kind of government and therefore the kind of internal peace that this country presently enjoys represents the exception rather than the rule. Our government operates under conditions, not wholly state-made, of widespread amity among most of the groups that are powerful enough to influence the course of domestic events. The government is recognized as legitimate by practically everyone and is ordinarily obeyed not because it has the force of coercion but because its authority is freely accepted. If one looks at the performance of other governments either in the contemporary world or in past periods of history, one finds no lack of examples of governments operating under quite different conditions and with quite different results.

Some governments are strong and ruthless enough to suppress the hostilities that would otherwise break out between warring factions, ethnic, social, or religious, but they do so by means of

---

[11] Some writers while agreeing that the ethical problems of political and private life are basically the same nevertheless stress the difference, if only quantitative, that makes international power politics the domain of evil *par excellence*. In his earlier works Reinhold Niebuhr stressed the peculiar selfishness and immorality of human communities including the state, as indicated by the title of his book, *Moral Man and Immoral Society* (Charles Scribner's Sons, New York, 1936). Later, however, he came to place more emphasis on the fact that all life is a "contest of power" and that international war and conflict are but a revelation of the general character of human existence and human sinfulness. (See his *Christianity and Power Politics*, Charles Scribner's Sons, New York, 1940, especially pp. 11, 12, 103.)

suppression which is often tyrannical or terroristic. Rather than eliminate Machiavellian practices, such governments merely monopolize them. To what extremes of behavior this may lead has been drastically demonstrated by the way modern totalitarian regimes have persecuted "enemies of the people." Other governments are too weak to control the forces of internal enmity: then there are bloody revolts or civil wars. When this happens enmity often reaches a degree of fierceness that relations between states rarely approximate. Machiavellian practices of the most extreme kind become the order of the day.

Government or statehood, whether national or world-wide, is therefore no panacea against those aspects of power politics that are morally deplorable. The real evil is enmity and its threat to values to which people are devoted.

The moralist, however, needs to be reminded that there is no sure way to eliminate the fateful circumstance of enmity and that at a given time there may be no way at all. Certainly the elimination of the multistate system itself, whether within a region such as Europe or on a world-wide scale, is not one of the objectives statesmen are free to choose and therefore they cannot be considered morally obliged to choose it under all circumstances. Even if a radical change in the existing order were morally desirable because there was reason to suppose that a regional federation or a world government would create circumstances of greater amity than exist today, the psychological prerequisites for a concerted move of major nations toward such a goal are beyond the control of any one government.

If statesmen cannot at all times choose to work for conditions of world-wide amity under world government, is it not their moral duty at least to promote amity at all times and at all costs? Once it is conceded that enmity requires and justifies sacrifices of value often of the most shocking kind, it would seem as if no price paid for amity could be considered too high. Yet, statesmen would be rendered incapable of maximizing value if they were forced to make the quest for amity the sole guide of their actions. Amity is a condition passionately to be desired; but there are times when efforts to bring it about can lead to disaster. It takes two to make friends. An attempt to establish bonds of friendship may be interpreted as a sign of weakness; the result may be aggression. Again the demands of the opponent may call for sacrifices of value greater than those connected with continued enmity. Firmness and even resort to force may under certain circumstances require less loss of life, less human suffering, less destruction of faith and principle than the most sincere attempt to eliminate the causes of hostility by concessions.

This is not the same as saying that power politics generally preclude the opportunity for persistent and active pursuit of amity—or of justice. There are many occasions when disputes can be settled peacefully and when enmity can be eliminated or avoided, provided one side at least has enough courage, imagination, and initiative. Sometimes a spirit of conciliation or even of generosity can do wonders in evoking a ready and sincere response. Whenever the lines of enmity are not irreparably drawn, there may remain room for moderation and self-restraint, for better understanding each of the other's true designs, and for fair compromise. While in the end it needs two to make friends, it is not always the other side that must take the first step.[12]

Only those who extol the value of national "virility" which is supposed to express itself in obstinate resistance to compromise, or those who are afraid of being the suckers will insist that the "necessity of state" is always on the side of toughness and unrelenting assertion of national claims. Harold Nicolson castigates Napoleon for being able to ascribe Castlereagh's "splendid moderation" only to treachery or corruption, to ignorance or folly.[13] Whether moderation is politically practical or suicidal depends on the circumstances. Those who feel called upon to give moral advice to statesmen must be ready, if they are to be true to the nonperfectionist ethic, to demand restraint of power, charity, and forgiveness in one situation, as when feelings of revenge and war passions run high, but to insist on a break with an opponent, if not on the use of violence, when weakness or procrastination threaten to bring on greater evils. If world government not only were practical but would, if established, temper enmities and help nations protect or

[12] Winston Churchill (*The Gathering Storm*, Houghton Mifflin Co., Boston, 1948, p. 320) testifies admirably to these opportunities for statesmanship. He says "those who are prone by temperament and character to seek sharp and clear-cut solutions of difficult and obscure problems, who are ready to fight whenever some challenge comes from a foreign Power, have not always been right. On the other hand, those whose inclination is to bow their heads, to seek patiently and faithfully for peaceful compromise, are not always wrong. On the contrary, in the majority of instances they may be right, not only morally but from a practical standpoint. How many wars have been averted by patience and persisting good will!"

[13] *The Congress of Vienna* (Constable, London, 1946), p. 236.

attain what they rightly value most highly, it would be the moral duty of statesmen to seek to bring it about. As things stand today, however, the obvious lack of consensus among the major nations about the desirability of world government; as well as about the kind of world government they would accept; makes any attempt to establish such a government more likely to lead to war than to reduce enmity.

The existence of enmity and the impossibility of eliminating it at a given moment would appear to dictate to statesmen a course of action often running counter to their moral preferences. Does this not mean that those exponents of *Realpolitik* are right who claim that the statesman, instead of being able to make moral choices, is left with virtually no leeway, having to bow instead to the dictates of the "necessity of state"?

It confuses the moral issue to state the case in this way. The "necessities" in international politics, and for that matter in all spheres of life, do not push decision and action beyond the realm of moral judgment; they rest on moral choice themselves. If a statesman decides that the dangers to the security of his country are so great as to make necessary a course of action that may lead to war, he has placed an exceedingly high value on an increment of national security.

Necessities of a similar kind are known to private citizens. Parents may decide that in order to save the family business they must try to get their son to enter the family firm. Although they know they are asking him to choose a career he abhors, they are ready to sacrifice his happiness to the necessity of family. A trade union leader who calls a strike which he knows will be ruinous to patrons to whom he is devoted makes and requires a painful sacrifice for the necessities of the labor movement. In every such case conflicting values, interests, and loyalties call for choices in which what is deemed to be the higher cause or value calls for submission to its necessities.

The necessity or reason of state is but another of these necessities of life which become compelling only as a particular pattern of values is accepted. If the position of the statesman differs from that of private citizens it is because he must take upon himself the responsibility for sacrifices of value in order that others, as a nation, may protect or attain the things they treasure. He may feel in duty bound to take responsibility for such sacrifices even though in a given instance he may disagree with the moral judgment of

those to whom he is responsible. In that sense if in no other it may
be justifiable to speak of the peculiar "demonic" quality of politics
and public office, as Max Weber and other writers frequently do.

There is good reason why the controversy about the relationship
between necessity of state and ethical standards should be rife in
our culture. The clash is between two sets of ethical standards, one
Christian or humanistic, the other nationalistic. Nationalistic ethics
place what are called vital national interests, and not national survival only, at the very pinnacle of the hierarchy of values. The
preservation or attainment of these values—territorial integrity,
colonial possessions, *lebensraum*, treaty rights, or economic interests
—are assumed therefore to justify the sacrifice of almost every other
value whether it be life, generosity, humane treatment of others,
truthfulness, or obedience to the law. The interests of other nations
count for little, if anything, on a nationalistic scale of values.

While those who adhere to nonperfectionist Christian or humanistic ethical views accept sacrifices of value as inescapable, as non-
nationalists they may in the case of any policy decision nevertheless
question whether a particular national interest is worth the sacrifices required or whether it could not be protected by a less costly
method. This may not seem to hold true when national survival
itself is unquestionably at stake. Because the multistate system rests
on the coexistence of a multitude of independent states, it is incompatible with any ethic that would forbid sacrifices necessary for
national survival. Moral advice not to submit to the necessities of
survival not only would be advice to commit national suicide but
would if followed tend to wreck the multistate system itself.[14]

----

[14] It is not surprising that authors who believe that international politics
are essentially a struggle for national survival should reach very pessimistic
ethical conclusions. Thus, Nicholas J. Spykman (*America's Strategy in World
Politics*, Harcourt, Brace & Co., New York, 1942, p. 12) bases his case on the
proposition that the "struggle for power is identical with the struggle for
survival" and that states can survive only by constant devotion to power
politics. Although the use of power "should be constantly subjected to moral
judgments," Spykman concludes that the "statesman can concern himself with
values of justice, fairness and tolerance only to the extent that they contribute
to or do not interfere with the power objective," meaning the quest for survival.
In his further statement that the quest for power is not made for the "achieve-
ment of moral values" he is taking issue with those exponents of nationalistic
ethics who place supreme moral value on national survival. See also in this
connection Mortimer Adler's statement in *How to Think about War and Peace*
(Simon & Schuster, New York, 1944, p. 78) that "so long as national self-
preservation remains the dominant end for which prudence must choose means,
the principles of morality cannot be reconciled with the counsels of prudence."

As a matter of fact, the controversy between exponents of nation-alistic and nonnationalistic ethical standards in our culture is not over the moral right to pay the price of survival. None but perfectionists or absolute pacifists deny a nation which is engaged in a life and death struggle the right to make and demand every sacrifice necessary for self-preservation.

The nonperfectionist does not have to capitulate before every alleged necessity of state. Nations engaged in international politics are faced with the problem of survival only on rare occasions. How otherwise could most of the nations that have attained independence in recent centuries have survived when surely most of them most of the time have been devoted to anything but an unrestrained quest for power? If ever any country did employ Machiavellian principles consciously and methodically it was Hitler's Germany, but as a result Germany lost its independence as conclusively as have few great nations.

As a rule, not survival but other "national interests" are at stake such as the preservation of outlying bases and possessions, the protection of treaty rights, the restoration of national honor, or the maintenance of economic advantages. While it is a prerequisite of the system that nations attach a high if not the highest value to their survival, the same cannot be said of all of these other national interests. As a matter of fact, the moral dilemmas constantly facing statesmen and their critics revolve around the question of whether in a given instance the defense or satisfaction of interests other than survival justifies the costs in other values. Does the expropriation of American investments abroad, for instance, justify the choice of military intervention rather than of unpromising negotiation? Is it morally preferable to risk a loss of prestige with its possible dangerous consequences for the safety of the country rather than to insist on maintaining a position that threatens to provoke hostilities? In every case the interpretation of what constitutes a vital national interest and how much value should be attached to it is a moral question. It cannot be answered by reference to alleged amoral necessities inherent in international politics; it rests on value judgments.

Even national survival itself, it should be added, is a morally compelling necessity only as long as people attach supreme value to it. In that sense the multistate system itself depends on a value pattern in which there is an element of nationalism. If at any time those who have the power to decide over the foreign policies of the major countries should come to attach higher value to the attainment of world government than to the preservation of independence, the psychological obstacle (though not necessarily all other practical obstacles) to world government would be removed.[15] Until that happens nations are likely to consent to all kinds of Machiavellian practices, however much they may abhor them, whenever their independence can be saved in no other way.

International politics offer some opportunities and temptations for immoral action on a vast and destructive scale; these opportunities tend to present themselves in the guise of "necessity of state." Statesmen in command of the machinery by which public opinion is manipulated may make it appear as if they were acting for the sake of objectives to which the people attach high value when in fact they are out to serve personal material interests or to satisfy personal ambitions for power. Where men wield as much power as they do in international politics there is room for an infinite variety of abuses for which the "necessity of state" can serve as a convenient cloak. Then again, statesmen may sincerely believe that vital national interests dictate a particular course of action; but judged by nonnationalistic standards of ethics they may be placing undue value on certain interests of their people or underestimating the value of things not pertaining to their nation which their policy would sacrifice.

While this makes moral criticism and self-criticism imperative, the difficulties standing in the way of such criticism's proper use in international politics need to be emphasized. If it is hard for policymakers to make proper moral choices, it is not any easier for others to do justice to the statesmen's conduct of foreign policy.

It is a baffling task, almost exceeding human capacity, to compare the value of an increment of national security with the value of human lives, or the value of a continued period of peace with the

---

[15] R.M. MacIver (*The Web of Government*, Macmillan Co., New York, 1947) suggests that these basic value judgments may change as the old myths of national sovereignty and national interests lose their grip on people, while Arnold Toynbee (*A Study of History*, Oxford University Press, New York and London, 1947, p. 229), passing moral judgment, denounces the "pagan worship of sovereign nation-states" calling it a "monstrous product of the impact of parochialism on the Western Christian Church." See also in this connection Harold Lasswell, *World Politics and Personal Insecurity* (McGraw-Hill, New York and London, 1935), who devotes Chapter XI, "In Quest of a Myth: The Problem of World Unity," to the problem of how, by the use of symbols, myths, and other practices, human value judgments might be changed in favor of world unity.

risks of a more destructive war in the future. Yet the statesman is faced with even more exacting and truly terrifying problems. Forced to make his choices whenever a decision is called for, he may have to compare the value of an uncertain chance of greater security with only roughly predictable risks of conflict and destruction. It may be easy with hindsight, years after the event, to condemn a statesman for having failed to maximize value; but it also becomes increasingly difficult as time goes on to do justice to the inevitable lack of knowledge and foresight under which the decision-maker labored at the time.

The trouble with much of the moral condemnation of foreign policies and with much of the moral advice tendered to statesmen goes back to a lack of appreciation of the kind of knowledge required for proper and useful moral criticism in international affairs. From a nonperfectionist point of view the circumstances, however technical, have to be taken into consideration; moral conviction and high ideals, much as they are needed to guide moral judgment, cannot by themselves offer an answer. Nor is this true in international politics only. One needs some knowledge of economics to judge whether an industrialist is exploiting his workers; he may be paying the highest wages the traffic will bear. One needs psychological understanding to decide whether in a particular situation divorce represents morally the least evil choice.

Similarly, in international politics where the circumstances are no less involved and technical, moral convictions cannot tell what roads are open to a statesman for the specific conditions under which he is forced to act, nor can they reveal what are likely to be the political consequences and therefore the relative costs in terms of value of any one of several courses of action. Will an alliance provoke war or will the failure to make a commitment tempt an aggressor? Will an appeal to the United Nations in a given case help bring about a peaceful settlement or instead create graver tension, perhaps even going so far as to destroy the organization? Disarmament may be morally the best choice under one set of circumstances; it may be downright evil in another set which places a nation—and small nations dependent upon it for their security—at the mercy of an ambitious conqueror. The same holds true for all the other panaceas or devices so dear to the hearts of those who are most quickly ready to give moral advice to policy-makers or to condemn them for their actions. In one context it may be right to offer concessions whereas in another the same concessions may constitute "appeasement" with all of its evil consequences.

The rule that no general principle can guide nonperfectionist moral judgment on all occasions may appear to have one exception. It might seem proper to assume that the "defensive" side is always right or that every action is justified, if it is necessary for the protection and preservation of values already possessed. Unfortunately, while individuals can disprove their guilt if they rightly can claim to have acted in self-defense, the case of nations is far more complex. Neither the nation's self nor its possessions are clearly circumscribed. May a nation defend as its self and its possessions only its territorial integrity and independence, or does the right of self-defense cover a way of life, national honor, living space, prestige, colonial possessions, and economic rights abroad? *Status quo* powers whose main concern is the preservation of the values they possess and the defense of the established order are prone to blame all Machiavellianism on those nations seeking to bring about change, whether it be revision of treaties, revolution of the social order, or liberation from foreign domination. Yet, the "offensive" side may have a valid case for insisting that it has a vital need for things withheld from it and rightly may value them to a point where any means of attaining them become morally justified. Those who refuse to make the sacrifices of change or who having brought about an unjust distribution of possessions and power, are unwilling to correct such distribution may be guilty of provoking enmity and aggression. Their opponents are not necessarily at fault, then, merely because they want change urgently or because they despair of any means short of violence. The *beati possidentes* may be more peaceful and less inclined to initiate open hostility, but their guilt may lie in their self-righteous and blind devotion to the *status quo* or in the resentment they evoke in others.

Despite the difficulties in doing justice to the statesman and in avoiding the pitfalls of politically dangerous as well as morally untenable condemnations, men who have nonperfectionist and non-nationalistic moral convictions dare not evade the task of moral judgment whether of their own political acts or of the acts of others. Where there is as much room for moral choice as there is in international politics and where the destiny of entire nations depends on the choice, attempts to evade, silence, or ignore moral judgment merely play into the hands of those who relish the uncriticized use or abuse of power. The Nazi leaders were helped by the climate of moral cynicism that prevailed in Germany; this made it easy for them to justify even the most brutal acts on the grounds of necessity of state and to glorify their freedom from any "decadent" moral inhibitions.

The world will not fail to suffer from the immoral acts of statesmen, as of other men, in the future as it has in the past. Nor does it look as though nations would soon be freed from the bitter consequences of international enmity, or from the appalling sacrifices inflicted and justified in the name of national interest and survival. A single powerful government engaged, for whatever reasons, in a policy of aggression and aggrandizement may force all others into line with its Machiavellian practices, provided these others have the will to survive. Moral exhortations and intentions will serve little unless the causes of such aggression and the dangers inherent in it are removed.

Yet international politics are not beyond the pale of nonnationalistic, nonperfectionist morality. Statesmen need not be fooling either themselves or others if they contend, as they frequently do, that in specific instances they have restrained their nation's quest for power; nor need they apologize if, on occasion, they choose a conciliatory or even a generous course of action when a more egotistical policy would promise more tangible national benefits. Despite the continued strength of nationalist sentiment in all parts of the world, there is no reason to assume that people value none but national benefits. They often attach a great deal of value to a good record of international collaboration and at times applaud a leader who takes risks for the good will, the amity, or the interests of other nations— or seeks to keep his own conscience and that of his people clear.

This explains why under certain circumstances a national government might receive the backing of its people even in sacrificing national independence itself, particularly if this were done for the purpose of establishing a better international order, perhaps by means of a regional federation. From the point of view of nonnationalistic ethics, national self-sacrifice for world government might also appear morally justified if there were assurance of enough amity and all-round consent to permit the establishment and functioning of an orderly and humane government of the world; national self-sacrifice would deserve to be condemned if it led to world tyranny or world anarchy. There are historical instances when such sacrifice of independence has justified itself in the eyes of almost everybody, as when the thirteen American states federated successfully.

Under the circumstances usually prevailing in a multistate system painful limitations are set on policies of self-negation, generosity, or restraint of power. It would be utopian to expect a drastic change in this respect. But to say that the field of international politics is reserved for selfishness, brutality, self-righteousness, or unrestrained ambition for power is not only cynical but manifestly unrealistic.

Chapter Five

THE GOALS OF
FOREIGN POLICY

IT MIGHT SEEM that the mere existence of a multitude of nation-states, each capable of independent decision and action, would suffice to explain the peaceless state of the world and the power struggles that fill the international arena. Undoubtedly, the anarchical condition inherent in any sytem of multiple sovereignty constitutes one of the prerequisites of international conflict; without it, there could be no international relations, peaceful or non-peaceful. Yet, in the last analysis, it is the goals pursued by the actors and the way they go about pursuing them that determine whether and to what extent the potentialities for power struggle and war are realized. This can be seen by imagining two extreme sets of conditions, both theoretically compatible with a multistate system, in which, as a consequence of the wide differences in the objectives pursued by the states in question as well as in the means they are willing to employ, the chances of peace would stand at opposite poles.

Starting at one pole, one can postulate a situation in which all actors are entirely satisfied with the established state of international affairs, and are content, therefore, to concern themselves exclusively with domestic matters. In this case, they would have no incentive to make or press demands on others. As a consequence, there would be no rational cause for conflict or for disturbances of the peace. Needless to say, this is a utopia. In some historical instances, however, conditions so nearly approached this extreme that to some observers the utopia appeared within reach, while in other times various schools of thought held it up as at least a goal toward which policy should be directed.

Thus, since the days of Cobden, free-traders have argued that if governments ceased to interfere with commercial activities across borders the chief source of international conflict would be removed. Others have pleaded instead for economic autarchy which, by eliminating the need for international economic intercourse altogether, would make economic demands on others unnecessary. Then again, the satisfaction of demands for national self-determination, one of the cornerstones of Woodrow Wilson's peace strategy, was expected to eliminate a potent cause of international conflict. If every nation had the government of its choice and if every ethnic group were united within the boundaries of a single state, demands for more territory or for independence, objectives most conducive to war, would lose their *raison d'être*. It might be added that some have advocated policies of isolation and neutrality on the same grounds: a condition of dissociation among nations would reduce their interdependence and thus minimize the occasions for conflict. My purpose here is not to determine whether such policies are practical or desirable, but to draw attention to the close relationship between foreign policy objectives and the incidence of tension that might lead to a resort to violence.

This close relationship appears confirmed if one moves to the other pole and postulates that nations are engaged in making exacting demands on one another and are prepared to fight rather than give in. Actually, to be able to predict very serious threats to the peace, one need only assume that a single powerful actor within a multistate system is bent on attaining goals of territorial expansion or dominion over others, because resistance to any drive toward acquisitive goals of this nature is almost certain to materialize. The stage is thus set for clashes that justify a high expectation of violence.

Before looking into the kinds of goals or objectives that nations tend to pursue in their external activities, one semantic hurdle must be taken. It is customary to distinguish between goals and means, a custom I intend to follow to a certain extent; yet it is impossible to draw a sharp line of demarcation between the two ideas. All means can be said to constitute intermediary or proximate goals, and few goals if any can be considered ultimate, in the sense of being sought as ends in themselves. Even when a nation aims for a goal as highly valued as national independence, it can be argued that the nation is seeking such independence as a means of providing its citizens with benefits other than national independence itself.[1]

To make things more complicated, what constitutes a means or intermediate goal in one context may be a remote if not ultimate goal in another, with specific objectives changing places from one instance to another. Thus, enhanced power may be sought as a means of obtaining more territory, while the acquisition of more territory in turn may be desired as a means of enhancing national power. In the case of Europe prior to the establishment of NATO, the question was whether what was needed most was higher productivity as a means of increasing defensive strength or conversely whether more defensive strength providing a greater sense of security was not a prerequisite of greater efforts toward higher productivity.

Because the objectives a nation seeks to reach can range from the most immediate means to the most remote or ultimate ends, all goals will be taken to fall within the scope of this chapter with the single exception of power and influence. The justification for this exception should become clear when the unique position of these two values as the means *par excellence* for the attainment of all other foreign policy goals is discussed.[2] The fact that power may be turned into an end in itself will be taken into consideration in that connection.

Despite the difficulties and complications arising out of the way ends can serve one another as means, it often becomes necessary to inquire whether a nation is seeking certain results from its policy primarily for the results' own sake or merely as means of reaching more remote goals. If a nation is helping others through economic aid to raise their standard of living, it may make a great deal of difference for the chances that such aid will be continued or extended whether the nation extending the aid considers economic improvement abroad as being desirable in itself, or promotes it merely for the sake of cementing its alliance with the assisted

[1] Percy Corbett, for instance, points out that "for democratic purposes it seems worthwhile to insist that the prime object of foreign policy . . . is the welfare of the individuals and groups organized as a national society" and goes on to conclude that "insofar as territorial integrity and political independence are judged to minister to that welfare, they may well be described as the mediate and instrumental objective to which foreign policy is especially directed." "National Interest, International Organization, and American Foreign Policy," *World Politics,* Vol. V, No. 1 (October, 1952) , p. 51.

[2] See Chapter 7, "Power and Influence: The Means of Foreign Policy."

country or of drawing that country over to its own side. To take another example, there has been uncertainty in Europe whether American support for European integration implies that the United States believes such integration to be a good thing in itself—worthy therefore of continued support, cold war or no cold war—or whether greater European unity is valued solely as a means of strengthening Western defenses. Then again, the importance of aim or purpose may be illustrated by a question that has led to much controversy. Some see the Soviet Union supporting revolutionary movements abroad because world revolution *per se* is the goal of Soviet policy; others maintain that the aim is to bolster the security of the Soviet Union as a nation-state, and the revolutions can count on Soviet support only when and where they are expected to enhance the power of the Soviet Union and its alliances. Frequently, of course, a single means can serve to promote two or more concurrent ends. The Soviet leaders being both the rulers of Russia and the leaders of world communism may be unable themselves to distinguish between their national and world revolutionary goals and interests.

As soon as one seeks to discover the place of goals in the means-end chain of relationships, almost inevitably one is led to probe into the dark labyrinth of human motives, those internal springs of conscious and unconscious actions which Morgenthau calls "the most illusive of psychological data." [3] Yet if one fails to inquire why actors choose their goals, one is forced to operate in an atmosphere of such abstraction that nothing is revealed but the barest skeleton of the real world of international politics.

It is understandable that historians have devoted so much time to probing the motives of actors. Although the success of an act such as an effort to pacify an area does not depend on the nature of the motivation, overt behavior remains unintelligible except in relation to motivation. An act of intervention may be the same in its outward appearance whether it is motivated by imperialist design or by the desire to help a people throw off the yoke of a tyrannical government. However, when other governments are making up their minds how to react to such intervention or deciding what to expect from the intervening nation in future contingencies, they cannot avoid seeking to discover what it was that prompted the particular action.

[3] Hans J. Morgenthau, *Politics Among Nations: The Struggle for Power and Peace* (3rd ed., Alfred A. Knopf, New York, 1960), p. 6.

If nations are seen to desire a wide variety of accomplishments and gains ranging all the way from such ambitious ends as empire or predominance to mere trade advantages, opportunities for cultural exchanges, or voting rights in international organizations, one might expect that whatever a nation values and can attain only from other nations will automatically be transformed into a foreign policy objective. This is not the case. Leading statesmen may give expression to hopes or ideals of their people, but these hopes do not, thereby, become what properly can be called policy goals. They will become goals only if the decision is reached that some national effort involving sacrifices, or the risk of sacrifices, is to be made for their realization. All goals are costly. Therefore an aspiration will not be turned into a policy goal unless it is sufficiently cherished by those who make and influence policy to justify the costs that its attainment is expected to require in terms of sacrifices. The American people, or influential Americans, may place high value on the liberation of satellite peoples; the question is whether such liberation is valued highly enough to turn it into an American foreign policy goal for which a high price possibly would be paid.

Picturing aspirations and goals at opposite poles is not accurate. One might better regard them as the two ends of a continuum that runs from mere hopes to goals of vital interest. "Liberation," declared a goal of American policy at the beginning of the Eisenhower Administration, is more than a mere hope as long as it is promoted by propaganda that risks enhancing East-West tension; when one speaks of peaceful liberation one implies that the goal is not considered vital enough to justify a resort to force. World revolution is not merely a hope, but a goal of Soviet foreign policy. Yet, while it may be close to the pole of vital goals usually assumed to justify the resort to violence, it may be sufficiently removed from this pole to keep Soviet policy-makers from initiating a war for the sake of its promotion. Statesmen are well advised to keep in mind that threats to the peace may arise if other nations are left uncertain whether or not national spokesmen who proclaim national aspirations have actually decided to turn a particular aspiration into a policy goal, possibly a goal deemed vital enough to warrant risking or sacrificing the peace.

In analyzing international politics, there would be no need to concern oneself with the problem of goals if nation-states were single-purpose organizations. If they were, states would never consent to make sacrifices for purposes—such as the promotion of peace

—that obviously do not constitute their sole objective. It should be added, however, that even if foreign policy were directed predominantly toward a single goal, such a goal would not monopolize the entire activity of states, except in the extreme emergency of a war. Always there would remain the many domestic goals which no government can ignore and which compete for resources with whatever external purposes the nation may be pursuing. Often these domestic objectives place the severest restraints on external aspirations, as one can gather from any parliamentary debate in which the demand for financial appropriations to meet the needs of external pursuits runs up against demands to increase social benefits or to reduce taxes.

Appearances to the contrary, there is no division of opinion among analysts of international politics about the fact that the policy of nations aims at a multitude of goals. Some exponents of realist thought have been misunderstood to hold that power or even maximum power represents the only significant goal. Authors like Nicholas Spykman and Hans Morgenthau have contributed to this misapprehension, the first by stating on one occasion that "the improvement of the relative power position becomes the primary objective of the internal and the external policy of states," [4] the latter by his statement that "the aspiration for power is the distinguishing element of international politics." [5] However, Morgenthau also stresses that power is only an immediate aim or chief means of foreign policy,[6] while Spykman, relating the quest for power to the task of survival, mentions the existence of other objectives that are "geographic, demographic, racial, ethnic, economic, social and ideological in nature." [7]

The goals of national independence, territorial integrity, and national survival which figure so large in the foreign policy of all nation-states are not uniform in scope or character and must, therefore, be treated as significant variables. Governments conceive of these cherished values in more or less moderate and in more or less ambitious and exacting terms. A good illustration is offered by colonial powers. Only those among them who insist that their "colonies"—or some of them—are not colonies at all but an integral part of their national territory are led to treat the preservation of

[4] Nicholas John Spykman, *America's Strategy in World Politics: The United States and the Balance of Power* (Harcourt, Brace & Co., New York, 1942) , p. 18.
[5] Morgenthau, *op. cit.*, p. 31.
[6] *Ibid.*, p. 27.
[7] Spykman, *op. cit.*, p. 17.

these areas as a requirement of national survival and thus as a vital goal that justifies almost any sacrifice. The new postcolonial states present another illustration of differences in outlook among different actors. Some insist that any continuing ties with the mother country are unacceptable because such ties would defeat the goal of sovereign independence; others favor "union" or commonwealth types of association in the interest of economic welfare, provided the goal of sovereign equality is attained.

The goal of national survival itself is given a wide variety of interpretations by different countries or countries facing different conditions. Nations intent upon keeping their involvement in international conflicts at a minimum are inclined to consider their survival at stake only when their own territory comes under the threat of attack or actually is attacked. The idea of "indivisible peace" which would require them to participate in collective action against any aggressor anywhere has little appeal to them. In contrast, a nation engaged in a global struggle, as the United States is today, will tend to regard any shift in the balance of power that favors its adversary as at least an indirect threat to its own survival. As a consequence, it may consider its survival at stake in a conflict over remote and intrinsically unimportant islands such as Quemoy and Matsu or over legal rights in West Berlin on the ground that, by an assumed domino effect or chain reaction, defeat at any one point will lead to defeat at every other point, until in the end all chances of survival are nullified.

No attempt will be made here to identify and classify all the many goals that nations set for themselves or may set for themselves in the framework of their foreign policy. Instead, I shall limit myself to a discussion of what appear to be particularly significant and persistent groups of contrasting goals. Most of them are in the nature of dichotomies; in the case of the goals pertaining to the national "self" and its accepted limits, however, a distinction into three categories has suggested itself. These will be treated in a later chapter as goals of national self-extension, national self-preservation, and national self-abnegation.[8]

One can distinguish goals pertaining, respectively, to national possessions and to the shape of the environment in which the nation operates. I call the former "possession goals," the latter "milieu goals." In directing its foreign policy toward the attainment of its possession goals, a nation is aiming at the enhancement or the pres-

[8] See Chapter 6, "The Pole of Power and the Pole of Indifference."

ervation of one or more of the things to which it attaches value. The aim may apply to such values as a stretch of territory, membership in the Security Council of the United Nations, or tariff preferences. Here a nation finds itself competing with others for a share in values of limited supply; it is demanding that its share be left intact or be increased. Because of the possessive nature of these goals, they are apt to be praised by some for being truly in the national interest, while condemned by others as indicating a reprehensible spirit of national selfishness or acquisitiveness.

Milieu goals are of a different character. Nations pursuing them are out not to defend or increase possessions they hold to the exclusion of others, but aim instead at shaping conditions beyond their national boundaries. If it were not for the existence of such goals, peace could never become an objective of national policy. By its very nature, peace cannot be the possession of any one nation; it takes at least two to make and have peace. Similarly, efforts to promote international law or to establish international organizations, undertaken consistently by many nations, are addressed to the milieu in which nations operate and indeed such efforts make sense only if nations have reason to concern themselves with things other than their own possessions.[9]

Milieu goals often may turn out to be nothing but a means or a way station toward some possession goal. A nation may hope to increase its prestige or its security by making sacrifices for the establishment and maintenance of international organizations. But this need not be its exclusive aim. Instead, the nation in question may be seriously concerned about the milieu within which it operates and may expect such organizations to improve the environment by making it more peaceful or more conducive to social or economic progress. Here for once the analogy with the behavior and interests of individuals should not be misleading. A man is rightly considered not merely selfish but shortsighted in terms of his own interests

[9] Dean Acheson expresses approval of the pursuit of such goals by the United States "so as to maintain an environment favorable to our interests" (*A Democrat Looks at His Party*, Harper & Bros., New York, 1955, p. 62). Writing in the same vein, Paul A. Nitze says that the United States "can no longer look merely to its narrow competitive interests within whatever structure happens, from time to time, to exist as a result of the policy and will of others or as a result of the chance operations of impersonal forces. If this is so, it follows that a basic objective of U.S. foreign policy is the creation and maintenance of a system of world order within which U.S. interests and U.S. security can find their satisfaction." (Annex A, "The Purpose of United States Military and Economic Assistance," from the *Study* submitted to the President's Committee to Study the United States Military Assistance Program, March, 1959).

if he puts all his efforts into the accumulation and protection of his possessions while remaining indifferent to the peace and order, the public health and well-being of the community in which he resides or works. These are aspects of his milieu, as the term is used here. It is one thing to be in good physical or financial condition within an orderly and prosperous community, but quite another thing to be privileged by the wealth of one's possessions in surroundings of misery, ill health, lack of public order, and widespread resentment. The difference need not be one only of greater or lesser security of acquired possessions; it may also signify a difference in happiness, in future opportunities, and perhaps in moral satisfaction.

Nations also face these differences in their milieu, although it is up to them to decide to what extent they wish to devote their resources to the benefits they may hope to derive from helping to preserve or improve conditions prevailing beyond their borders. There is bound to be competition here with the demands that their goals of possession, some of them pressing and vital, make on the limited national resources. Statesmen and peoples called upon to allot priorities among goals that belong to these two categories often face trying dilemmas. Recent debates on aid to underdeveloped countries supply ample material to illustrate these dilemmas. Is it desirable to divert, to the promotion of a more friendly environment or to the satisfaction of a generous public impulse to help underprivileged peoples, funds that otherwise might go into the build-up of military forces?

In considering this question, one might be tempted to substitute for "milieu goals" the term international goals. There is, however, danger in using the word international here because it might suggest either that these goals are not in the national interest or that governments can and should pursue goals other than those concerning the national interest.[10] The likelihood of milieu goals' being

[10] Thomas Cook and Malcolm Moos (*Power Through Purpose: The Realism of Idealism as a Basis for Foreign Policy,* The Johns Hopkins Press, Baltimore, 1954, p. 138), declaring that nations should substitute "international interests" for the traditional interests, claim that the American people's "root concern" and "ultimate concept" is the "spreading and sharing . . . of its societal blessings." They are pleading, in other words, for "milieu goals" as a substitute for national possession goals on the ground that the latter consist exclusively of the goals of national glory and aggrandizement, values alien to the American people. They disregard the fact that no nation could hope to survive if it failed to be concerned about its own independence and territorial integrity, core possession goals of all nation-states.

also in the national interest of other countries does not make them
less valuable; it only points up that nations find themselves sharing
common interests. If some critics of milieu goals expect their country always to be the loser if it engages in costly efforts by which
others benefit, they fail to realize that any promotion of peace or
international lawfulness, any fight against the trade in narcotics or
the spread of epidemics, to cite only a few examples, depends on
concerted efforts by many nations—and such efforts are not likely
to be forthcoming unless they are in the common interest.

Not all criticism of efforts directed toward milieu goals can, however, be discounted in this fashion. Frequently enthusiasm for
such goals stems from an inclination to downgrade certain values
that nations cherish highly—and need not be ashamed to cherish—
such as adequate national security and its military prerequisites.
Thus, nations have been advised to act on the principle of collective
security, in the strict sense of the term, in order to help create a
milieu in which threats to national possessions will cease to arise.
But even assuming that such a milieu would be created, it is at
best a long-run goal. In the meantime much can happen to a nation
that diverts its limited military power from the task of protecting
itself against immediate and specific threats to the task of "police
action" in places where its survival is not at stake.

Another case of what may turn out often to be excessive zeal for
a milieu goal takes the form of advice to wealthy countries to concentrate on lessening mass poverty and economic maldistribution
throughout the world. Here again, immediate needs of self-preservation, which include the need for internal unity and public support
of the government, place limits on the extent to which the pursuit
of this goal is rational under given circumstances.

It has been argued that it is incompatible with the essence of
national statehood to devote efforts to the creation of a "better
world for all to live in." There is nothing, however, in the functions the nation-state performs to prevent it from engaging in acts
of altruism if its people or its rulers so desire and if in the judgment
of its leaders it can afford to do so. A government that had assured
its country of adequate security would not be violating its duties
if it extended help to friendly nations without concern for the
advantages its own country might expect to gain in return. Whether
such altruistic acts are likely to occur, or whether, if a government
claimed credit for them, its motives would be found to have been
as pure as one were asked to believe, is another question. Acts of

national foreign policy expressing a generous and sympathetic impulse—as was surely the case when the United States launched the Marshall Plan—usually will be found to have served the national security interest or economic interest of the donor as well. The same is true, too, of many acts of individual generosity and charity which may pay high "dividends" to the donor and yet be a moral credit to him. But while an altruistic act by an individual is likely to benefit the actor more if he is not conscious of serving his own interests too, usually when nations are involved suspicion of hypocrisy will be easily aroused; self-righteous claims of pure benevolence, by hurting the pride of others, will diminish the desirable effect of greater amity. For this reason it is wise for governments and peoples to be aware of—and in fact to stress—the element of national self-interest, however farsighted, that leads nations to improve the milieu by rendering services to others.

Another distinction between contrasting goals has been touched upon earlier: the distinction between goals arising from interests of the citizens as private individuals and from state interests, respectively.[11] While it was denied that state interests were the interests of a nonhuman Leviathan, nevertheless a significant difference exists between goals meant primarily to serve the nation as a state or territorial entity and goals that are of prime interest to individual citizens or groups of citizens in their private capacity. If the latter benefit the nation as a whole, this can only be in an indirect fashion. Therefore, I call the first "direct national goals," the second, "indirect national goals."

Some goals like national independence or national security unmistakably are direct national goals. They have no meaning for men as private individuals except as these individuals identify themselves with their nation-state. The erection of tariff barriers, on the contrary, is of interest primarily to those private groups that expect to profit from tariff protection and it may or may not be advantageous to the nation as a whole. When tariff protection is made the objective of national policy it becomes an indirect national goal.

There is no yardstick by which to decide whether the promotion of any particular interest of larger or smaller groups of citizens deserves to be turned into a national goal, but it would be absurd to maintain that no goal can be in the national interest unless it is of the direct type. In a democratic society the state is not regarded

[11] See Chapter 1, "The Actors in International Politics."

as an end in itself or as an absolute good. We assume that the state must justify itself by its ability to insure such values as liberty, welfare, and happiness to its citizens. Although in promoting such values the nation usually will benefit some people more than others and frequently even serve some at the expense of others—as in the case of tariffs, subsidies, or bars to immigration—this inequity does not in itself militate against such promotion. It greatly increases the difficulty, however, of deciding what is and what is not in the interest of the nation as a whole. Not everything that is good for General Motors—or for the auto workers—is good for the nation, but it can be.

It should be pointed out that indirect national goals are not a peculiarity of democratic foreign policy although they are alien to Communist countries in which private interests have no place at all. But a difference between democratic and autocratic countries may show up in the kind of private interests believed worthy of becoming an object of national concern. While in modern mass democracies the interests assumed to be those of the general public (or the common man) are likely to qualify for national support, in more stratified societies it is the interests of certain minorities, ruling groups, or economic elites that will tend to be identified with the interests of the nation.[12]

Indirect national goals present a problem similar to the milieu goals. They, too, can absorb more of a nation's efforts and resources than is compatible with the vital needs of national security or power. The danger is particularly serious in the case of indirect goals because of the influence that subnational pressure groups are capable of exerting on their behalf.

There is bound to be controversy in instances in which, in the absence of a clear-cut national emergency, the question of priority arises with respect to possession and milieu goals or to direct and indirect national goals. Such controversy reflects differences in value patterns as well as in estimates of what the situation requires. Nowhere more than here does it become evident how little guidance policy-makers can gain simply from being referred to the "national interest." Countries presently partitioned offer a striking illustra-

---

[12] Charles Beard in *The Open Door At Home: A Trial Philosophy of National Interest* (Macmillan Co., New York, 1935) discusses under the labels "industrialist statecraft" and "agrarian statecraft" the way powerful sections of the population succeed in making the promotion of their special interests the goal of a policy parading as a policy of the national interest.

tion of the dilemmas governments and nations face when setting these priorities. Reunification has become a pressing possession goal for these partitioned countries. The core value of territorial integrity is at stake. Yet most Germans seem to agree with the official view of the West German government according to which the goal of preserving the freedoms West Germans enjoy under a democratic constitution—an indirect national goal—should be given precedence over German reunification. If the restoration of the former territorial integrity of the country enjoyed top priority among German national goals, West Germany could bring it about at the price of turning Communist and joining the Soviet camp.

There come to mind other circumstances in which an indirect national goal might gain precedence even over what were formerly regarded as national core values. In the case of a threat of nuclear devastation some governments might be led to decide—or be forced by public opinion to decide—that surrender rather than defense offers the only chance for the nation to survive in any meaningful sense of the term. Here, then, the indirect national goal of keeping citizens alive and their possessions intact would have won over the goal of national self-preservation in the traditional sense.

One further pair of contrasting categories of goals deserves attention. It makes sense, especially in our era, to distinguish between ideological or revolutionary goals on the one hand and traditional national goals on the other. The example that comes to mind is that of Communist governments which, it is widely assumed, engage their countries in efforts to promote the universalist goal of worldwide victory for Communism whether or not their countries as nation-states with a territorial base and with distinct security interests stand to gain by such efforts. There is no way of proving, however, that the Soviet Union while claiming to promote the cause of international Communism actually consents to sacrifices that would not be justified by the way in which its leaders interpret the Soviet national interest. In assisting "wars of liberation," for instance, the Soviet Union may hope to gain friends or allies for itself while simultaneously helping history along its predestined path toward a Communist world. The Soviet leaders themselves may not be able to distinguish between their national goals and their revolutionary or universalist goals because ever since Lenin declared Russia to be the "Fatherland of the Revolution" they have been able to claim, sometimes to the dismay of Communists abroad, that what was good for Russia—and only what was good for Russia—

was good for Communism. It seems evident, however, that Communist doctrine colors Soviet thinking so strongly that the interpretation of what constitutes a Soviet national interest as well as the Soviet image of the outside world are strongly affected by the doctrine.

The Communist governments are not the only governments that are influenced by universalist ideological causes and are therefore ready to engage in efforts unappealing to nation-states of nineteenth-century European vintage. Some of the more revolutionary neutralist leaders, as will be discussed in a later chapter,[13] carry on their fight against colonialism even after their own countries have gained independence. When this happens these leaders place their states in the service of the transnational cause of abolishing Western colonial rule everywhere. Similarly, and even prior to Woodrow Wilson, the United States has engaged in policies directed toward spreading democracy abroad, especially by promoting the institution of free elections in other countries.[14] While much of the declaratory policy by which governments claim to be pursuing such lofty ends as self-determination for all peoples, or a world safe for democracy, may be either hypocritical or a matter self-delusion, it would be as difficult to argue that Woodrow Wilson was acting in behalf of specific American interests when he struggled to get the Covenant of the League of Nations into the Versailles Treaty as it would be to assert that Lenin after becoming head of the Russian government placed its power and prestige exclusively in the service of national as against world revolutionary objectives. However, although men like Lenin and Wilson who were motivated to an exceptional degree by revolutionary or ideological fervor were able to inject a universalist element into the policy of their respective countries, events in their own lifetimes demonstrated the persistent predominance of the concern with strictly national interests: it was not long before the Soviet Union, following its Czarist predecessors, was to struggle to keep the Dardanelles open to Soviet shipping and before the United States was to refuse to join the League of Nations.

[13] See Chapter 14, "Allies, Neutrals, and Neutralists."
[14] See Theodore Wright's discussion of this policy in his article on "Free Elections in the Latin American Policy of the United States," *Political Science Quarterly*, Vol. LXXIV, No. 1 (March, 1959).

Chapter Six   THE POLE OF POWER
AND THE POLE OF
INDIFFERENCE

IN INTERNATIONAL RELATIONS, two opposing schools of thought have fought each other throughout the modern age.[1] Ever since Machiavelli published *The Prince,* his "realist" views have shocked "idealist" thinkers. As a battle of the mind, fought by and large outside the political arena, the dispute between the two schools was of great concern to philosophers and moralists; but not until Woodrow Wilson set out to transform utopia into reality did it become a political issue of the first magnitude. For the first time, the responsible head of one of the leading powers acted as though the world were on the verge of crossing the threshold from sordid "power politics" to a "new era" in which the admonitions of the idealist philosophers suddenly would become the political order of the day.

No amount of disillusionment has been able to wipe out the deep marks left by the outburst of idealist enthusiasm which Woodrow Wilson's leadership evoked. Today more than ever American statesmen and the American public find themselves torn between the conflicting pulls of idealist and realist thought. Often the same event—as the war in Korea vividly demonstrated—is interpreted simultaneously in terms of both schools: as an incident in the age-old struggle for power on the one hand, as a great venture in community action against an aggressor on the other.

This puts the theoretical analyst in something of a predicament. When interest in a theory of international politics became alive in

[1] This chapter is reprinted, with minor changes, from *World Politics,* Vol. IV, No. 1 (October, 1951) , by permission of the publisher.

81

the United States in the mid-thirties, it did so as part and parcel of a reaction which set in at the time against the prevailing optimistic Wilsonian school.[2] Machiavelli rather than Wilson became the patron saint of the new venture. But today the "realist" engaged in theoretical pursuits finds himself swimming against the stream, and a powerful stream it is when leaders of both political parties insist that American foreign policy centers on the United Nations and collective security. There is little in realist thought—beyond the tools to debunk many popular idealist notions—to suggest that organizations and ideologies transcending national boundaries deserve more than marginal attention. The theorist has all the more reason, then, to reassess his own position in relation to the two schools and to seek to discover whether there may be some unexplored terrain lying beyond their controversy.[3]

The realist image of the world has been presented in its essential features by a number of authors concerned with the theory of international politics. In its pure form the realist concept is based on the proposition that "states seek to enhance their power." In this brief statement are implicit the major assumptions of realist thought.

States are conceived of as the sole actors in the international arena. Operating as a group of sovereign entities, they constitute a multistate system. The analogy of a set of billiard balls or chess figures comes back to mind. All the units of the system behave essentially in the same manner; their goal is to enhance if not to maximize their power. Each of them must act with a single mind and single will, in this respect, resembling the princes of the Renaissance about whom Machiavelli wrote. Like them, too, the states are completely separate from each other, with no affinities or bonds of community interfering in their egotistical pursuit of power. They are competitors for power, engaged in a continuous and inescapable struggle for survival. This makes them all potential if not actual

[2] See William T.R. Fox, "Interwar International Relations Research: The American Experience," *World Politics*, Vol. II, No. 1 (October, 1949), pp. 67-79.

[3] Not all authors can be classified as belonging clearly to one of the two schools, because the views which will be presented in sharp contrast are often found to shade over into each other. Still, it is not difficult to discover in what direction a writer's main inclination lies. E.H. Carr (*The Twenty Years' Crisis*, Macmillan Co., 1st ed., London, 1940) makes a deliberate attempt to synthesize the tenets of both schools, which he calls utopian and realist. (See particularly p. 125.) I think it can be said, however, that he lets the realist come out on top.

enemies; there can be no amity between them, unless it be an alignment against a common foe.

Under these conditions the expectation of violence and even of annihilation is ever present. To forget this and thus fail in the concern for enhanced power spells the doom of a state. This does not mean constant open warfare; expansion of power at the expense of others will not take place if there is enough counterpower to deter or to stop states from undertaking it. Although no state is interested in a mere balance of power, the efforts of all states to maximize power may lead to equilibrium. If and when that happens, there is "peace" or, more exactly, a condition of stalemate or truce. Under the conditions described here, this balancing of power process is the only available "peace" strategy.

While few would deny that the picture presented in these sweeping generalizations resembles the world we are living in at this time, this same picture would not have passed for more than a caricature at other times. International relations within the Western world in the twenties or within the inter-American system today cannot fully be understood in terms either of balanced power or an all-out struggle for survival. This does not preclude the possibility that the "pure power model" of the realists can render service at least as an initial working hypothesis. The actual world might never fully comply with the postulates of the model, yet to the extent it did, consequences deduced within its context would apply to the real world. Countries engaged in a race to enhance their power could be expected, for example, to align themselves in disrespect of earlier "friendships" or ideological affinities; expansion would be sure to take place wherever a power vacuum existed.

Of course, no such approximation of reality to pure power conditions can be taken for granted. It presupposes the basic "realist" contention about state behavior to be truly realistic. If an insatiable quest for power were not the rule, but instead represented an abnormality or marginal case, developments in the world might deviate drastically from those which the model leads one to expect. Peace strategies other than the balancing process might have a chance of success.

Realist scholars have sought to explain why states do in fact behave as postulated or why they are compelled to so behave. They have offered two different explanations. According to the first, human nature is such that men, as individuals and as nations, act like beasts of prey, driven by an insatiable lust for power or *animus dominandi.* Their will to power, moreover, when transferred from small and frustrated individuals to the collectivity of the state, takes on greater dimensions and generates an all-round struggle for survival.[4]

According to the second explanation, which is gaining adherents, the quest for power is due not to any desire for power as such, but to a general human craving for security.[5] The insecurity of an anarchical system of multiple sovereignty places the actors under compulsion to seek maximum power even though this may run counter to their real desires. By a tragic irony, then, all actors find themselves compelled to do for the sake of security what, in bringing about an all-round struggle for survival, leads to greater insecurity. This "vicious circle theory" makes statesmen and people look less vicious than the *animus dominandi* theory; what it does is to substitute tragedy for evil and to replace the "mad Caesar," as Harold Lasswell calls the *homo politicus* of the pure power model, with the "hysterical Caesar" who, haunted by fear, pursues the will-o'-the-wisp of absolute security.

The validity of these explanations of an alleged uniform behavior of states toward power need not be discussed here, because the realist scholars who started out with the assumption of such uniformity have not stuck to it after descending from the high level of abstraction of their initial propositions to the lower levels where the shape of actual things can be apprehended. All of them have found it necessary to "deviate" from their original assumption to the point of distinguishing between at least two categories of states with different attitudes toward power.

Few have stated more emphatically than Hans Morgenthau that in international relations "power is pitted against power for survival and supremacy." [6] But more recently he has drawn a sharp distinction between two types of states, the *"status quo* powers" and the "imperialist powers." Of the former, he says their policy tends "toward keeping power and not toward changing the distribution

---

[4] See Hans J. Morgenthau, *Scientific Man vs. Power Politics* (University of Chicago Press, Chicago, 1946) , Chapter VII, "The Moral Blindness of Scientific Man," especially pp. 191-201, "selfishness and lust for power."

[5] John H. Herz (*Political Realism and Political Idealism,* University of Chicago Press, Chicago, 1951, p. 4) , who expounds the theory of what he calls the "security dilemma" with much skill and vigor, says that "basically it is the mere instinct of self-preservation which . . . leads to competition for ever more power." This is the view held by Thomas Hobbes, which C.J. Friedrich discusses in *Inevitable Peace* (Harvard University Press, Cambridge, Mass., 1948, p. 126) .

[6] *Op. cit.,* p. 71.

of power"; of the latter, they aim "at acquiring more power." [7] Similarly, Frederick Schuman starts out with the assertion that "power is sought as an end in itself" in international politics, but then goes on to differentiate between "satiated" and "unsatiated" states. His statements that "each state left to itself tends to extend its power over as wide a field as possible" and that "enhancement of state power is always the goal" are contradicted, it would seem, by his subsequent contention that states which benefit from the established *status quo* naturally seek "to preserve that from which they benefit," in contrast to states "which feel humiliated, hampered and oppressed by the *status quo*." [8] The authors of another recent text, Strausz-Hupé and Possony, follow a similar line. After stating at the outset that "foreign policy aims at the acquisition of optimum—and sometimes of maximum—power," the optimum remaining undefined, they go on to define, as a special type, the "natural aggressors" who in contrast to other states are "driven by a particularly pronounced dynamism, i.e., urge toward power accumulation." [9] Finally, Nicholas Spykman, who did much to introduce the pure power hypothesis into the contemporary American discussion, deviates from his opening statement, according to which "the improvement of the relative power position becomes the primary objective of the . . . external policy of states," by speaking of the "dynamic state" which, as he puts it, "rarely sets modest limits to its power aims." [10] This implies that nondynamic states, on the contrary, do set such "modest limits." [11]

[7] Hans J. Morgenthau, *Politics Among Nations* (Alfred A. Knopf, New York, 1948), p. 21. Actually, he adds a third type, described as a nation pursuing a policy of prestige. Prestige, however, in contrast to maintenance and acquisition of power, "is but rarely an end in itself," he says (p. 50); "it is rather an instrument through which the other two ends can be achieved."

[8] *International Politics* (3d ed., McGraw-Hill, New York, 1941), pp. 262-63, 274-75, 279.

[9] Robert Strausz-Hupé and Stefan T. Possony, *International Relations* (McGraw-Hill, New York, 1950), pp. 2, 9.

[10] *America's Strategy in World Politics* (Harcourt, Brace & Co., New York, 1942), pp. 18, 20.

[11] Max Weber emphasizes the difference between more "isolationist" and more "expansive" powers, as well as their changing attitudes in this respect. (See *From Max Weber: Essays in Sociology*, trans. and ed. by H.H. Gerth and C. Wright Mills, Oxford University Press, New York, 1946, Chapter 6 on "Structure of Power.") "For general reasons of power dynamics *per se*," he writes, "the Great Powers are often very expansive powers." "But," he continues, they "are not necessarily and not always oriented toward expansion." See also William T.R. Fox (*The Super-Powers*, Harcourt, Brace & Co., New York, 1944) who distinguishes between the "quest for security (power not to be coerced)" of some nations and the "quest for domination (power to coerce)" of others.

One consequence of distinctions such as these is worth mentioning. They rob theory of the determinate and predictive character that seemed to give the pure power hypothesis its peculiar value. It can now no longer be said of the actual world, for example, that a power vacuum cannot exist for any length of time; a vacuum surrounded by "satiated" or *"status quo"* states would remain as it is unless its existence were to change the character of these states and put them into the category of "imperialist," "unsatiated," or "dynamic" states.

The idealist model, if such there be, cannot be as easily derived from writings or statements of exponents of the idealist school itself. This school has been anything but theory-minded. Its attention has been focused on peace strategy and on blueprints for a better world. However, it would have made no sense for idealists to proffer advice on policy if they had not held general views about the existing world which permitted them to regard as practical the policies they sought to promote. As a matter of fact, Woodrow Wilson himself, with his predilection for broad generalizations, has expressed on one occasion or another all the main tenets of the "Wilsonian" school.

One feature of the idealist image strikes the eye because of its contrast to the realist view. Here the basic propositions deal not with states, but with individuals, with peoples, or with mankind. The idealist seems to be looking out not on a multistate system with its separate national entities, but on a nascent world community and the people who make it up. This precludes placing the emphasis on national quests for power or on the struggle for power among nations. Instead, the accent is either on the "common purpose of enlightened mankind" [12] or on the common values which men hold as individuals. Because the vast majority of men are assumed to value the same things—individual freedom, the right to govern themselves, the safety of their homeland, and above all the absence of violence—it is concluded that there can exist no basic conflict between them even as nations. If it were not for extraneous interference, and a remediable measure of ignorance and misunderstanding, there would be harmony, peace, and a complete absence of concern for national power. "I sometimes think," said Wilson, "that . . . no people ever went to war with another people." But he goes on to say that "governments have gone to war" with one another, thereby pointing to the darker side of the idealist picture.[13]

[12] *The Public Papers of Woodrow Wilson: War and Peace,* ed. Ray S. Baker and William E. Dodd (Harper & Bros., New York, 1927), p. 259.

[13] *President Wilson's State Papers and Addresses,* introd. by Albert Shaw (George H. Doran Co., New York, 1918), p. 177.

Only a dreamer could mistake for the existing order that vision of a world of independent nations in which there is no conflict, nor any drives for power. The idealist school does not do so. It not only fully recognizes the continued presence or threat of "power politics," but considers this discrepancy between "what is" and "what should and will be" as the crucial moral and political issue of international relations. The explanation for the discrepancy is believed to lie in the operation of evil forces which violate the peace and law of the community.

There is no doubt about the character of these forces. They are conceived of as anachronistic remnants of an age—now coming to an end—in which autocratic rulers rather than the peoples themselves controlled the destiny of nations. It was these rulers who were "playing the game of power," as Woodrow Wilson put it; their ambitions, not the interests of their peoples, were in conflict which plunged the world into power politics and the struggle for survival. Whenever and wherever such autocracy asserts itself, or reasserts itself through a relapse into a bygone age, the community of peace-loving nations falls victim to the onslaught of aggressive power and violence.

One might suspect that when such aggression occurs, the world would return to conditions very much like those portrayed by the pure power model. The only difference would seem to be in the power of aggressors now being pitted against the collective power of peace-loving nations. The idealist denounces such a comparison as superficial and dangerously misleading. It would be no less inappropriate, he maintains, to speak of a struggle for power or a balancing of power process when describing the defense of international peace and lawfulness than it would be to apply these same terms to the actions of a national police force engaged in fighting individual criminals.

According to idealist thought, then, the quest for collective international police power has taken the place of the obsolete quest for national power as far as the majority of the actors is concerned. One would be tempted, by way of contrast, to call this idealist image by some such name as the "pure solidarity model" were it not for the emphasis placed on the continued threat or presence of aggressive antisolidarity forces.

The idealist school has been taken to task by its critics for the illusory character of much of its interpretation of the existing world, especially for its *a priori* optimistic assumptions concerning human nature and the harmony of interest, as well as for its narrow explan-

ation of the phenomenon which it terms aggression.[14] The validity
of such criticism should become clearer, at least by implication, from
what will be said later. It is more important, here, to point to some
of the insights which the idealist approach suggests to the theoretical analyst.

By distinguishing from the outset between two types of behavior
toward power, rather than introducing discrimination as an after-
thought or deviation, the idealist has been more aware of the problems arising from this lack of uniformity. (If anything, he may be
too much inclined to take the lack of uniformity for granted, for
example, when asserting categorically that democracies behave differently from dictatorships in foreign affairs.) Because of the important role he assigns to individuals and their values as well as to
bonds of community transcending national boundaries, the idealist
has an eye for aspects of reality—such as the relative ease with which
the English-speaking world has learned to collaborate—which are
hard to reconcile with the image of a "billiard ball world."[15]

These remarks are not intended as a recommendation to scholars
to take the pure solidarity model as their initial hypothesis. If they
did, they would find themselves in all probability in the position
of an economist who sought to gain an understanding of the Soviet
economy by starting with the *laisser faire* assumptions of the classical economists. He might reach his goal in the end, but only by
an arduous detour.

The two schools, realist and idealist, are obviously far apart if
not diametrically opposed on many issues. Yet, despite striking differences, their views are closely related to each other at least in one
significant respect. Both approach international politics on the same
level which briefly might be called the power level, though they

---

[14] For criticism of idealist thought in international relations, see Carr, *op. cit.*;
Morgenthau, *Scientific Man, op. cit.*; Reinhold Niebuhr, *The Children of Light
and the Children of Darkness* (Charles Scribner's Sons, New York, 1944).

[15] Frederick S. Dunn (*War and the Minds of Men,* Harper & Bros., New
York, 1950) emphasizes the importance of supplementing the picture of international affairs that reveals itself when attention is focused on interstate relations by one that places social or human relations between individuals in the
center of the scene (p. 12). He warns, however, against the illusion that a
shift to the goals and values of individuals will help us to escape "from the
sickening recurrence of international crises and war." "Political conflicts," he
rightly insists, "arise from the existence of competing values among sovereign
states."

approach it from opposite ends.[16] By way of simplification, it can be said that while the realist is interested primarily in the quest for power—and its culmination in the resort to violence—as the essence of all politics among nations, the idealist is concerned above all with its elimination. On this level there can be no meeting of the minds. But the question arises whether to start off with the quest and struggle for power does not mean tying up the horse at its tail.

Normally, power is a means to other ends and not an end in itself. Where it becomes an end, as in the case of the "mad Caesars," one is faced with what Toynbee would call an "enormity." To treat the quest for power, positively or negatively, outside the context of ends and purposes which it is expected to serve, therefore, robs it of any intelligible meaning and also makes it impossible to judge its appropriateness or excessiveness. It is as if an economist, in developing economic theory, were to concentrate on the accumulation and expenditure of money. He could not avoid painting a picture of a world of misers or spendthrifts, as the political scientist on the power level can see little but a world of insatiably power-hungry or unconditionally power-hostile political actors.[17]

A very different picture develops, as the further discussion should show, if one considers first the values and purposes for the sake of which policy-makers seek to accumulate or use national power, as they may also seek alternative or supplementary means.

This suggests beginning with a "theory of ends" and proceeding from there to the analysis of the quest for power as it develops in conjunction with and under the impact of the ends it is meant to promote. Keep in mind, however, that one is not dealing with a

[16] The term "power" is used here and throughout this chapter in the restricted sense in which it occurs in the popular use of such word combinations as "power politics" or "struggle for power," meaning to cover the ability to coerce or, more precisely, to inflict deprivations on others. This leaves out other ways of exerting influence, e.g., by bestowing benefits which are not ordinarily connected with or condemned as "power politics." (See Harold and Margaret Sprout, in *Foundations of National Power,* 2d rev. ed., D. Van Nostrand Co., New York, 1951, p. 39, where they explain their reasons for choosing a much broader definition.) The term "resort to power" will be used to mean reliance on the ability to inflict deprivations, "resort to violence" to mean actual coercion by the use of physical force.

[17] Some political scientists would exclude by definition from what they call "political" anything but the problems of power. But the consequence is that a "foreign policy" must then be called political in one respect and non-political in all others, the latter including all policy ends other than power itself.

simple cause and effect relationship. The degree to which power is available or attainable frequently affects the choice of ends. Prudent policy-makers will keep their ends and aspirations safely within the power which their country possesses or is ready and willing to muster.[18] Statesmen with a respect for moral principles, or under pressure from people who have such respect, may hesitate to pursue goals which demand the sacrifice either of these principles or of other values in the process of power accumulation or use.[19]

There is little reason to expect all actors on the international stage to orient themselves uniformly toward one and the same goal, whether it be peace, security, or "power as an end in itself." However, they may be operating under some form of "compulsion" forcing them in the long run to fall in line with each other.

States are not single-purpose organizations like hospitals, golf clubs, or banking establishments.[20] At one and the same time people expect from their states not only external security, but such widely differing things as colonial conquest, better control over foreign markets, freedom for the individual, and international lawfulness. Among goals such as these, relatively scarce means must be parceled out in order of preference and by a constant process of weighing, comparing, and computing values. Because policy-makers, like all men, seek to maximize value in accordance with everfluctuating value patterns, one would anticipate great variation in their choice unless something compelled them to conform.[21]

[18] Walter Lippmann has consistently advocated such prudence. "The thesis of this book," he says in reference to his *U.S. Foreign Policy: Shield of the Republic* (Little, Brown & Co., Boston, 1943), "is that a foreign policy consists in bringing into balance, with a comfortable surplus of power in reserve, the nation's commitments and the nation's power. The constant preoccupation of the true statesman is to achieve and maintain this balance."

[19] For some of the ethical problems involved, see Chapter 4, "Statesmanship and Moral Choice."

[20] In speaking of the actors on the international stage, I shall use the term "states" as a means of abbreviation. The real actors are aggregates of decision-makers acting in the name of states or nations, including in a varied order of influence such persons as statesmen, legislators, lobbyists, and common citizens. There are also, today, as there were in medieval times, actors other than states, like the Vatican, the United Nations, or the Anglo-Iranian Oil Company, which one could not afford to ignore in any complete theory of international politics. One might call them subnational, transnational, and supernational centers of influence and often of power.

[21] As Harold D. Lasswell and Abraham Kaplan put it in *Power and Society: A Framework for Political Inquiry* (Yale University Press, New Haven, 1950): "No generalizations can be made *a priori* concerning the scale of values of all groups and individuals. What the values are in a given situation must in principle be separately determined for each case."

The number of conceivable ends is much larger than is indicated by broad categories such as security, aggrandizement, or international order. Policy-makers must decide whether a specific increment of security is worth the specific additional deprivations which its attainment through power requires. However, for purposes of analysis it is permissible to limit the discussion to a few representative types of goals. It need only be kept in mind that these typical bundles of related ends are not sharply divided from one another and that no actor is likely to be found pursuing a single type of objective all the time. He may be out for security today, for conquest tomorrow.

The goals of foreign policy as they refer to the national "self" can be classified under the three headings of goals of national self-extension, goals of national self-preservation, and goals of national self-abnegation. For actors other than states, corresponding categories would have to be chosen.[22]

The term "self-extension" is not used here in a derogatory sense, although some goals which belong in this category may deserve moral condemnation. It is meant to cover all policy objectives expressing a demand for values not already enjoyed, and thus a demand for a change of the *status quo*. The objectives may vary widely. The aim may be more "power as an end in itself" or domination over other peoples or territorial expansion; but it may also represent a quest for the return of lost territory, or the redress of legitimate grievances, such as termination of unjust discriminations,

---

[22] There will be little room in the following to discuss the factors that account for the choice of goals by the decision-makers. There is need for much more study of these factors. Growing awareness that policy cannot arise except through choices and decisions of individuals has led recently to a tendency to stress the psychological factor. But it is probable that the understanding of national foreign policies, as well as any long-run predictions concerning such policies, will be found to depend on knowledge of actions' antecedents that are more general and more constant than the psychological traits and predispositions of frequently changing individuals, or even of groups, elites, and nations. Spykman's prediction of 1942 (*op. cit.*, p. 469) that "a modern, vitalized and militarized China . . . is going to be a threat not only to Japan, but also to the position of the Western Powers in the Asiatic Mediterranean," which sounded almost blasphemous to some of his critics when it was made, could not have been made if it had depended on knowledge of the future political fortunes, the psychology, and the doctrine of one who was then a little-known Communist agitator with the name of Mao Tse-tung.

the emancipation from foreign control or imposition on others of an ideology or way of life.[23]

Self-preservation is meant to stand for all demands pointing toward the maintenance, protection, or defense of the existing distribution of values, usually called the *status quo*. The term "self-preservation" is not without ambiguity. The national "self" which states seek to preserve can undergo a wide variety of interpretations. It may be considered to include only national independence and territorial integrity of the homeland; or it may be held to embrace a whole catalogue of "vital interests," from safety belts and influence zones to investments and nationals abroad. Another variable makes the notion of self-preservation even more elusive and therefore often a convenient cloak for other purposes. To preserve possessions does not mean merely to defend them when they are actually under attack. *Status quo* powers regularly demand that the threat of such attack be reduced at least to the point of giving them a reasonable sense of security.

Thus the quest for security—the preservation goal *par excellence* —points beyond mere maintenance and defense.[24] It can become so ambitious as to transform itself into a goal of unlimited self-extension. A country pursuing the mirage of absolute security could not stop at less than world domination today.[25] A change to self-extension in the name of security often occurs at the close of a war.

---

[23] The literature on the causes of imperialism is extensive. Studies have also been made bearing on such problems as the relationship between dictatorship and expansionist foreign policies; but one would wish studies like that of Edmond N. Cahn (*The Sense of Injustice,* New York University Press, New York, 1949) to be extended to the international field. For where is the "sense of injustice" more "alive with movement and warmth" (p. 13) and where is the "human animal" more "disposed to fight injustice" (p. 25) than in international relations? *Status quo* countries will continue to live in a fool's paradise if they fail to understand the deep and manifold causes which account for demands for change and self-extension even through violence.

[24] I am employing the term "security" as it is used in the everyday language of statesmen to signify not "high value expectancy" generally—as Lasswell and Kaplan define the term (*op. cit.,* p. 61) —but high expectancy of value *preservation.* The two authors may have had the same thing in mind, because they specify that security means a realistic expectancy of *maintaining* influence. One would not say that Nazi Germany either came to be or came to feel more secure as her expectancy of successful self-*extension* through conquest of territory increased.

[25] The degree of security-mindedness of different countries and of groups within countries depends on many circumstances which would be worth studying. Looking at the United States and France in recent times, it would seem as if countries become more ambitious in their desire for security either for

Victims of attack who were entirely satisfied before hostilities started are rarely content, if victorious, to return to the *status quo ante.*

Self-abnegation, finally, is meant to include all goals transcending if not sacrificing the "national interest," in any meaningful sense of the term. It is the goal of those who place a higher value on such ends as international solidarity, lawfulness, rectitude, or peace than they place even on national security and self-preservation. It is also the goal of individuals, groups, or regimes who at the expense of the nation as a whole use their influence within the decision-making process to promote what might be called "subnational" interests.

This may appear to be a category which only a utopian could expect to find in international politics, at least as far as idealistic self-abnegation is concerned. How could any nation dare indulge in altruistic pursuits—or allow its interests to be sacrificed to the interest of a group—and yet hope to survive? While the discussion of compulsion and penalties must be further postponed, it is worth pointing out nevertheless that the United States was powerful enough in 1918 to permit Woodrow Wilson to indulge in self-abnegation goals without much harm to American interests and that little Denmark, too weak to seek self-preservation through power, limited its foreign policy largely to humanitarian causes and yet in the end survived Hitler's conquest. There is also the case of governments like that of Communist Czechoslovakia which for the sake of party doctrine and power are ready to promote the transnational cause of world Communism, though it means sacrificing all but the outward appearances of national sovereignty and independence. Highest devotion to national interests and aspirations, even if spread over the globe more widely today than ever, is not the only possible attitude of actors in international affairs. Exponents of world government are not necessarily utopians for hoping that peoples and governments some day will commit an act of radical national self-abnegation and abdicate as sovereign entities in favor of a world state.

---

having enjoyed a high degree of it over a long period or for having had much and recent experience with the sad consequences of insecurity. James Burnham in *The Struggle for the World* (John Day Co., New York, 1947, pp. 134 ff.) argues that in the atomic age, there can be no security short of world empire, with only two candidates for such empire available today. "In the course of the decision," he says, "both of the present antagonists may . . . be destroyed. But one of them must be."

Cases in which self-abnegation goals have precedence over national self-preservation may be rare in an era in which nationalism and the ethics of patriotism continue unabated.[26] This does not preclude the possibility, however, that where influential groups of participants in the decision-making process place high value on a universal cause such as peace, pressures exerted by these groups may affect the course of foreign policy. It may lead to a more modest interpretation of the national interest, to more concern for the interests of other nations, to more concessions for the sake of peace, or to more restraint in the use of power and violence. Whether the nation will profit or suffer in the end from the success of such "internationalist," "humanitarian," or "pacifist" pressures depends on the circumstances of the case; whichever it does, the abnegation goals will have proved themselves a reality.

Now let us suppose that a government has picked its objective or objectives and also has decided to rely on the accumulation and use of power as the chief means of reaching its goal. We can then ask ourselves what will determine the scope of its quest for power. Does it not stand to reason—provided the government in question is acting rationally—that it would seek to preserve or acquire as much power as appeared adequate to assure the success of its policy? It would not aim at a higher level of power, because every increment adds to the burdens the country has to bear, cuts down on the chances of attaining other objectives, and tends to provoke counteraction. To seek less than adequate power would mean giving up the chance of attaining one's goal.

Because adequacy is a matter of subjective estimates, the factors which influence these estimates are of major interest. Two countries having the same goals and acting under similar circumstances may differ widely in their views on adequacy of power. But this need not invalidate some general theses concerning the relationship between the main categories of policy goals and the quest for power.

---

[26] As Hermann Göring is reported to have said, cynically (see G.M. Gilbert, *The Psychology of Dictatorship*, Ronald Press, New York, 1950, p. 117): "Voice or no voice, the people can always be brought to do the bidding of the leaders. That is easy. All you have to do is to tell them they are being attacked and denounce the pacifists for lack of patriotism . . . ."

According to Charles A. Beard (*The Idea of National Interest*, New York, Macmillan Co., 1934), the interest of the nation as a whole, if it can be defined at all, is constantly being sacrificed to the interests of groups which are powerful enough to have their special interests pass for the "national interest." If he were right, most countries would be engaged most of the time, involuntarily, in a process of national self-abnegation—and still survive.

Goals of national self-abnegation, provided they are not set by subnational groups parading their interests as the national interest, call for the approval and support of more than a single nation. Accumulation, show, or use of national power are likely to defeat rather than to promote such ends. Nations' pursuing ends falling into this category—including the goal of eliminating power politics! —will tend to play down their own national power or to reduce it. "Disarmament by example" pursued by Great Britain prior to 1932 was a way of trying to promote world peace by a policy of self-abnegation.

Obviously, cases will be rare in which for the sake of goals of self-abnegation a nation refuses to resort to power even when the inner core of the national self comes under serious threat of attack. Under stress, therefore, self-preservation usually gains the upper hand. Even then, however, idealistic pressures at home in favor of self-denying policies may persist and either delay or reduce the effort to enhance defensive national power.

Statesmen and peoples who hold (or profess to hold) strong beliefs in universal causes, religious or ideological, are not always found to minimize reliance on national power. On the contrary, striking cases have become only too familiar in this age of revolutionary and ideological strife, in which goals appearing to be of a self-transcending kind have revealed themselves as the most ambitious goals of self-extension. Whenever a nation goes out on a "crusade" for some universal cause, claiming to have a mission of imposing its ideas and institutions on others, there is practically no limit to the enhancement of national power it deems necessary. National power is looked upon or advertised here as the chosen instrument with which to bring salvation to mankind.

Goals of self-extension generally place an extremely high premium on the resort to power as a means. The chances of bringing about any major change in the international *status quo* by means other than power or even violence are slim indeed. Because it is also true that self-extension is often sought passionately if not fanatically and by actors of various sorts and motivations, the tendency is toward frequent and intensive quests for enhanced power by nations belonging to this category. No phenomenon in international politics calls for more study and attention.

Adequate power, in this instance, means power deemed sufficient to overcome the power of resistance put up by those who desire to preserve things which they possess and cherish. Where such resistance is expected to be feeble, as it is when the demand is directed against weak or complacent and isolated countries, the nation seeking self-extension may be expected to be satisfied with far less than the maximum power for which it has potentialities. However, since other and stronger countries, as a rule, are awake to their interest in preserving well beyond their own borders the established distribution of values, resistance to change is usually not easy to break. It may be so forbidding as to deter countries from making the attempt. Thus, fervently "revisionist" Hungary after 1919 was sufficiently impressed by the power and resolution of the Little Entente not to attempt to regain her lost territories by means of power. The whole idea of the balance of power as a guarantor of peace rests on the assumption that the costs of adequate power for self-extension may at a certain point become excessive or prohibitive.

Many a "satisfied" country would better be called a country "resigned to nonextension," as can be seen whenever easy opportunities for gain present themselves. Not many belligerents, even if they were victims of attack when the war started, fail to come forth with "historic claims" and strategic demands once they are victorious. It would be exaggerated, however, to say that self-extension will always take place where no resistance is expected, or where no serious costs are involved. While Switzerland may stand alone in having refused to consider an increase of territory, even as a gift, it is well known how consistently influential groups in the United States Senate, and in the American public at large, have opposed territorial annexations.

Because self-extension almost invariably calls for additional power, countries that seek self-extension tend to be the initiators of power competition and the resort to violence. Herein lies the significant kernel of truth in the idealist theory of aggression.[27] Cases are conceivable, of course, where the initiative rests with a country concerned with self-preservation which starts enhancing its defensive power for fear of an imagined threat; the resort to violence, too, may be the preventive act of a nation that believes itself to be menaced by an attack on its own values or those of its friends.[28] If two countries are both eager to gain advantages at

[27] See also Strausz-Hupé and Possony, *op. cit.*, p. 9.

[28] ". . . A government with no appetite whatsoever," writes W.T.R. Fox ("Atomic Energy and International Relations," in *Technology and International Relations,* ed. W.F. Ogburn, University of Chicago Press, Chicago, 1949, p. 118), "may start a conflict if its leaders feel sure that the opponent has for a long time been unscrupulously trading on their general unwillingness to start a war."

each other's expense, or are both haunted by fears and suspicions, it may be difficult to decide where the initiative lay and where the first move was made that led to a race for higher levels of power and ultimately to war.

Turning, finally, to the goals of self-preservation, one finds this category to be most elusive when it comes to setting up general hypotheses concerning its effect on the quest for power. Depending on the circumstances, countries in this category may run the whole gamut from a frantic concern with the enhancement of power at one extreme to complete indifference to power at the other. Great Britain offers an excellent example of the pendulum's swing from complacency under Baldwin and Chamberlain to spectacular and heroic total mobilization of power under Churchill.

Self-preservation calls forth such a variety of attitudes toward power because countries which are satisfied to let things stand as they are have no immediate incentive for valuing power or for wishing to enhance it. Whether they become interested in power at all, and the extent to which they do, depends on the actions they expect from others. It is a responsive interest which takes its cue from the threats, real or imagined, directed at things possessed and valued. If policy is rationally decided, the quest for power here increases and decreases in proportion to these external threats.

One can bring forward the peculiarities of this responsive attitude most clearly if one starts out by postulating a situation in which all of the major actors are assumed to be concerned with nothing but self-preservation. In the mid-twenties, when the "revisionist" nations were still impotent, this situation was closely approximated. Under such conditions, policy-makers are inclined toward keeping the costs of power at a minimum and toward avoiding any move which might provoke a race for power from which, after all, they have nothing to gain. If there were no reason to fear that one or more within the group might switch to goals of self-extension, and particularly if there were no danger of dissatisfied and potentially strong countries outside the group regaining actual power, the estimates of what constitutes adequacy would drop very low. The unguarded border between Canada and this country serves as a striking reminder of the indifference to power in the relations between two nonextension-seeking and nondistrustful neighbors.[29]

[29] W.T.R. Fox (*The Super-Powers, op. cit.,* p. 11) points out that "one state's security is not necessarily every other state's insecurity. . . . Greater security . . . is an objective toward which it is at least conceivable that all states can move simultaneously."

The conditions postulated here describe a configuration in which peace strategies such as the idealist school advocated in the twenties would have an excellent chance of success, provided no country feared the early ascendancy of a presently impotent and dissatisfied nation. All would be interested in a disarmament to the lowest level compatible with internal security; all would be interested in the promotion of mutual confidence and understanding and in the collective organization of "watchfulness." Only hysteria could produce a race for power within a group of countries intent upon self-preservation. The high degree of security which they would believe to be enjoying probably would lull them into a state of such indifference toward power that they might be overtaken by a self-extension-seeking outsider—so slow is the "security dilemma" in catching up with those who are content with mere security!

In history conditions of all-round satisfaction are neither frequent nor persistent. Certainly they are not in our age which has produced, among other ways of creating dissatisfaction, a surprising contempt for the art of satisfying defeated enemies. As a consequence, threats to the established order are almost constantly forcing those who seek preservation of cherished values to muster power of resistance if they wish to assure the success of their defensive objective. In this sense, one can say that their quest for power is the result of external "compulsion."

This compulsion is not some kind of mechanical force, however, which would rob the actors of their freedom of choice. No decision-maker is forced by anything except his own value preferences or his conscience to defend by means of power either national independence or any other threatened values. Plenty of Europeans today—and maybe European governments tomorrow—prefer to risk their country's freedom and institutions rather than embark on a policy of armed resistance which they consider hopeless or too costly. What the penalties are for not ceding to the "compulsion" is another question.

Those who interpret international politics as being essentially a struggle for survival, similar to the survival of the fittest in business competition or in the Darwinian world of competing animal species, are thereby suggesting that the penalty consists in the loss of independent existence. This has been true in some instances; but there is plenty of historical evidence to show that a threat to "existence," of great powers at least, has occurred only in the exceptional though cataclysmic eruptions of revolutionary or imperialist ardor characteristic of a Napoleon or a Hitler.[30] In our era such eruptions have become not only frequent but also capable of spreading out over the entire globe and of drawing all nations into a single struggle for survival. There have been other times—and they cover much of the maligned history of European power politics—when the demands for self-extension, though ubiquitous as far as the major powers of the time were concerned, have remained limited in scope. Even when these demands for self-extension were successful, the penalties on the loser rarely ranged beyond such deprivations as the loss of a strip of territory or the shift of a neighboring country to a less friendly dynasty. Whether such limitation was imposed solely by the lack of means for more ambitious self-extension, or whether it also expressed a prudent and conservative spirit on the part of the decision-makers, cannot be discussed here. In any case, the contrast with the "struggles for survival" of an age of revolutionary and total wars is striking.

Even when the penalty is not annihilation—and defeat today, as in remote ages, may actually mean physical extermination—countries usually feel compelled by their judgment and conscience not to allow possessions they value to go by default. They may enhance and use their power in defense of everything from prestige and colonies to free institutions and moral principles. The loss of values for which a people is ready to fight and die becomes a compelling penalty. Collective security, as practiced recently, can be understood as an effort not only to equal in scope and speed the power drive of the initiators, but to bring the free peoples to a point where they will identify their "selves" with the entire non-Communist world and its institutions and feel compelled to fight for the preservation of their larger "selves."

In the preceding pages I have suggested an approach to international politics that differs from that both of the idealist and the realist school by the emphasis it places on policy goals and the functional relationship existing between these goals and the quest for power. It would be tempting to compare the results to which one is led by this approach with the results attained by those of the two traditional schools of thought, especially in matters pertaining to policy. I can intimate only some of the differences here,

[30] See Morgenthau, *Scientific Man, op. cit.,* p. 107, on the difference between the "great international conflicts" and the "secondary conflicts."

leaving the consequences for a theory of peace strategy to be treated in detail on a later occasion.[31]

The idealist school is correct in stressing the value that men generally place on peace and in insisting that such evaluations can affect the decisions of policy-makers. Whether of their own volition or under pressures from more peace-minded groups of the population, statesmen under certain circumstances will desist from pressing national demands through means of power or will limit their demands. Realists would not be so eager, as was Machiavelli himself, to impress their governments with the "necessity" of playing the game of power politics as consistently as their opponents, were it not for fear that their governments might act with too much restraint.

The idealists, however, refuse to recognize that while peace-loving peoples wish for peace, they also wish to preserve what in the past they as individual nations have acquired or helped to establish. When their valued possessions come to include a wide circle of values reaching far beyond the national boundaries, as they do in the days of ideological or religious conflict, the occasions for power competition and violence are further enhanced.

Idealists are right in stressing that policy goals transcending the national interest (as traditionally interpreted) and affinities transcending national boundaries not only exist, but can be promoted by suitable policies. Nations defending common values and interests may come to form such bonds of friendship that their relationship ceases to be merely that of a temporary and expedient alliance in a balancing of power process; in the end they may merge or federate. However, if this process of amalgamation—clearly not compatible with the image of a world of billiard balls—takes place, as it usually does, in the context of a common conflict with an "outgroup," such national self-abnegation within the "in-group" does not diminish the intensity of power politics in the world at large; it may increase it. Thus, if the "free world" or the North Atlantic group of powers of Western Europe were drawn ever more closely together and learned to act as an organized community in accord with commonly accepted laws, it would still depend on the intensity of the East-West struggle how deeply the nations of the world were engaged in "power politics."

[31] See Chapter 9, "Peace Strategies of Deterrence and Accommodation."

The extent to which there is a struggle for power is decided, then, by what might be called the "relationship of major tension," rather than by the attitude that nations not engaged in conflict take toward one another. In the same sense, the degree of power competition and the expectation of violence rest not upon the behavior of countries concerned with self-preservation, but upon that of the "initiator." Idealist optimism in regard to the elimination of "power politics" is out of place, therefore, as long as the trend toward major tensions and toward the eruption of new and ambitious demands for self-extension is not reversed.

The drastic change that has taken place over the last twenty-odd years in the attitude of the idealist school itself toward peace strategy bears witness to the deterioration in the prospects for enduring peace. While the emphasis earlier was on conciliation and disarmament, it has come to be placed almost exclusively on "force behind the law" and "enforcement of peace." This means a swing to the realist view that nothing but counterpower and counterforce— although this be the collective power and force of the peace-loving community acting under the rules of an international organization —can safeguard the peace. This is the old idea of the balance of power, if within a new institutional frame. The change of attitude has gone so far that other means of peace strategy, such as the negotiation of concessions to satisfy demands of potential "initiators," are now often condemned without qualification as imperialist deals, appeasement, or rewards for aggression. This is not said in a critical vein. The idealist school may prove to be realistic in recognizing our being caught at present in a situation of such extreme tension and incompatibility of goals that anything other than the display of adequate defensive force on our part will merely serve to encourage offensive resort to violence on the part of others.

The realist school has merited its name for having appreciated the role that the quest for power plays in international politics, although it has devoted little attention to the policy goals from which this quest for power springs. It has recognized that a multistate system—a term that still properly designates the outstanding feature of contemporary international politics—is heavily slanted toward struggles for power. Lying somewhere within a continuum that stretches from the pole of an all-out struggle for power to the pole of an all-round indifference to power, the actual world tends to be pulled more strongly toward the former. This is true, whether the realist *a priori* assumptions concerning a universal human hunger for power or of a "security dilemma" arising from *la condition humaine* are correct or not. The main reason lies in the ever-recurring new incentives to demands for change and the equally strong incentives to throw power in the path of such change. By a curious irony, the same readiness to resist through power which is the prerequisite of any competition for power may, if strong, quick-moving, and determined enough, prevent the struggle from degenerating into violence. This is what the realists have in mind when placing their hopes for peace on the balance of power.

Quite possibly most of the great drives toward national and revolutionary self-extension which at intervals have thrown the world into struggles of sheer survival could not have been prevented by any means available to man. One can hardly escape a sense of fatalism if one asks oneself retrospectively whether the rise and aggressions of a Hitler could have been avoided. But this does not mean—as realist thought would seem to imply—that no influence can be brought to bear on policy-makers that would serve the interests of peace. Anything bearing on their value patterns and preferences, on their estimates of gains and deprivations, or on the scope of their identifications will, in principle, be able to affect the course of policy upon which they decide to embark.

It may be utopian to expect that the causes accounting for resorts to power and power competition could ever be wholly eliminated, as it is utopian to believe that defensive counterforce could be consistently held at sufficient strength to prevent the actual resort to violence; but there need be no resigned acceptance of the "enormity" of a continuous all-round struggle for survival. Through suitable policies, pressures, and appeals designed to attack the causes of intensive drives for enhanced power, the pulls toward the pole of all-round indifference to power can be strengthened. The main task of those engaged in developing a realistic theory of peace strategy is to discover policies and practices that offer most promise of turning nations away from goals pointing toward power competition and violence.

Chapter Seven   POWER AND
INFLUENCE:
THE MEANS OF
FOREIGN POLICY

BEFORE DISCUSSING the role of power in international relations it is necessary to establish how the term is to be used. If power is defined broadly as the ability to move others, or to get them to do what one wants them to do and not to do what one does not want them to do, then logically all foreign policy—the purpose of which is to make others conform to one's wishes—comes under the heading of power politics. But such a broad definition of power politics runs counter to common usage of the term which like "struggle for power" evokes the image of coercion and not of measures such as foreign aid or cultural exchanges that are common to present-day foreign policy and also affect the behavior of others. It is appropriate, therefore, to distinguish between power and influence, the first to mean the ability to move others by the threat or infliction of deprivations, the latter to mean the ability to do so through promises or grants of benefits.[1] The distinction between power and influence or "power politics" and "influence politics" does not mean that the two can be clearly separated in practice; as a rule they will

[1] Lasswell and Kaplan, who draw the same distinction, suggest an even stricter definition of power to include only cases of "serious deprivation." But the term "serious" causes difficulties of demarcation, and also there is merit in making the term "power politics" applicable both to the use of the small stick (threat of credit withdrawals, for instance) and to the use of the big stick (in the extreme case, use of nuclear weapons) in order to steer clear of the hypocritical notion that a nation is not using power to achieve its ends unless it is resorting to the open use of military force. Harold D. Lasswell and Abraham Kaplan, *Power and Society: A Framework for Political Inquiry* (Yale University Press, New Haven, 1950), p. 76.

be found to go hand in hand. It is also an oversimplification to say that power operates exclusively through coercion while influence relies entirely on persuasion. In practically every instance in which these means achieve significant political results, there is present both an element of persuasion and an element of pressure or constraint bordering on coercion. The best way to demonstrate the relationship between the two is to consider the wide spectrum from almost pure coercion to almost pure persuasion into which one can fit the actual means used by nations in pursuit of their foreign policies.

If, at the close of a war, a defeated country agrees to unconditional surrender, one might be inclined to say that the country was coerced into submission. In fact, however, it was persuaded to prefer surrender to further punishment. Japan's surrender in 1945 was not achieved by "moving" those whose lives were destroyed by the force of atomic bombs but by the persuasive effects of the destruction of Hiroshima and Nagasaki on that country's leaders. For the victim of extreme deprivation, it is true, the leeway for choice may be reduced almost to the vanishing point at which, in a not quite literal sense, he is forced to comply with the demands made on him.

Turning to the other extreme, a condition of sheer persuasion would seem to exist whenever a nation is led to make concessions in return for highly attractive gratifications. Yet, in most instances, there is present also an element of external pressure operating in a more or less overt and more or less coercive form which reduces the opportunity for choice. The pressures upon the decision-makers may originate with domestic groups especially interested in obtaining the particular benefits offered by the other nation; or they may result from threats of deprivation implicit in the offer of benefits. Thus, even if no strings are attached to foreign aid, the recipient government is likely to be, or believe itself to be, under pressure to conform to the wishes of the donor, if it wants to qualify for further aid in the future. When strings are attached explicitly, the operation clearly falls into the category of power politics. The realization of have-not countries that dependence on foreign aid subjects them to some degree of foreign power frequently dampens their gratitude toward the donor and may even induce them to refuse the grants.

While power and influence differ in many respects—in effectiveness, for instance, or in the sacrifices they impose—they share the role of being the means *par excellence* of foreign policy. No country that has any external objectives can hope to attain them and yet operate without some degree of power and influence. All the other instrumentalities of foreign policy can be judged by the way in which they enhance national power and influence though, like these, nations may come to value them as ends in themselves. In the case of armaments and alliances the fact that they have value only if they enhance national power is not likely to be forgotten because the costs and embarrassments connected with their establishment and maintenance prevent them from becoming desirable in themselves. The case of international organizations is different. While they are meant, originally, to help nations influence the behavior of others, either in the direction of co-operative action or of conformity with established rules, enthusiasm for international organizations *per se* may lead a nation to support them irrespective of whether it gains or loses influence as a consequence of the way the organizations operate. A change from the role of means or proximate goal to that of an ultimate goal may take place in the case of territorial objectives too. A nation that originally covets a strip of territory because its possession would enhance its strategic position or security may in the course of time come to cherish the territory for sentimental reasons, even though in the meantime it has become a drain on power rather than an asset.

In many respects, power and influence play the same role in international politics as money does in a market economy. In such an economy, money is indispensable for the purchase of goods both for consumption and production. For most people, therefore, acquiring money is a proximate goal, a steppingstone to things valued for their own sake or usefulness. But a second group of people, a minority, are skillful or fortunate enough to be able to accumulate financial reserves. These reserves are useful in an unforeseen crisis or opportunity, raise a man's credit, and give him a sense of economic security and freedom of action. There is finally a third group, the misers, who lose sight of the service money can render as a means to other ends and come to value it as an end in itself. Such men spare no effort or sacrifice in their unlimited quest for the accumulation of money.

In seeking influence and power, nations fall into three groups similar to those encountered among money-seekers. Most nations fall into the first category for which influence or power is an exceedingly scarce commodity strictly limited by the external prerequisites of its enhancement and by the sacrifices involved in its attainment.

For these nations, then, power and influence are instruments by which to satisfy at least their most urgent national needs. A second group comprises nations in the fortunate position of possessing some reserves of influence or power not immediately needed in the service of specific goals. A nation may have military forces or alliances in existence at times when no threat to its security nor any desire for new assets has yet materialized. The centuries-old British-Portuguese alliance can be placed in this category. Finally, as in the case of money, rulers or nations at times develop a lust for power or influence as ends in themselves. Here, as for the miser, the drive for their enhancement propels a nation to unlimited exertions and unlimited demands on others; a rational drive has become a pathological urge; a quest for power adequate to attain national ends turns into a quest for maximum power irrespective of circumstances.

Differences in purpose for which power is sought—as a means for the satisfaction of specific demands, as a reserve for future contingencies, as a value in itself—account for some of the great variations in the scope and intensity of the quest for influence and power, both among different nations and in the case of a single nation from one period to another. Other factors enter in and further enhance these differences. Much depends on the value that nations attach to the goals they seek to attain through influence or power. The higher this value, the greater the incentive to bear higher costs for an increase in power. Much depends also on the estimate of the amount and kind of power that will be required to satisfy one's demands. The uncertainty here is greater than in the case of money because there are no price tags to indicate what it takes to "buy" a desired success in foreign policy. Another, and in some instances the crucial, factor is the difference in value governments and nations attach to the assets, financial and other, that have to be sacrificed if influence or power is to be attained, preserved, or enhanced. Despite these many variables, some predispositional or subjective in character, the quest for influence or power is as universal in the international arena as is the quest for money in a market economy. Nations have little chance of surviving as independent units if they fail to attain some degree of coercive power: influence without power is not likely to carry far. Having to rely on their own strength for almost all the things they cherish, including their very survival, nations set limits below which they dare not drop in their quest for power and influence and their resort to power.

So far the emphasis has been on what power and influence have in common. Now it must be stressed that the two can be worlds apart in their effectiveness and in the way they affect the actors. It stands to reason that for the country that is to be moved, it is far preferable to be subjected to influence than to power. But the country seeking to obtain its objectives will as a rule also much prefer to use influence provided this promises net benefits similar to those attainable through power. After all, the exercise of coercive power is bound to be costly and risky, and usually far more costly than the use of persuasion. Therefore it is almost a truism to say that a government would rather obtain its objectives by negotiation than by war. Except in the case of a bloodthirsty tyrant, the question is whether the objective can be obtained without coercion or whether avoidance of the costs and risks of coercion justifies sacrificing part, or the whole, of the objective.

Unfortunately, in most of the situations in which nations are inclined to go to great lengths to attain highly valued objectives, resort to coercive power promises to be far more effective than influence. Only under quite exceptional circumstances have nations found it possible, without at least the threat of coercion—and usually the threat of military action—either to bring about serious changes of the established order or to prevent such changes when the demand for them was intense. The cases of "peaceful change" of any substantial kind are known to be very rare. Can anybody imagine that England could have been persuaded to give independence to its thirteen American colonies by any benefits they could have offered the mother country, that Alsace and Lorraine could have been reunited with France through the exercise of French influence, or that any of the colonial empires could have been liquidated short of the threat or use of large-scale violence? Because there is no substitute for coercion—even less for the threat of coercion—to bring about or prevent a change of control over assets to which both parties to a dispute attach great value, it is hypocritical to say that one has no quarrel with the objectives of nations seeking change but condemns only their resort to force. Given the conditions of the multistate system and the value patterns of nations it is not surprising that no nation possessing adequate power has managed consistently to get along without threatening deprivations on others and only few have managed without actually resorting to military coercion on occasion. In our era of cold war and nuclear deterrence the threat of force, implicit or explicit, is a constant accompaniment of the foreign policies of the major powers. Peace cannot become more stable unless nations decide to cut out or downgrade some of the demands that lead them into severe clashes with others.

Influence usually comes out second best in its competition with power. Yet its usefulness as an instrument of policy is far from negligible and in some situations, especially where demands are to be made on friendly nations, it outstrips power. A nation can often be persuaded by its ally to see the common interest more clearly, or to yield for the sake of benefits to be obtained from continued solidarity. Instead, if an ally threatens to withdraw from an alliance unless he gets what he wants, he may come to be regarded as so unreliable that his associates lose interest in his continued participation. In cases of serious conflict, particularly when relations have become inimical and the promise or grant of net benefits to the other side is uninviting, influence is limited to the kind of persuasion that diplomats can exercise in negotiations or around the conference table. Here diplomacy may succeed or fail according to its own intrinsic capacities. Lord William Strang has dealt with this aspect of persuasion thoroughly, and his words deserve to be quoted in full:

> Apart altogether from effective military power or the prestige that rests on military potential, there are factors which can weigh substantially in the diplomatic scales. One of them is sheer diplomatic skill. Power of exposition, choice of timing, the appeal to reason or to good faith or to international comity and morality, or to personal relationship, or to self-interest; the canvassing of support, the judicious threat, the dangled inducement, the hint of support or opposition on other issues, the sagacious estimate of the other minister's standing with his colleagues or with his sovereign, or with his public, or of the strength and standing of the other government: as between well-matched adversaries, these skills can play a substantial part.

In common with Sir Harold Nicolson, Strang also stresses the value of a "well-founded reputation for fair-dealing, for truth-telling, and a liberal regard for the common interest."[2]

Yet after all is said about the possibilities of moving others by persuasion, it is necessary to remind oneself—and to remind diplomats—that "coercive power in the background" usually deserves a

[2] Lord William Strang, *Britain in World Affairs: The Fluctuations in Power and Influence from Henry VIII to Elizabeth II* (Frederick Praeger, New York, 1961), p. 153.

major part of the credit for successful negotiation. One need not think of the kind of open and clumsy threats of force that instead of being persuasive may merely antagonize friends or stiffen the resistance of the opponent. But if any diplomat should doubt the assistance he gains from the mere existence of power in the hands of his government and from the threat of forceful action implicit in such power, he need only ask himself whether he would expect equal success in negotiating with a strong opponent if he were representing Iceland instead of the United States.

Turning to power, little need be said about the potentialities for moving others by the threat or infliction of deprivations. It is the limitations on the effectiveness of power that are not self-evident and therefore require analysis. If professional diplomats are often inclined to place undue confidence in their peculiar skills, military men are no less inclined to consider the instruments at their disposal a panacea for the ills besetting their countries. While both groups are indispensable to the conduct of foreign policy, both need to be protected, less against their own illusions than against those they may evoke in others who, expecting miracles from negotiations or force as the case may be, turn bitterly against their leaders whenever failure occurs. The most skillfully conducted negotiations may lead nowhere except to disillusionment, and very powerful countries may suffer exasperating frustrations if unaware of the limits of their capacity for effective coercion.

Consideration of what to expect from the threat or application of power in making others behave as one desires them to do must focus not on power in general but on particular types of power. From a natural desire to minimize military violence many people have been led to wishful thinking about what nonmilitary types of power can achieve. After World War I the tendency, as the League of Nations Covenant indicates, was to place great confidence in economic coercion; the threat and use of economic sanctions were hailed as substitutes for war. When sanctions actually were applied, however—against Italy after her attack on Ethiopia—members of the League discovered that getting agreement among the large number of nations whose participation was needed to make economic sanctions effective was extraordinarily difficult, and that economic sanctions were insufficient unless supplemented by the willingness to move on to military action in case the victim of the sanctions should resort to military force. After World War II a similar illusion about another alleged substitute for military power became widespread. Verbal or propagandistic coercion now took the place of economic sanctions. No doubt propaganda, by exerting a subversive influence, can under certain circumstances inflict serious deprivations. But if exponents of a "dynamic policy" call for propaganda and subversion as a substitute for military superiority, the Hungarian Revolution should have taught them a lesson: it may be possible by encouragement from outside a country to trigger a rebellion which might otherwise have been delayed, but nothing short of intervention by superior military power can save the rebels —if they get into trouble—from brutal suppression by their own government.

It is a prerequisite of rational policy that coercion be kept at the minimum required to attain desired results. And both humanitarian considerations and concern for public opinion give nations an additional interest in keeping the deprivations they inflict on others at a minimum. Power operates, however, by frightening others or by inflicting pain and it can be effective only if the pain anticipated or suffered is greater than the opponent is willing to tolerate. How much pain it takes to move him depends among other things on his vulnerability to a specific type of coercive measure. Nations differ in their vulnerability or immunity to subversion or to economic blockade, to severance of diplomatic relations or to bombardment. What may be a pinprick in one case may be a calamity in another. While a blockade may suffice to bring one country to its knees, it is a blunt weapon against another country that is economically self-sufficient. Mao Tse-tung may be convinced that his country would have a better chance of surviving a nuclear war than a foolproof blockade; blockade threats are not likely to make much impression on Khrushchev. In every instance, the value of coercive power hinges on the particular deprivations it can inflict on a particular actor under a particular set of circumstances, and also on the costs to its user when employed under these circumstances.

Despite the unique services the threat and use of coercive force can render, it is a fallacy to equate an array of even the most impressive instruments of coercion with effective national power. A nation with large, well-equipped, and well-commanded military forces may still suffer frustration in foreign policy. There are several reasons for the frequent discrepancies between the appearance of power and its actual performance: one is the relativity of power, another is the gap between the estimate of power and its reality, and a third is the specificity of power, which means that it takes specific types of power to bring results under specific circumstances. I shall briefly discuss these three sources of limitation and frustration.

Because the power of one country has to be measured against the power of its opponent, absolute figures relating to a nation's military strength prove nothing. This was obvious to military planners prior to the nuclear age, when strategic calculations were based on the estimated relative strength and stamina of the opposing forces in the field. In a confrontation of nuclear powers, the problem at first sight appears different. Here the power of a nation possessing the means to "kill off" its opponent in a first strike is not diminished by the prehostilities power of its victim which, if the assumption holds, will not survive the initial attack. The assumed ability of one country to disarm another in a first strike gives it an absolute advantage by eliminating any power its opponent possessed prior to the encounter. However, as soon as both sides have nuclear power that can survive an initial attack, the element of relativity reappears, though in somewhat different form from that existing under nonnuclear conditions. Because the power of the potential initiator of nuclear war must be measured against the surviving retaliatory strength of its victim rather than against his prehostilities strength, a comparison of their prehostilities strength in terms of numbers of megatons and carriers does not indicate their relative nuclear power in war and is, therefore, misleading.

There is one familiar phenomenon in international relations that seems to run counter to the suggested relativity of power. It could be called the paradoxical "power of the weak"—vividly demonstrated by the success with which a score of very shaky new states have gained advantage from the world's superpowers, and especially by the ways in which tiny Cuba and tiny Albania, each on at least one occasion, were able to reject pressures from overwhelmingly powerful close neighbors. Here lies the source of some of the worst irritations and frustrations of the major powers. The chief reason for this "power of the weak" stems from the relationships among the great powers themselves. Even for them power is a scarce commodity which they need to husband with care. This means placing priorities on its use. Therefore, whenever two great powers are locked in serious conflict they can spare little if any of their coercive strength to deal with minor offenders and to impose their will on them over issues that have no direct bearing on the major struggle in which they are involved with their equals. Weak countries awake to their own interests and to conditions favorable to them do not fail to appreciate the advantages accruing to them, without their doing, whenever major powers are forced to concentrate on struggles among one another. The current heyday of small power influence on world affairs is not likely to come to a close as long as the parties to the cold war remain rather evenly balanced or stalemated.

Not all the success of the "weak," however, is thus borrowed from others. Relatively weak countries as a rule are not lacking coercive power assets of their own. One such asset is the solidarity that usually prevails among the lesser countries and makes all of them sensitive to the "bullying" of any one of them. The potential hostility of a large number of lesser countries, some of which may be allies or close friends, is a deprivation that any nation setting out to impose its will on a weaker country must take into consideration. Further power accrues to a weak country if it can credibly threaten to switch its allegiance from one side to the other. The mere belief on the part of one great power that it would suffer a serious loss if a weak country with which it was dealing shifted either from one camp to the other or from alignment to neutrality gives the weak country a far from negligible coercive asset, sometimes called the power of blackmail. The United States has added immeasurably to the influence of the many neutralist states that have arisen in the postcolonial era, and even to the influence of some of its allies, by making plain that it would consider it a major deprivation if any non-Communist country were to fall into the hands of a Communist regime or to move closer to the Sino-Soviet bloc.

Under nuclear conditions, discrepancies between the estimates of two opponents' power distribution and the actual distribution tend to have particularly serious consequences, though erroneous power estimates have plagued nations at all times and have been the cause of many national calamities. Usually the error consists of underestimating the relative power of one's opponent. Overestimation of the strength of an opponent may be detrimental too: it discourages action or resistance where it would actually be rational. Neither the difficulties nor the importance of accuracy in the estimates of power can be exaggerated, but it is a mistake to conclude that the inevitability of particularly wide margins of error under nuclear conditions makes it senseless to continue thinking in terms of a balancing of power process. The statement that a "balance of power" is assuring mutual deterrence means that under given conditions each side estimates the forces its respective opponent will bring into play in case of war to be too great to engage except in desperation. A nation is more likely to be deterred the more it overestimates its opponent's relative power and willingness to carry through his threats. The error or accuracy of the estimates will not be revealed unless deterrence fails and the actual opposing forces become locked in battle.[3] But it does not follow that bluffing with great power and massive threats is a safe means of deterrence. Whether the bluff will be called and deterrence fail depends on how much self-punishment the threatened nation assumes its opponent expects to suffer should he execute his threat, and also on what the initiator believes his opponent to be ready to suffer for the values at stake for him in the particular confrontation. A threat that is not credible is no deterrent.

The problem of credibility arises also in connection with the third cause of frustration mentioned above, to which I applied the term specificity of power. Not all forms of power can be applied with equal success under all conditions. Thus, even the most impressive array of strategic nuclear forces has little deterrent value if it is incredible to the opponent that the country possessing those forces would sacrifice possibly tens of millions of its people to counter a relatively moderate provocation. Here, less destructive weapons offering a chance of less mutual punishment, may represent a more effective deterrent.

Because of the need for a wide variety of means of coercion and of persuasion, a nation is best prepared for future contingencies if it is equipped with a whole arsenal of means appropriate to varying uses. But the accumulation and maintenance of such means is costly in terms of other values even to nations with great resources and great willingness to make sacrifices for the attainment of their national goals. The question they constantly are asked—or ask themselves—is whether to hold their goals to limits set by their power or, instead, to enhance their power to the extent required for their goals. There is no general answer that can serve as a guide to rational policy under all conditions. Nations have been able to make good on the saying that "where there's a will there's a way" and have mustered a wholly unexpected degree of strength when cherished values were at stake. Not always have the sacrifices and

[3] This problem will be discussed more fully in Chapter 8, "The Balance of Power in Theory and Practice."

exertions been regretted or condemned afterward. But defeat and disillusionment are ahead for those who blind themselves to the limits that conditions are bound to place on the enhancement of power at some point—and frequently at a point far below what megalomania or dreams of glory suggest. The limits need not be absolute; they operate whenever, in terms of the values that prevail in a society, and are respected by the government, the costs of further enhancing power exceed the advantages it promises to provide. Rational policy-makers will seek to bring policy ends—and commitments to pursue them—in line not necessarily with existing power but with the potential power that can be actualized at sacrifices they judge to be justified by the national interest. One can speak, therefore, of a relationship of mutual dependence between ends and means.[4]

If nations were not so eager to obtain things they do not possess or so keen to hold on to rights and possessions acquired in the past, power politics would cede more place to influence politics; nations would forego objectives and relinquish possessions the attainment and maintenance of which are dependent on the threat or use of coercion. But there is no indication, despite the prohibition of resort to force in treaty after treaty, that a development away from power politics is taking shape. As in the past, nations satisfied with the *status quo* live in fear of new initiations of violence by others and nations that urgently, if not in blind fanaticism, demand change have little hope of bringing it about peacefully. But there are some promising signs of greater caution and self-restraint wherever a resort to coercion threatens to trigger the great strategic nuclear forces. Particularly the great powers themselves, who would bear the responsibility for a nuclear holocaust, seem to have recognized that at the level of large-scale nuclear destructiveness war ceases to be a rational instrument of policy. It remains to be seen whether this recognition will lead these powers—and lead all of

[4] Speaking of the "determinative importance of means," Charles Burton Marshall in *The Limits of Foreign Policy* (Henry Holt & Co., New York, 1954, p. 31) says: "It is important—nay, necessary—to maintain balance between those portions of ends chosen as purposes for action and the means available . . . . Regard for this necessity of balance between means and purposes is the heart of foreign policy." On the same point, Walter Lippmann in *U.S. Foreign Policy: Shield of the Republic* (Little, Brown & Co., Boston, 1943, p. 10) says of a statesman that "he must . . . bring his ends and means into balance. If he does not, he will follow a course that leads to disaster."

them equally—to downgrade the value of assets they can expect to acquire or to hold only by means of force, or whether the result will be to place an ever-increasing premium on coercive measures short of the kind of wars that might escalate to the nuclear level.

Chapter Eight   THE BALANCE OF
                    POWER IN THEORY
                    AND PRACTICE

AS LATE AS THE outbreak of World War II, any suggestion
that the United States was—or should be—concerning itself with the
world balance of power was distasteful to Americans, many of
whom considered the suggestion almost cynical.[1] The term "balance of power" was linked in people's minds with those features of
the old European state system that seemed most objectionable: the
struggle for power, the division of the world into hostile blocs, the
unending series of wars. Today, on the contrary, there are constant
references in the press and in official statements to the American
policy objective of preserving or restoring the world balance of
power and to the dangers of Soviet threats to this balance. Far from
being a subject of purely theoretical interest, the concept of the
balance of power has thus become intimately related to matters of
immediate practical import for the United States and its allies.

Investigating the manner in which the balance of power concept
can illuminate the current problems of American policy or even
guide American decision-makers, it is necessary first to examine the
age-old debate among theorists on the meaning of the term and on
the phenomena to which the term most usefully applies. Much
confusion arises from different interpretations. While it is obvious
that the term refers somehow to the distribution of power among
nations, it is taken in some instances to be synonymous with the
distribution of power generally, and in other instances to imply
the superiority of one country over another—a surplus of power on

[1] This chapter is a revised version of an article originally appearing in *The
Naval War College Review*, Vol. XI, No. 5 (January, 1959) and is reprinted
here by permission of the publisher.

117

one side comparable to the balance on the credit side of a book-keeping account. Most frequently, however, the term signifies the equilibrium of an evenly balanced scale.

In order to cut the semantic knot at the start; I choose the last meaning and shall speak of the balance of power as meaning an equilibrium or a roughly equal distribution of power between two opponents, the opposite, then, of hegemony or domination. To draw a distinction between balanced and unbalanced power does not suggest, however, that there is any sure way of measuring and comparing the relative power of nations and thus of deciding how great is the unbalance or how close the balance. Even the extent of a nation's military power (which is but one, albeit the most important, part of its total power) can be tested only in war; but if it comes to such a test, then the balance of power has failed in its purpose of preserving the peace. Nevertheless, it makes sense to speak of an existing balance of power—or of a fair approximation to such a balance—whenever there are indications that two opposing nations, or blocs of nations, are being deterred from putting their opponent's total power to the test. In peacetime one can speak of a balance of "mutual deterrence" which today when nuclear power is involved has been called not very accurately a "balance of terror." It presupposes that in the estimates of both sides the respective opponent possesses and is ready to employ more coercion than he is willing to suffer.

Using this definition of the balance of power, one can examine theories on the merits of an equilibrium of power among adversaries and on the process by which such equilibrium is established, preserved, or upset. I shall discuss four such theories—three of long standing, one of recent vintage—and inquire into their significance for contemporary foreign policy. One theory regards the balance of power as the ideal distribution of power; a second considers it the automatic outcome of developments inherent in the multistate system; to a third, the balance of power represents a goal of foreign policy that some policy-makers find useful to pursue; according to a fourth theory of mid-twentieth century origin, it has become an obsolete notion which is misleading to anyone concerned with contemporary international affairs.[2]

[2] E.B. Haas, who in his articles, "The Balance of Power as a Guide to Policy-Making" (*Journal of Politics*, August, 1953) and "The Balance of Power: Prescription, Concept or Propaganda" (*World Politics*, July, 1953), made valuable contributions to the discussion of the balance of power concept, drops all mention of it in the textbook (and its index) published with A.S. Whiting

Presumably, very few people in this country would consider seriously the kind of glorification of balanced power found in earlier centuries. While the idea of checks and balances, intimately associated with the American Constitution, is still regarded as a valuable device in domestic affairs, equilibrium on the world stage arouses grave misgivings today particularly because it implies the continued coexistence of a free world and a communist world, with each side holding the other in check. Such a concept could hardly be said to conform with our ideals of the world in which we would wish to live. At best then, a balance of power between the two main opponents of today's world may be found acceptable as the least evil or objectionable distribution of power presently attainable.

But even without the cold war, many people in the West would refuse to consider international equilibrium an ideal distribution of power. Current predilections run toward what is called "collective security." This theory assumes that the peace of the world depends not on having the power of all nations balanced and checked by the power of others but, on the contrary, on making overwhelming power available to those who are ready to oppose potential aggressor nations or to punish actual aggressors. By the rules of collective security, the "peace-loving nations" of the world cannot have too much power since they can be expected never to abuse their supremacy. The stronger they are, collectively, the better their chances of deterring or, if necessary, of punishing potential violators of the peace. On this premise, the ideal situation is one in which the assumed defenders of the peace and law of the world community enjoy unchallengeable hegemony.

Without being able to do justice here to the arguments for and against collective security which will be discussed in later chapters,[3]

---

in 1956 (*The Dynamics of International Relations*, McGraw-Hill, New York). Only in two sentences, with an "of course" here and a "simply" there, does the function of a power equilibrium receive attention implicitly. These sentences read: ". . . The ability of the potential enemy to inflict losses and damage is, of course, the primary feature which induces a given interest group to assume the attitude of restraint. On the basis of this tendency, then it may be concluded that a rough equality of power may act as a restraining force simply because neither side can be confident of an easy victory" (p. 50). It looks as if Haas, like some other "modernists" in political science, has become so absorbed with the trees (subnational groups and individual decision-makers) that the forest of power distribution and power conflict among nation-states has dropped out of sight.

[3] See Chapter 11, "Collective Security and the War in Korea," and Chapter 12, "Collective Defense versus Collective Security."

I cannot refrain from pointing to some recent events that have cast doubts on the ideal of hegemony for the peace-loving nations.

In World War II the Soviet Union, an ally of the West in its struggle against the "aggressor nations" of the Axis coalition, became labeled as one of the peace-loving nations. Consequently, it was assumed that there was no need for concern about the postwar distribution of power between the Soviet Union and its Western Allies. In fact, President Roosevelt was incensed when Churchill raised the old bogy of the balance of power to warn against a strategy that would place Vienna under the control of the Soviet Union. Implicit in the Allied demand for unconditional surrender, moreover, was the desire that Germany and Japan should be impotent after their defeat in spite of the fact that the complete elimination of their power was bound to have an unbalancing effect in Eurasia. In its efforts to prevent a no longer "peace-loving" Soviet Union from dominating the entire world island of Eurasia, the United States has since discovered how costly and dangerous indifference to the distribution of power can prove.

The Suez crisis of 1956 struck another and more serious blow at the notion that some nations can be classified as falling regularly into the peace-loving category and can be assumed therefore to need no external checks and balances. Great Britain and France, two of the chief pillars of the United Nations collective security system, and democratic Israel turned up on the side of aggression. As a result, of all the great powers that have existed in this century, so far the United States alone has escaped condemnation as an aggressor by an international organization. Thus, from the point of view of preserving the peace—although not necessarily from the point of view of promoting justice—it may be a valid proposition that a balance of power placing restraint on every nation is more advantageous in the long run than the hegemony even of those deemed peace-loving at a given time.

It has been said that even those statesmen who have been the foremost verbal champions of equilibrium never really regarded it as an ideal. The British, in particular, have been accused of hypocrisy for advocating the balance of power as a universally beneficial principle when their country was deriving unique benefits from its observance. Britain, by seeking an equilibrium between her continental rivals rather than between herself and potential enemies was able to assume the role of "balancer" with all the advantages of that position.

Preference for equilibrium need not, however, be a mere rationalization of national interest. In fact, it is deeply rooted in what today would be called conservative thought which characteristically embodies the pessimistic view of human nature that found classical expression in the writings of Machiavelli and Hobbes. This pessimistic view sustains Lord Acton's expectation that "power corrupts and absolute power corrupts absolutely." Men with a conservative bent of mind need find nothing shocking, therefore, in the suggestion that all nations, including their own, should be restrained by counterpower and thereby be spared temptations as well as prevented from abusing their power.

The suggestion that all nations need the restraint of the balance of power does not mean that the same amount of power is required to deter an aggressive would-be empire builder or megalomaniac dictator from initiating violence as is required to prevent a satisfied nation from doing the same, especially if it is a democratic country operating under strong internal restraints. In any "balance of deterrence," different estimates have to be taken into account both of the power distribution and of the willingness of the opponents to use force and to take risks. A fanatical government bent on conquest will tend to overestimate its own power and underestimate that of its "decadent" opponents; revolutionary governments consider violence a necessary part of the historic process of change. Nobody could seriously praise a balance of power as a safeguard against war, therefore, except on the assumption that it is of a kind that promises to place effective restraints even on the least self-restrained of the parties.

The potential restraining effect of the balance turns would-be conquerors—the Napoleons or Hitlers—into its most violent critics, making them strange bedfellows of the idealistic exponents of collective security who share this hostility towards the concept of a power equilibrium. The Nazis were vociferous in their accusation that Britain espoused the "ideal" of a balance of power merely to prevent potential continental rivals from challenging her predominance. Generally, countries in revolt against the *status quo* oppose balanced power because it bars the way to change. Equilibrium tends to prevent change by force, usually the only means through which major changes can be brought about.

For the exponents of the second theory of the balance of power, the controversy between those who contend that the balance of power is a good thing and those who condemn it makes no sense.

They assert that equilibrium of power is not a matter of choice; instead, it is brought about automatically by a competition for power among nations that is inherent in the multistate system. According to this view, a mechanism is at work, similar to the "invisible hand" the classical economists detected in a market economy and which they expected would tend automatically to produce an equilibrium between supply and demand. Theorists have constructed a model of a multistate system in which, similarly, equilibrium results without any deliberate choice by the actors. While today such a model is not regarded as more than an abstract initial working hypothesis, the conditions existing in the nineteenth century gave it the character of a rather striking portrait of reality. After the end of Napoleon's continental hegemony, world power was distributed among five or six major European nations. All of them were jealous of their relative power positions, all were keenly aware of changes in the distribution of power, and all were eager to prevent any one of the others from stepping into the shoes of Napoleonic France. Therefore, in order to render impossible, or to defeat, any incipient hegemony, two or more powers could be counted upon to line up almost intuitively against any power that threatened to become their superior. In their "game of power politics" they were united by a common interest not to allow the balance to be tipped against them. Competition for allies and competition in armaments were the chief instruments of a balancing process in which the realities of European power politics came to resemble an automatically balancing system.

Even in that period of the nineteenth century, however, the expectation of an equilibrium of mutual deterrence resulting without any deliberate and intelligent efforts on the part of governments had visible flaws. Again and again, a country believing it had attained a position of superiority struck out against its rivals, or another country fearing an increasingly adverse balance initiated war before the balance had tilted too far against it. In such instances, war was the instrument by which the breakdown of equilibrium was overcome or prevented, a method of adjustment hardly comparable with the relatively smooth-working price mechanism of the market economy. Innumerable historical cases could be cited to show how far the success of the balancing process depended on the choices made by statesmen of the countries involved. British statesmen were faced with a momentous choice when, prior to the outbreak of war in 1914, they had to decide whether or not to give advance British backing to France and Russia as a means of deterring the Central Powers. There was no automatism in operation to prevent them from making the wrong choice. Similarly, when three years later Germany had hegemony almost within its grasp, there was nothing automatic about the decision of the United States to enter on the side of the hard-pressed Allies. In fact, by resuming unrestricted submarine warfare early in 1917, Germany itself was largely responsible for speeding up a decision that might otherwise have been reached too late to tilt the balance of power against Germany before the Allies were defeated.

While it makes little sense to use the term "automatic" literally, as if human choices and errors were irrelevant to the establishment, preservation, or destruction of a state of equilibrium, there nevertheless is a significant element of truth in the theory of "automatism" which is valid even today. If one may assume that any government in its senses will be deeply concerned with the relative power position of hostile countries, then one may conclude that efforts to keep in step in the competition for power with such opponents, or even to outdo them, will almost certainly be forthcoming. If most nations react in this way, a tendency towards equilibrium will follow; it will come into play whether both sides aim at equilibrium or whether the more aggressive side strives for superiority. In the latter case, the opposite side is likely to be provoked into matching these aggressive moves. Forces appear therefore to be working "behind the backs" of the human actors, pushing them in the direction of balanced power irrespective of their preferences.

In the light of recent events, it is also worth noting how nations seem to be drawn into the balancing process almost without conscious choice or deliberation. The policy of the United States since World War II offers a particularly striking illustration. Despite its long-established policy of resisting all pressures and temptations toward involvement in the peacetime balancing of power process, the United States reversed its traditional stand without hesitation when no other country was in a position to contain the ascending Soviet Empire or to restrain it by means of counterpower.

Other countries also have reluctantly become concerned about the balance of power in recent years. Yugoslavia, for instance, although strongly committed by the ideology of its regime to remain on the Soviet side, has repeatedly given signs of appreciating the security it enjoys through the existence of Western counterpower.

Fearing Soviet predominance, Yugoslavia has sided with the West on several occasions and conceivably might throw its military weight on the side of the camp whose ideology it rejects. Here again an almost irresistible pull toward equilibrium appears to exist.

There are other instances, however, in which the "automatic" reaction fails to materialize. Some weak countries seek safety by getting on the bandwagon of an ascending power, hoping somehow to escape complete subjugation once their powerful "friend" has gained supremacy. Other countries are so absorbed with their internal affairs or so unheeding of national power that the effects of their policies on the distribution of power, whether helping to preserve or upset the balance, are purely accidental. Therefore, while not slighting the ability of the "invisible hand" to aid power equilibrium, one may expect more insight from a theory that does not ignore the effects of variant human intentions and actions.

The question is whether nations under certain circumstances do or should, as a matter of expediency, make power equilibrium rather than power superiority the target of their efforts. If equilibrium is their objective, they must assume it to be a practical policy that will serve the best interests of their country. Frequently, the original intention to preserve or achieve superiority will be dropped only after the competitive race has proved superiority to be unattainable. Then equilibrium—or stalemate, as it is often called today—may be accepted not without resignation as the least detrimental goal. Both sides, in fact, may come to realize that a race for superiority is leading nowhere except to mutual exhaustion or provocation, and so they may agree to settle, tacitly at least, for the less ambitious and less costly goal of balanced power.

As indicated earlier, what some governments mean when they claim to make the balance of power their aim is, rather, a balance between the power of other nations that will place their country in the enviable position of "balancer." Countries too weak to become active balancers can merely hope that an equilibrium which will make them more secure even if they can do nothing to promote it will be established between their stronger neighbors. Up to 1914, the United States was one of the passive beneficiaries of the balance of power which Britain did so much to maintain on the Continent. Today, the United States stands out as the country most able to keep other nations, especially within the free world, in a state of equilibrium. Not a few American moves have been directed towards this goal. The United States is interested in the maintenance of peace among its many non-Communist friends and allies. Therefore, it acts true to the traditions of the state system when seeking, for instance, to keep Israel and its Arab neighbors in a condition approximating balanced power.

No country faced with grave external danger, as the United States is today, would willingly forego superiority of power over its opponent if such superiority were attainable at acceptable costs. A sigh of relief would go up if a technical break-through in the arms race were suddenly to give us indubitable military supremacy. However carefully estimated and maintained, equilibrium can give nothing like the security that would follow such supremacy. Nevertheless, the United States and most of its allies can afford to resign themselves without much trepidation to a policy of mere equilibrium if they are rightly classified as *status quo* powers.

The term *"status quo* power" is used here for nations that either desire to preserve the established order or that, while actually desiring change, have renounced the use of force as a method for bringing it about. In their position what they need is power—or more correctly counterpower—sufficient to deter or stop an opponent who is believed to seek change even at the price of war. For such deterrence, power equal to that of the opponent is sufficient; neither deterrence nor defense requires superiority of power or supremacy.[4] Although the United States is thoroughly dissatisfied with a world order in which some countries have suffered partition and others are in bondage as satellites, it nevertheless qualifies as a *status quo* power because it has renounced the use of force as a means of remedying the iniquities of the *status quo*. Therefore, acceptance of power equilibrium as the goal of American policy means not that the United States has sacrificed its defensive objective, but only that it has forfeited the greater security that *status quo* powers can obtain from a position of superiority.

The other category of nations, formerly called "revisionist" countries, which are bent on changing the *status quo* by force if necessary, are in a less favorable position. They can accept balanced power only with utter resignation since they know that only in quite exceptional cases can the established order be seriously modi-

---

[4] Equilibrium is not always assured by equal numbers of forces for both sides. Under circumstances in which the offensive side gains an increment of power from the fact of being able to choose the time and place of its attack, the defensive side needs correspondingly larger forces to avoid a disadvantage.

fied without at least the threat of a force so preponderant that it will overcome the resistance of the opposing side. Thus, for these states to give up the goal of superior power in favor of balanced power means renunciation of their ultimate national goal: a substantial change in the existing order. If the Soviet Union and Red China fall into the category of revisionist countries, as everything indicates they do, their power goal must be assumed to be superiority of power rather than balanced power.

There are many Americans who deplore the acquiescence of their country in the position of a *status quo* power. But their demands for a more offensive policy which would seek to break Soviet resistance to changes favoring the non-Communist world must nevertheless face the question whether American superiority of power of the kind required for such a policy is or could be brought within practical reach. Moreover, a quest for mere equilibrium may offer some advantages that will compensate partly for the failure, serious even for *status quo* powers, to attain the kind of security that only a safe margin of superiority can offer.

If a country is able to give convincing evidence of seeking only equilibrium, it will not as a rule be suspected of aggressive intentions. By obviously seeking to attain defensive capabilities only, it will appeal to those of its friends and allies who belong in the category of *status quo* powers and will disappoint only its "revisionist" friends. There is a chance, too, that the more modest power goal will have some effect on the behavior of the opposing side—in this case of the Sino-Soviet bloc. Should the Soviets become convinced that the chance of gaining a significant edge on the United States and its allies in terms of military power is slim and at the same time should come to believe that their opponents are seeking a balance of power only, they might in time resign themselves to equilibrium rather than continue an unrewarding race for superiority.

Any suggestion that the United States might make a reasonable balance of power between East and West a target of its foreign policy and the standard by which to measure its efforts in the power field runs counter to the last of the four theories mentioned earlier according to which the whole notion of a balancing of power policy has been rendered obsolete by radical changes in the conditions of international politics. While, in former times, the balance may have been a condition both of peace and of the continued independence of many nations, the exponents of the theory assert that because of the impact of a number of new factors with which statesmen did not formerly have to contend, it has ceased to be a practiced goal today.

One of these factors, strongly emphasized at the close of World War II, was the rise of the United States to a leading position in world politics. Many argued that the newcomer was little fit for the task of playing the balancing game. Was it possible to expect a country so little accustomed to or inclined towards power calculations in foreign affairs to be able to switch sides from former friends to former enemies if such a move were necessary for the restoration of the world balance of power? Would the United States agree to "entangling" itself in alliances? The record of American policies since World War II has laid these misgivings to rest and has thoroughly disproved the alleged ineptitude of the United States in the matter of the balancing of power process. With speed that came as a shock even to many Europeans supposedly reared in the traditions of the power game, America's enemies of World War II became her military allies, and soon the United States was to emerge as the center of a peacetime alliance system of unprecedented breadth. Statesmen in Washington quickly became aware of the need for establishing a balance between the power of the East and the West. Concepts such as containment and deterrence, soon catchwords of the day, pointed to equilibrium as a minimum American objective. Therefore, rather than confirming the theory of obsolescence, this first factor appears to demonstrate the continuing primacy of balancing of power considerations.

A second new factor, the so-called "bipolarity" of the postwar world, was thought to be of even greater consequence. After all, the balance of power system of the nineteenth century rested on the simultaneous existence of five or six major powers. Now only two were left; the remaining lesser powers were able to throw so little into the scales against a potentially ascending state that their influence could not become decisive. Here too, however, experience has merely added significance to the contention that whenever there is more than one sovereign power in the world, the balancing process will operate. Even had it been true that all significant power was to remain vested in the U.S.A. and the U.S.S.R., their competition in armaments and in economic development could have led to a balance of power between them that might have been maintained by their efforts alone. But the condition of the extreme bipolarity of 1945 has been steadily on the decline as other centers of not inconsiderable power have arisen or reasserted themselves in many parts of the world. As the situation stands today, these lesser powers can throw their weight to one side or another and significantly affect the distribution of power between the two main opposing camps. Moreover, regional balancing of power is under way among some of the lesser countries; for instance, between the Arab countries and Israel, or between Pakistan and India.

Neither bipolarity nor the rise of new states, then, has resulted in the disappearance of traditional policies. On the contrary, one of the striking characteristics of the present situation is the manner in which some of the new states have come to throw their weight around in the world balancing process, although one might have expected them to be preoccupied with their thorny internal problems. Sometimes, as in the case of Yugoslavia, they act for the obvious purpose of preventing one of the superpowers from becoming too mighty in a particular area.

A third novelty rightly attracting attention is the ideological note that has been introduced into the world's major power struggle. Some observers predicted the growth of such strong ideological affinities and antagonisms that nations would become unwilling to leave the camp of their ideological preference whatever the requirements of the balancing process. If this had occurred, the distribution of power in the world would have been at the mercy of ideological competition. Undoubtedly, ideological appeals have affected the orientation of some countries toward East or West, but in such cases one cannot say that efforts to establish a balance of power have necessarily ceased. Indeed, whenever ideological power has shown a tendency to gain the upper hand over other forms of power, competition between East and West does not disappear but is transferred to the field of ideology, propaganda, and subversion. We can see evidence of this competition on all sides today, and we may have to conclude that the United States will have much trouble balancing Soviet power if it fails to match the ideological pull the Communists are able to exert in many areas today.

Ideology has not, however, come to reign supreme. There have been instances to show that the "blood" of national security and military power considerations can still run thicker than the "water" of ideological sympathy. As mentioned earlier, Communist Yugoslavia lined up with the West when it felt threatened by Soviet military superiority, and countries with no Communist bias like Nasser's Egypt have taken full advantage of opportunities to swing toward the Soviet side when, for reasons of national interest, they wished to weaken or blackmail the Western camp. If ideology interferes with the relatively smooth functioning of the traditional balancing process, it is most likely to do so by blinding ideologically fanatical leaders and elites to threats emanating from the camp of their ideological preference. When statesmen jeopardize national security interests in this way, one can speak of a kind of "ideological stickiness" in favor of certain alignments even when they run counter to the requirements of equilibrium.

Finally, there is the new factor of nuclear weapons. The question has been raised whether the conditions of the nuclear age, with its weapons of unprecedented destructiveness and its revolutionary developments in weapons technology, does not defeat all efforts at rational power calculation and comparison. If it did, governments would be unable to aim at a particular world power distribution, balanced or unbalanced, or to know even approximately whether equilibrium exists at any given time. Thus, it would be hopeless for them to attempt to rely on the balance of power for the security of their countries or for the preservation of peace.

No one can deny that the art of estimating power—one's own and that of one's adversary—the source of so many tragic errors even in prenuclear days, has been complicated immensely by the introduction of ever new and untried instruments of war. Yet, despite this new element of uncertainty, there probably has never been a time in which more effort has been exerted towards estimating comparative military power, strategic nuclear striking power included. All the talk of a stalemate on the strategic plane would be meaningless if these estimates had become a matter of sheer guesswork. In time of peace, it must be remembered, it is the balance of mutual deterrence that is important, and deterrence rests not on the *actual* relative strength of the two sides—which only war can reveal—but on what governments *believe to be* the existing distribution of power. In fact, the more both sides overestimate the relative power position of their opponent, the more likely it is that they will be deterred from using their power. Since the chief danger in the past has been an underestimation of enemy strength and determination, the advent of nuclear weapons has had the effect of buttressing the deterrent value of the balancing process in situations in which the threat of a nuclear strike appears credible. Even a megalomaniac will not easily discount enemy nuclear retaliatory power, provided he has the slightest reason to believe that his opponent might use that power to counter his moves. If credible, the threat of retaliation even with less than equal nuclear force may suffice for deterrence provided enough of the lesser force is expected to survive a first strike to be capable of causing intolerable damage to the attacker.

What makes it particularly difficult and costly for the United States to balance the Soviet Union today lies not on the level of strategic nuclear forces but on other levels of power competition. The strategic nuclear capabilities of the United States and the Soviet Union may come to neutralize each other and thus to drop out of the scale as a positive balancing factor. The balance will then depend on power relationships all the way down the ladder from somewhere below massive retaliatory power to the respective capacities for limited war, for conventional war, for subversion, and for ideological or economic appeal. The balance already depends on these factors in all confrontations in which the nuclear threat lacks credibility. On at least some of these less elevated rungs of the ladder, the Sino-Soviet bloc is superior at this time. While unable to end the balancing of power process or to rob it of its former functions, the nuclear factor merely adds to the difficulties of manipulating the process in such a way that a reasonable degree of equilibrium can be attained, ascertained, and preserved.

One last remark should be made about the alleged obsolescence of the balance of power and balancing of power process. Those who accept the obsolescence theory must ask themselves whether any practical alternative course is open to nations. An organization like the United Nations, despite its provisions for collective security, cannot put the balancing process to rest because it leaves all coercive power in the hands of its members. There can be only one alternative: the elimination of all military power from the control of individual nations, which, if it occurred, would obviously relieve governments of the need to concern themselves with the world distribution of power among nations. With the monopoly of military power in the hands of a single world authority—though only in the case of such a monopoly—international politics itself, and with it the whole balancing of power process, would disappear. Nations embroiled in conflict with one another would have no more reason to worry about the power position of other nations than a Rhode Island or an Oklahoma need have about the power of larger and potentially more powerful neighboring states of the Union.

Unfortunately for those who would like to see such a world authority established, it must be said that there is nothing to indicate a chance of its being established in the foreseeable future. Can anyone imagine the United States and the Soviet Union subordinating themselves voluntarily to an authority over which their chief opponent might come to exercise supreme control? If they did, they would make themselves as impotent as any state in the Union is as compared to the federal government. Moreover, if ever the two superpowers had enough confidence in each other not to mind being ruled by a world authority possessing a monopoly of military power that might come under the control of the other, there would be no need for such a world authority. Under such ideal conditions of mutual confidence, the two together could rule supreme in the world though their chances of preserving such mutual confidence and of agreeing on the use of their power would be greater if they preserved a high degree of equilibrium between themselves. Rather than making a world authority more practical today than it has been in earlier periods, ideological conflict, concentration of power in the hands of two antagonistic superpowers, and the introduction of nuclear weapons have deepened the gulf between nations and made world unity more remote. Under these circumstances the balance of power, while far from ideal, suggests itself as an acceptable and practical substitute for the supremacy in the world that the United States with all its actual and potential power cannot presently hope to attain for itself.

Chapter Nine

PEACE STRATEGIES
OF DETERRENCE
AND ACCOMMODATION

IN THE PRECEDING chapters peace was discussed only incidentally, as one environmental goal among others, for instance, or
as the desired outcome of a balance of power policy conducted by
status quo powers. Yet policies dealing with peace, or with the prevention of war, occupy a prominent place in the foreign policy of
most nations much of the time. It would be distressing if this were
not so, particularly now that war threatens unprecedented destructiveness and, at least in the case of unrestricted war between two
nuclear powers, has ceased to be a rational instrument of policy.

Despite the widespread public clamor for peace and the unending
stream of official professions of peaceful intent, it is often said that
peace itself is never the actual goal of foreign policy. This contention rests on the misapprehension that in order to qualify as a goal,
peace would have to be regarded as an absolute value for which
all other values would be sacrificed. But few objectives, even the
protection of such a core value as territorial integrity, are absolute
in this sense: Czechoslovakia, for example, ceded much of her territory to Hitler in 1938 in order to save the rest. Peace too competes
with other values, with justice in one instance, with honor in
another. It may therefore be sacrificed if avoiding war would require resigned acceptance of intolerable injustice or the violation of
solemn pledges. As a rule, only a nation facing defeat will "buy"
peace at the extreme price of an unconditional surrender which
means placing itself and all it values at the mercy of the enemy.
Between this contingency and the opposite extreme at which a
nation prefers war to making any sacrifice—or actually cherishes
war as a value in itself—lie the wide range of choices by which

133

nations decide what losses to incur or what gains to forfeit in order to restore, preserve, or consolidate peace.

It stands to reason that peace is valued most by nations for whom war and violence can promise nothing but loss and destruction. The more satisfied nations are with the established order, or the weaker they are compared to their potential enemies, the more they can be expected to be "peace-loving," i.e., willing to make sacrifices to preserve the peace. But even powerful dissatisfied countries will sometimes be found on the peace-loving side; the restraint of these countries, which are capable of contesting the *status quo* through force but instead accept the conditions that provoke their dissatisfaction, is all the more praiseworthy.[1] Of course, under present nuclear conditions such resignation is not difficult for countries that could not hope to change the *status quo* except by resort to a war of devastating self-destruction. Germany's resignation to partition, at least for an indefinite time, or the resignation of the United States to Moscow's continued rule over Eastern Europe can be better explained by their realization of the costs of the alternative to peace than by either a passionate desire for peace or a condemnable indifference to the injustices of the *status quo*.

The varying value different men and nations attach to the blessings of peace and to the lives and property that war would destroy are not irrelevant in accounting for their respective propensity to resort to war, whether offensively, to change the *status quo,* or defensively, to preserve it; but if, in times ahead, the readiness to initiate war should decline, it will be less for greater love of peace or greater indifference to unjust conditions than for greater fear of nuclear destruction. Evidence of this has not been lacking since the dawn of the nuclear age. In places such as Indochina, Suez, Tibet, and Goa, where the danger of nuclear weapons' being used, or of escalation of war to the nuclear level, was considered small, nations and factions within nations have demonstrated no unusual restraint in the resort to violence and even less in the use of threats of war—not all bluff—for purposes of both deterrence and blackmail.

---

[1] George Kennan suggests that Americans, particularly, are prejudiced in favor of the *status quo* and peacefulness. He points out that "to the American mind, it is implausible that people should have positive aspirations, and ones that they regard as legitimate, more important to them than the peacefulness and orderliness of international life," and goes on to say that "we tend to underestimate the violence of national maladjustments and discontents elsewhere in the world." *American Diplomacy, 1900-1950* (University of Chicago Press, Chicago, 1951) , p. 96.

When governments do concern themselves with the promotion of peace, they are faced with a wealth of suggestions and an ever growing volume of literature on how peace can be attained or made to endure.[2] Most of the advice on peace addressed to the problem of how to order the world—legally, politically, and militarily—to make wars among nations impossible fails to spell out how national governments responsible for the security of their countries could go about creating such an order.

The plans of exponents of world government offer the most striking example of the dichotomy between the ideal and the practical peace strategy. In maintaining that a world authority enjoying a monopoly of military power would make war impossible, they are stating a truism. The important question is whether national governments are in a position to replace the multistate system with a single sovereign power possessing unchallengeable authority over the entire political world. To affirm this as a practical possibility the exponents of world government point out, correctly, that sovereign nations have on occasion merged their independence into a union or federation with others, forfeiting their separate control over military forces and thus their ability to resort to war. This argument fails to consider, however, the amount of amity and mutual confidence necessary among nations to make their merger conceivable. Wherever peace is endangered and conflict and enmity reign as they do, for instance, in the cold war today, peace through world government—and thus its greatest purpose, the elimination of the danger of nuclear war—presupposes that the two opposing power blocs agree on its establishment. Such agreement, however, as mentioned earlier,[3] assumes willingness on the part of the opposing blocs to place their countries in the hands of an authority wielding a monopoly of power over which their opponent might later manage to gain control.

Here lies the utopian joker. If ever the United States and the Soviet Union gained such boundless confidence in each other, no world government would be needed. For a nation to favor world

---

[2] See the elaborate and useful bibliographies and research proposals published by the Institute for International Order (11 West 42 Street, New York 36, New York). These include the quarterly bibliographical publication *Current Thought on Peace and War,* and five "Research Designs for Peace." Also prominent in the field of nonutopian peace research is the Center for Research on Conflict Resolution of the University of Michigan, which publishes the quarterly *Journal of Conflict Resolution.*

[3] See Chapter 8, "The Balance of Power in Theory and Practice."

government even in the absence of such mutual confidence, on the ground that the envisaged constitutional or legal provisions and commitments would make it impossible for the other nation to seize control, would be to demonstrate an almost inconceivable degree of ignorance on the part of responsible leaders about the limits of the power of law under conditions in which a deeply rooted consensus on major issues and a genuine community among the parties are conspicuously absent.

Some other well-known peace proposals or panaceas for peace are similarly utopian in that they lie beyond the range of practical policies open to the "powers that be." Peace would be safer, for instance, if human nature could be changed so as to bring all statesmen to value peace more than anything their countries could hope to attain or defend by a resort to force. Similarly, there would be no danger of war if all governments could be made to abide by a rule of law prohibiting war's initiation. The question is how governments interested in peace could effect not only in their own people but also in their opponents the radical switch in psychology and behavior that would be required. If the answer is that nations who failed to change the nature of their citizens or went to war in violation of the law should be punished by the ones who have been reformed, the result still would be war even though it would be called enforcement of the peace, police action, or military sanctions.

Yet another set of ideas about peace is put forth with at least implicit advice that they be made the basis of national peace policies, in this case policies of a domestic type. As was mentioned earlier,[4] many of the social scientists who have digressed from their chief field of interest and competence into the field of relations between nations have treated international war as an event originating in the minds of psychoneurotic men characterized by abnormal aggressiveness, dogmatism, or hatred of other peoples. From this assumption—of which, to my knowledge, no empirical verification has ever been attempted—it follows that the prevention of war calls for measures designed either to cure the unbalanced minds of the men who are in a position to initiate war, to prevent such men from attaining power, or, best of all, to combat the causes of psychoneuroses within the society itself.

[4] See Chapter 3, "The Determinants of Foreign Policy," and especially fn. 3 thereto.

I do not propose to inquire here into the validity of the under-lying psychological thesis, which reminds one of the similar ethical thesis ascribing all initiation of war to the action of evil men. No doubt many wars have been the work of mad or vicious men; but I would argue that the Hitlerian wars of the "mad Caesars" are the exception rather than the rule. Yet even if the "neurosis thesis" were correct, it is hard to see how governments to whom it might appeal could go about eliminating the disease or seriously reducing it even at home, if one considers the number of neurotics in every nation from whose ranks future "mad Caesars" and their followers could be drawn. It is impossible, moreover, to envisage how these same governments could hope to affect the incidence and influence of men of a neurotic type in countries other than their own. Prob-ably the promotion of nonaggressiveness in some countries would merely strengthen other countries that are more inclined toward war and therefore opposed to the suggested reforms or therapy. The result would be a unilateral psychological disarmament and a dan-gerous undermining of peace efforts based on deterrence.

Leaving aside, then, both utopian and domestic policy proposals recommended as peace strategies, I shall turn to the practical ways in which governments concerned with peace can express their con-cern in a manner compatible with the pursuit of the nation's inter-ests as traditionally conceived. They can express this concern and indeed have done so again and again by measures designed to pro-mote peace. Three different objectives of such measures can be distinguished: first, the restoration of peace after it has been broken, or "peacemaking"; second, the preservation of peace by prevention of war; and third, the consolidation or stabilization of peace.

If it had not been amply proved before that peacemaking is one of the most ticklish tasks of diplomacy, the two world wars should have removed all doubts. Even if both sides become keenly inter-ested in ending hostilities, they often continue to fight because there is more at stake for them than peace, the price of which in terms of other values may change with every turn of the war. Moreover, even within the camp that sees a chance of victory there is fre-quently passionate controversy between those who advocate a puni-tive peace and those who prefer to settle for a conciliatory peace. The goal of both factions is an "enduring peace," but the proper road to that goal is not clear. Those who would continue the fight may be sincerely convinced that only total defeat will deter the enemy from ever renewing the war; those who advocate reconciliation hope thereby to remove some of the dissatisfactions that origi-nally provoked the resort to force. Because the kind of order estab-lished at the close of a war may become the chief cause of a subsequent war, one would wish that more of the "peace research" to which scholars are dedicating themselves would focus on the problems raised by peacemaking.

Policies designed to preserve the peace form a regular and often predominant part of the foreign policy of nations that consider themselves exposed to military attack. If they see no way to change the intention of the would-be attacker, and are unwilling to sur-render to such an attack, they must seek to prevent it. This means engaging in a policy known as deterrence; it is designed to frighten off the opponent or to dissuade him from carrying out his intention to fight. Nuclear deterrence is only one form of this policy, but one in which the means of causing fright are particularly awesome. If effectiveness means no more than that hostilities are avoided or postponed, deterrence can be an effective peace strategy. But while the opponent has been prevented from carrying out his aggressive intentions, neither his intentions, nor his means of putting them into practice, nor the underlying conflict between the opponents has been altered. Peace remains no less precarious for having been preserved in this fashion and may continue to be what today is called the cold war.

Because governments concerned with peace are interested in going beyond the mere prevention of open hostilities, much of their foreign policy or peace strategy is aimed at consolidating and sta-bilizing the peace. Since as in the case of the restoration of peace, deterrence is not, or not by itself, sufficient, consolidation calls for accommodation in its broadest sense. Deterrence, to preserve the peace, and accommodation, to consolidate it, then, are the chief peace strategies of nations and they usually can be pursued simul-taneously. While they may at times get into each other's way, neither strategy is likely in the long run to achieve satisfactory results alone. Nations that have neither the means to deter nor the means to accommodate their opponents must rely on others for their protection from war. They are incapable of any policy that would deserve the name of peace strategy, although they may mistake pro-fessions of peaceful intent or the advocacy of sweeping universal schemes for peace, such as total disarmament, as substitutes for such a strategy.

Deterrence through military power is as old as the multistate system itself: *si vis pacem para bellum* was a classic commentary. It is a prominent aspect of the balancing of power process because it defines the purpose of the balancing operations of countries seeking to prevent the initiation of war by their opponents.[5] Most of the discussion on deterrence lies beyond the scope of the present study which concerns international politics without extending into the field of military policy and strategy.[6] The relationship between deterrence policy and peace preservation deserves some consideration here, however. It is often claimed that preparations for war (for that matter, preparations for any coercive action), which are inherent in all military deterrence, increase rather than reduce the danger of war. For this reason the United States has been criticized for an alleged overemphasis on deterrence and thus on military preparedness or "positions of strength." There is some truth in the contention that what is intended to deter an opponent may instead provoke him and thus lead to the war it was supposed to prevent. This may happen even when there is no unnecessary sabre-rattling and no lack of communications between the parties. No government can ever be certain that a build-up of forces and weapons systems by the other side is not a preparation for offensive action, or that it will not turn into such preparation even if not originally so intended. Under nuclear conditions a strong suspicion on this count might even trigger a pre-emptive strike.

Yet, however serious the risks inherent in polices of deterrence, particularly when the full intensity of nuclear brinkmanship is reached, the alternative involves risks of far more ominous proportions. It means placing oneself at the mercy of an actual or potential opponent, who as a rule will not fail to justify to himself, if

[5] For further consideration of this point see Chapter 8, "The Balance of Power in Theory and Practice."

[6] The present author has contributed to the discussion of military and especially nuclear deterrence in the following articles: "The Atomic Bomb in Soviet-American Relations," in *The Absolute Weapon*, ed. Bernard Brodie (Harcourt, Brace & Co., New York, 1946); "Could a War in Europe be Limited?" *The Yale Review*, Winter, 1956; "Europe and the NATO Shield," *International Organization*, No. 4, 1958; "Limits on Disengagement" in *East-West Negotiations*, published by the Washington Center of Foreign Policy Research, 1959; "Nuclear Restraint: A Two-Edged Sword," *Marine Corps Gazette*, May, 1960; and by his part in the report of the Washington Center of Foreign Policy Research to the Committee on Foreign Relations of the United States Senate entitled, "Developments in Military Technology and Their Impact on United States Strategy and Foreign Policy," December, 1959, of which he was a coauthor and the responsible editor.

not to others, actions designed to take advantage of his superiority. Instead of being provoked, opponents are being tempted here by the lack of resistance they expect to meet.

But while deterrence is indispensable, it can be accepted as the sole peace policy only when chances of accommodation at a tolerable price are nonexistent. After all, at best deterrence can affect the underlying dispute only by "laying it on ice" for a more or less prolonged period. Occasionally such postponement of hostilities may allow the old conflict to be superseded by new preoccupations and consequently to fade away. Some people in the West, for instance, cherish the hope that during a prolonged Soviet-Western stalemate, Red China will develop into a major threat to the Soviet Union and that this will induce Moscow eventually to lose interest in communizing the West. As a rule, peace resting on deterrence alone, whether it be deterrence of only one party or mutual deterrence, leaves nations in a state of conflict and thus in the precarious position of sitting on the lid of a boiling kettle. This is particularly true in an age troubled both by fanatical demands for change and by profound fears for the security of national core values.

Accommodation is no more a panacea for peace than is deterrence. It takes two to accommodate just as it takes two to make war. If one side cannot be deflected from the demands that produce conflict and, therefore, threaten violence no matter what compromises the other is in a position to offer, the only remaining alternatives to war are either deterrence or surrender. But even if successful, accommodation cannot guarantee enduring peace and it may, in fact, have an unstabilizing effect. There is no way of telling in advance whether concessions will satisfy the other side or merely whet its appetite. If accommodation takes the form of unequal or unilateral concessions, it becomes "appeasement" in the invidious sense the term has taken on since Munich, which implies that it will call forth new demands. To point to the dangers of the chain reaction or domino effect of such appeasement does not mean, however, to rule out accommodation by unilateral concession under all circumstances. To give up untenable positions with a view to creating better chances of effective deterrence and accommodation further in the rear, as belligerents frequently have done with success, may be the lesser of two evils.

Leaving aside the case of unilateral concessions, accommodation aims at compromise in which the difference between the parties is split at a point acceptable to both. Most of the work of diplomacy and of international organizations such as the United Nations consists of efforts at accommodation. Not only do parties to disputes rarely offer inflexible resistance to accommodation, which usually requires direct negotiation at some point, but "third parties" that are prepared to get into the act if given an opportunity are even more rarely lacking, although the role of the mediator is known to be neither easy nor thankful. Their overriding incentive is to moderate or resolve conflict between others before it erupts into violence and destroys the peace, the benefits of which all parties share. Left to their own devices, conflicting parties engaged in measuring their respective strength encounter great difficulties initiating a policy of accommodation because they become exposed to the suspicion of weakness. This explains why the mediator almost invariably is a crucial figure in accommodation.

The question of what makes a successful mediator deserves much more attention than it has received. A reputation for impartiality may be only one characteristic of the suitable mediator, but it is indispensable; therefore the present lack of genuinely neutral countries or of individuals in these countries recognized as neutral by both sides—Khrushchev has even denied that there can be such individuals—seriously reduces the chances for effective mediation and thus for peace through accommodation. The United Nations, though in many respects an ideal mediator, is no substitute for individuals or individual nations with a reputation for impartiality: it cannot set up acceptable mediatory boards or committees unless at least chairmen can be found who are recognized as neutrals by both parties.

The most serious obstacle to any accommodation that is not merely a verbal cloak for the surrender of one party is the depth of the gulf that separates parties whose conflicts constitute a threat to the peace. It would be defeatist, however, provided a balance of coercive power is maintained on all levels of confrontation, to assume *a priori* that maximum demands and counterdemands cannot be whittled down and compromised or that the issues are as indivisible as the political labels used to characterize them would indicate. Of course, mediation and negotiations may fail, as they have frequently failed in the past. But while their failure should serve as a warning to those who would sacrifice or jeopardize deterrence for the sake of the more "peaceful" road of accommodation, nations with a vital stake in the prevention of war have strong reason to wish to meet their opponents part way whenever there is any chance of resolving conflict by agreement. Those seeking change may be induced to accept less than they originally demanded—or to resign themselves to no change at all—particularly if a determined and credible show of counterpower or the odium of initiating violence makes the price of forceful change appear high. It may prove more difficult to induce a nation defending its established rights and possessions to negotiate away any part of the *status quo* both because the use of force in response to an attack is unlikely to provoke moral condemnation and because the impression of weakness is deeply feared as a threat to the security of all of a nation's rights and possessions. Stringent advance commitments to take or to hold add further obstacles to peaceful change. Yet without such change nations can hope at best for the "peace" of a tenuous stalemate or truce.

No mention has been made so far of arms control or disarmament as instruments of peace strategy, although in the public mind they hold a key position among such instruments. Disarmament proposals are not necessarily utopian, although of course they may be. On many occasions nations have cut back their armaments unilaterally, often because the danger to their security declined, sometimes because they could no longer afford to continue their previous military efforts. But only in rare cases have limitations and reductions of armaments been agreed upon, either tacitly or formally, by two or more nations. This phenomenon calls for some explanation here because of its discouraging implications for a peace strategy of agreed disarmament.

Arms control agreements, if they turn out to be practical, can bridle an arms race that aggravates tensions by heightening the fear of both accidental and offensive war. The dangers arising from a nuclear arms race are particularly serious because a nation might strike preventively if it foresaw a change in its relative power position arising from technological advantages gained by its opponent in the field of decisive weaponry. The most formidable practical obstacle to arms control agreements is the justified fear that mutual reduction or abolition of military establishments will destroy an existing distribution of military power on which deterrence rests. It can be taken for granted that no nation locked in conflict with another will consent to a change in its relative military power position by an arms control agreement, yet the difficulties posed by the technical problem of making reductions proportional in their effect on the power of the opposing parties tends to defeat even the most serious efforts at accommodation in this field.

The question has been raised whether general and complete disarmament would not obviate the need for proportionality. If both sides reduce their forces to zero how, it is asked, can one of them then increase its relative military strength—remembering that by the terms of the agreement it retains none? Here, however, the problem of reliable inspection is raised, in a most acute form. As others have pointed out, instability would be vastly increased under nuclear conditions if one side could gain a monopoly of nuclear power merely by hiding a limited number of warheads and missiles in contravention of an agreement. Nor is this the sole objection to total disarmament as a peace strategy. Under the best of circumstances it would take time to cover the road to total disarmament. Every step in the process, therefore, raises the same problem of proportionality as is encountered in the case of less than total disarmament or arms control measures. Then too, nations considering the total elimination of military forces and weapons must ascertain whether such elimination would leave intact their remaining relative power position. The country with superior capabilty for coercion short of war, or for more rapid rearmament, would by total disarmament improve and under certain circumstances decisively improve its relative power position.[7]

It can be concluded that tacit or formal agreements for the proportional reduction of military power if faithfully carried out would tend to consolidate the peace by reducing the dangers inherent in an arms race, although in leaving the underlying conflict unresolved, such agreements could not by themselves eliminate the precariousness of peace nor would they make efforts at accommodation beyond the field of armaments superfluous. Total disarmament, however, presents such difficulties under nuclear conditions in terms both of proportionality and inspection that it can be ruled out as impractical and relegated to the category of utopian schemes.

[7] For an imaginative exploration of problems that total disarmament would not solve, see T.C. Schelling, "The Stability of Total Disarmament," Study Memorandum Number 1, Special Studies Group, Institute for Defense Analyses, Washington, D.C., October 6, 1961.

II.

The Pursuit of National Security

Chapter Ten   NATIONAL SECURITY
                          AS AN
                          AMBIGUOUS SYMBOL

STATESMEN, PUBLICISTS, and scholars who wish to be considered realists, as many do today, are inclined to insist that the foreign policy they advocate is dictated by the national interest, more specifically by the national security interest.[1] This should not be surprising. Today any reference to the pursuit of security is likely to strike a sympathetic chord.

When political formulas such as "national interest" or "national security" gain popularity they need to be scrutinized with particular care. They may not mean the same thing to different people. They may not have any precise meaning at all. Thus, while appearing to offer guidance and a basis for broad consensus, they may be permitting everyone to label whatever policy he favors with an attractive and possibly deceptive name.

In a very vague and general way "national interest" does suggest a direction of policy which can be distinguished from several others presenting themselves as alternatives. It indicates that the policy is designed to promote demands that are ascribed to the nation rather than to individuals, subnational groups, or mankind as a whole. It emphasizes that the policy subordinates other interests to those of the nation. But beyond this, it has very little meaning.

When Charles Beard's study of *The Idea of National Interest* was published in the early years of the New Deal and under the impact of the Great Depression, the lines were drawn differently from those of today. The question at that time was whether American foreign policy, then largely economic in scope and motivation, was aimed not at promoting the welfare interests of the nation as a whole but

[1] This chapter is reprinted, with minor changes, from *Political Science Quarterly*, Vol. LXVII, No. 4 (December, 1952), by permission of the publisher.

instead at satisfying the material interests of powerful subnational interest or pressure groups. While it was found hard to define what was in the interest of national welfare or to discover standards by which to measure it, there could be no doubt as to what people had in mind: they desired to see the makers of national policy rise above the narrow and special economic interests of parts of the nation to focus their attention on the more inclusive interests of the whole.

Today, the alternative to a policy of the national interest to which people refer is of a different character. They fear policymakers may be unduly concerned with the "interest of all of mankind." They see them sacrificing the less inclusive national community to the wider but in their opinion chimeric world community. The issue, then, is not one of transcending narrow group selfishness, as it was at the time of Beard's discussion, but rather one of according more exclusive devotion to the narrower cause of the national self.

There is another difference between the current and the earlier debate. While it would be wrong to say that the economic interest has ceased to attract attention, it is overshadowed today by the national security interest. Even in the recent debates on the St. Lawrence Seaway, clearly in the first instance an economic enterprise, the defenders of the project, when seeking to impress their listeners with the "national interest" involved, spoke mainly of the value of the seaway for military defense in wartime while some opponents stressed its vulnerability to attack.

The change from a welfare to a security interpretation of the symbol "national interest" is understandable. Today we are living under the impact of cold war and threats of external aggression rather than of depression and social reform. As a result, the formula of the national interest has come to be practically synonymous with the formula of national security. Unless they explicitly state some other intent, spokesmen for a policy which would take the national interest as its guide can be assumed to mean that priority shall be given to measures of security, a term to be analyzed.[2] The question is raised, therefore, whether this seemingly

[2] Hans Morgenthau's *In Defense of the National Interest* (Alfred A. Knopf, New York, 1951) is the most explicit and impassioned recent plea for an American foreign policy which shall follow "but one guiding star—the National Interest." While Morgenthau is not equally explicit in regard to the meaning he attaches to the symbol "national interest," it becomes clear in the few pages devoted to an exposition of this "perennial" interest that the author is

more precise formula of national security offers statesmen a meaningful guide for action. Can they be expected to know what it means? Can policies be distinguished and judged on the ground that they do or do not serve this interest?

The term national security, like national interest, is well enough established in the political discourse of international relations to designate an objective of policy distinguishable from others. We know roughly what people have in mind if they complain that their government is neglecting national security or demanding excessive sacrifices for the sake of enhancing it. Usually those who raise the cry for a policy oriented exclusively toward this interest are afraid their country underestimates the external dangers facing it or is being diverted into idealistic channels unmindful of these dangers. Moreover, the symbol suggests protection through power and therefore figures more frequently in the speech of those who believe in reliance on national power than of those who place their confidence in model behavior, international co-operation, or the United Nations to carry their country safely through the tempests of international conflict. For these reasons it would be an exaggeration to claim that the symbol of national security is nothing but a stimulus to semantic confusion, although used without specifications it leaves room for more confusion than sound political counsel or scientific usage can afford.

The demand for a policy of national security is primarily normative in character. It is supposed to indicate what the policy of a nation should be in order to be either expedient—a rational means toward an accepted end—or moral, the best or the least evil course of action. The value judgments implicit in these normative exhortations will be discussed.

Before doing so, attention should be drawn to an assertion that is implicit if not explicit in most appeals for a policy guided by national security. Such appeals usually assume that nations have made security their goal except when idealism or utopianism of their leaders has led them to stray from the traditional path. If such conformity of behavior actually existed, it would be proper to infer that a country deviating from the established pattern of con-

---

thinking in terms of the national security interest, and specifically of security based on power. The United States, he says, is interested in three things: a unique position as a predominant power without rival in the Western Hemisphere and the maintenance of the balance of power in Europe as well as in Asia, demands which make sense only in the context of a quest for security through power.

duct would risk being penalized. This would greatly strengthen the normative arguments. The trouble with the contention of fact, however, is that the term "security" covers a range of goals so wide that highly divergent policies can be interpreted as policies of security.

Security points to some degree of protection of values previously acquired. In Walter Lippmann's words, a nation is secure to the extent to which it is not in danger of having to sacrifice core values, if it wishes to avoid war, and is able, if challenged, to maintain them by victory in such a war.[3] This definition implies that security rises and falls with the ability of a nation to deter an attack, or to defeat it. This is in accord with common usage of the term.

Security is a value, then, of which a nation can have more or less and which it can aspire to have in greater or lesser measure.[4] It has much in common, in this respect, with power or wealth, two other values of great importance in international affairs. But while wealth measures the amount of a nation's material possessions, and power its ability to control the actions of others, security, in an objective sense, measures the absence of threats to acquired values, in a subjective sense, the absence of fear that such values will be attacked. In both respects a nation's security can run a wide gamut from almost complete insecurity or sense of insecurity at one end, to almost complete security or absence of fear at the other.[5]

[3] Walter Lippmann, *U.S. Foreign Policy: Shield of the Republic* (Little, Brown & Co., Boston, 1943), p. 51.

[4] This explains why some nations that seem to fall into the category of *status quo* powers *par excellence* may nevertheless be dissatisfied and act very much like "imperialist" powers, as Morgenthau calls nations with acquisitive goals. They are dissatisfied with the degree of security they enjoy under the *status quo* and are out to enhance it. France's occupation of the Ruhr in 1923 illustrates this type of behavior. Because the demand for more security may induce a *status quo* power even to resort to the use of violence as a means of attaining more security, there is reason to beware of the easy and often self-righteous assumption that nations which desire to preserve the *status quo* are necessarily "peace-loving."

[5] Security and power would be synonymous terms if security could be attained only through the accumulation of power, which will be shown not to be the case. The fear of attack—security in the subjective sense—is also not proportionate to the relative power position of a nation. Why, otherwise, would some weak and exposed nations consider themselves more secure today than does the United States?

Harold D. Lasswell and Abraham Kaplan in *Power and Society* (Yale University Press, New Haven, 1950), defining security as "high value expectancy," stress the subjective and speculative character of security by using the term "expectancy"; the use of the term "high," while indicating no definite level, would seem to imply that the security-seeker aims at a position in which the events he expects—here the continued unmolested enjoyment of his possessions—have considerably more than an even chance of materializing.

The possible discrepancy between the objective and subjective connotations of the term is significant in international relations although the chance of future attack can never be measured "objectively"; it must always remain a matter of subjective evaluation and speculation. However, when the French after World War I insisted that they were entitled to additional guarantees of security because of the exceptionally dangerous situation which France was said to be facing, other powers in the League expressed the view that rather than submit to what might be French hysterical apprehension they should objectively evaluate the relative security of France. It is well known that nations, and groups within nations, differ widely in their reaction to one and the same external situation. Some tend to exaggerate the danger while others underestimate it. With hindsight it is sometimes possible to tell exactly how far they deviated from a rational reaction to the actual or objective state of danger existing at the time. Even if for no other reason, this difference in the reaction to similar threats suffices to make it probable that nations will differ in their efforts to obtain more security. Some may find the danger to which they are exposed entirely normal and in line with their modest security expectations while others consider it unbearable to live with these same dangers. Although this is not the place to set up hypotheses on the factors which account for one or the other attitude, investigation might confirm the hunch that those nations tend to be most sensitive to threats that have either experienced attacks in the recent past or, having passed through a prolonged period of an exceptionally high degree of security, suddenly find themselves thrust into a situation of danger.[6] Probably national efforts to achieve greater security would also prove, in part at least, to be a function of the power and

[6] The United States offers a good illustration and may be typical in this respect. For a long time this country was beyond the reach of any enemy attack that could be considered probable. During that period, then, it could afford to dismiss any serious preoccupation with security. Events proved that it was no worse off for having done so. However, after this happy condition had ceased to exist, government and people alike showed a lag in their awareness of the change. When Nicholas J. Spykman raised his voice in the years before World War II to advocate a broader security outlook than was indicated by the symbol "Western Hemisphere Defense" and a greater appreciation of the role of defensive military power, he was dealing with this lag and with the dangers implied in it. If Hans Morgenthau and others raised warning voices after World War II, seeming to tread in Spykman's footsteps, they were addressing a nation which after a new relapse into wishful thinking in 1945 had been radically disillusioned and was now swinging toward possibly excessive security apprehensions.

opportunity that nations possess to reduce danger through their own efforts.[7]

Another and even stronger reason why nations must be expected not to act uniformly is that they are not all or constantly faced with the same degree of danger. For purposes of a working hypothesis, theorists may find it useful at times to postulate conditions wherein all states are enemies—provided they are not allied against others—and wherein all, therefore, are equally in danger of attack.[8] But, while possibly in the living world, too, no sovereign nation can be absolutely safe from future attack, nobody can reasonably contend that Canada, for example, is threatened today to the same extent as countries like Iran or Yugoslavia, or that the British had as much reason to be concerned about the French air force in the twenties as about Hitler's *Luftwaffe* in the thirties.

This point, however, should not be overstressed. There can be no quarrel with the generalization that most nations, most of the time—the great powers particularly—have shown, and had reason to show, an active concern about some lack of security and have been prepared to make sacrifices for its enhancement. Danger and the awareness of it have been and continue to be sufficiently widespread to guarantee some uniformity in this respect. But a generalization that leaves room both for the frantic kind of struggle for more security which characterized French policy at times and for the neglect of security apparent in American foreign policy after the close of both world wars throws little light on the behavior of nations. The demand for conformity would have meaning only if it could be said—as it could under the conditions postulated in the working hypothesis of pure power politics—that nations normally subordinate all other values to the maximization of their security. This, however, is obviously not the case.

There have been many instances of struggles for more security taking the form of an unrestrained race for armaments, alliances,

[7] Terms such as "degree" or "level" of security are not intended to indicate merely quantitative differences. Nations may also differ in respect to the breadth of their security perspective as when American leaders at Yalta were so preoccupied with security against the then enemy countries of the United States that they failed or refused to consider future American security vis-à-vis the Soviet Union. The differences may apply, instead, to the time range for which security is sought as when the British at Versailles were ready to offer France short-run security guarantees while the French with more foresight insisted that the "German danger" would not become acute for some ten years.

[8] For a discussion of this working hypothesis—as part of the pure power hypothesis—see Chapter 6, "The Pole of Power and the Pole of Indifference."

strategic boundaries, and the like; but one need only recall the many heated parliamentary debates on arms appropriations to realize how uncertain has been the extent to which people will consent to sacrifice for additional increments of security. Even when there has been no question that armaments would mean more security, the cost in taxes, the reduction in social benefits, or the sheer discomfort involved have militated effectively against further effort. It may be worth noting in this connection that there seems to be no case in history in which a country started a preventive war on the grounds of security—unless Hitler's wanton attack on his neighbors be allowed to qualify as such—although there must have been circumstances where additional security could have been obtained by war and although so many wars have been launched for the enhancement of other values. Of course, where security serves only as a cloak for other more enticing demands, nations or ambitious leaders may consider no price for it too high. This is one of the reasons why very high security aspirations tend to make a nation suspect of hiding more aggressive aims.

Instead of expecting a uniform drive for enhanced or maximum security, a different hypothesis may offer a more promising lead. Efforts for security are bound to be experienced as a burden; security after all is nothing but the absence of the evil of insecurity, a negative value so to speak. As a consequence, nations will be inclined to minimize these efforts, keeping them at the lowest level that will provide them with what they consider adequate protection. This level will often be lower than what statesmen, military leaders, or other particularly security-minded participants in the decision-making process believe it should be. In any case, together with the extent of the external threats, numerous domestic factors such as national character, tradition, preferences, and prejudices will influence the level of security that a nation chooses to make its target.

It might be objected that in the long run nations are not so free to choose the amount of effort they will put into security. Are they not under a kind of compulsion to spare no effort provided they wish to survive? This objection again would make sense only if the hypothesis of pure power politics were a realistic image of actual world affairs. A quick glance at history is enough, however, to show that survival has only exceptionally been at stake, particularly for the major powers. If nations were not concerned with the protection of values other than their survival as independent states, most of them most of the time would not have had to be seriously worried about their security, despite what manipulators of public opinion engaged in mustering greater security efforts may have said to the contrary. What "compulsion" there is, then, is a function not merely of the will of others, real or imagined, to destroy the nation's independence but of national desires and ambitions to retain a wealth of other values such as rank, respect, material possessions, and special privileges. It would seem to be a fair guess that the efforts for security by a particular nation will tend to vary, other things being equal, with the range of values for which protection is being sought.

In respect to this range there may seem to exist a considerable degree of uniformity. All over the world today peoples are making sacrifices to protect and preserve what to them appear as the minimum national core values: national independence and territorial integrity. But there is deviation in two directions. Some nations seek protection for more marginal values as well. There was a time when United States policy could afford to be concerned mainly with the protection of the foreign investments or markets of its nationals, its "core values" being out of danger, or when Britain was extending its national self to include large and only vaguely circumscribed "regions of special interest." It is a well-known and portentous phenomenon that bases, security zones, and the like may be demanded and acquired for the purpose of protecting values acquired earlier; and they then become new national values requiring protection themselves. Pushed to its logical conclusion, such spatial extension of the range of values does not stop short of world domination.

A deviation in the opposite direction of a compression of the range of core values is hardly exceptional in our days either. There is little indication that Britain is bolstering the security of Hong Kong although colonies were once considered part of the national territory. The Czechs lifted no finger to protect their independence against the Soviet Union and many West Europeans are arguing today that rearmament has become too destructive of values they cherish to be justified even when national independence is obviously at stake.

The lack of uniformity does not end here. A policy is not characterized by its goal—in this case, security—alone. To establish its character, the means used to pursue the goal must be taken into account as well. Thus, if two nations were both endeavoring to maximize their security but one were placing all its reliance on armaments and alliances, the other on meticulous neutrality, a policy-maker seeking to emulate their behavior would be at a loss where to turn. Those who call for a policy guided by national security are not likely to be unaware of this fact, but they take for granted that they will be understood to mean a security policy based on power, and on military power at that. Were it not so, they would be hard put to prove that their government was not already doing its best for security, though it was seeking to enhance it by such means as international co-operation or by the negotiation of compromise agreements—means which in one instance may be totally ineffective or utopian but in others may have considerable protective value.

It is understandable why it should be assumed so readily that a quest for security must necessarily translate itself into a quest for coercive power. Since security is being sought against external violence—coupled perhaps with internal subversive violence—it seems plausible at first sight that the response should consist in an accumulation of the same kind of force for the purpose of resisting an attack or of deterring a would-be attacker. The most casual reading of history and of contemporary experience, moreover, suffices to confirm the view that such resort to "power of resistance" has been the rule in nations grappling with serious threats to their security, however much the specific form of this power and its extent may differ. Why otherwise would so many nations which have no acquisitive designs maintain costly armaments? Why did Denmark with her state of complete disarmament remain an exception even among the small powers?

But again, the generalization that nations seeking security usually place great reliance on coercive power does not carry one far. The issue is not whether there is regularly some such reliance but whether as between nations there are no significant differences concerning their over-all choice of the means upon which they place their trust. The controversies concerning the best road to future security which are so typical of coalition partners at the close of victorious wars throw light on this question. France in 1919 and all the Allies in 1945 believed that protection against another German attack could be gained only by means of continued military superiority based on German military impotence. President Wilson in 1919 and many observers in 1945 were equally convinced, however, that more hope for security lay in a conciliatory and fair treatment of the defeated enemy, which would rob him of future incentives to renew his attack. While this is not the place to decide which side was right, one cannot help drawing the conclusion that, in the matter of means, the roads that are open may lead in diametrically opposed directions.[9] The choice in every instance will depend on a multitude of variables, including ideological and moral convictions, expectations concerning the psychological and political developments in the camp of the opponent, and inclinations of individual policy-makers.[10]

After all that has been said little is left of the sweeping generalization that in actual practice nations, guided by their national security interest, tend to pursue a uniform and therefore imitable policy of security. Instead, there are numerous reasons why they should differ widely in this respect, with some standing close to the pole of complete indifference to security or complete reliance on nonmilitary means, others close to the pole of insistence on absolute security or of complete reliance on coercive power. It should be added that there exists still another category of nations which cannot be placed within the continuum connecting these poles because they regard security of any degree as an insufficient goal; instead they seek to acquire new values even at the price of greater insecurity. In this category must be placed not only the "mad Caesars" who are out for conquest and glory at any price, but also idealistic statesmen who would plunge their country into war for the sake of spreading the benefits of their ideology, for example, or of liberating enslaved peoples.

The actual behavior of nations, past and present, does not affect the normative proposition, to which we shall now turn our attention. According to this proposition nations are called upon to give priority to national security and thus to consent to any sacrifice of

[9] Myres S. McDougal, "Law and Peace," *American Journal of International Law,* Vol. 46, No. 1 (January, 1952), pp. 102 ff. He rightly criticizes Hans Morgenthau for his failure to appreciate the role that nonpower methods, such as legal procedures and moral appeals, may at times successfully play in the pursuit of security. But it is surprising how little aware McDougal appears to be of the disappointing modesty of the contributions which these "other means" have actually made to the enhancement of security and the quite insignificant contributions they have made to the promotion of changes of the *status quo.* This latter failure signifies that they have been unable to remove the main causes of the attacks that security-minded peoples rightly fear.

[10] On the problem of security policy *(Sicherheitspolitik)* with special reference to "collective security," see the comprehensive and illuminating study of Heinrich Rogge, "Kollektivsicherheit Buendnispolitik Voelkerbund," *Theorie der nationalen und internationalen Sicherheit* (Berlin, 1937), which deserves attention despite the fact that it was written and published in Nazi Germany. It bears a distinctly "revisionist" slant.

value that will provide an additional increment of security. It may be expedient, moral, or both for nations to do so even if they should have failed to heed such advice in the past and are not living up to it today.

The first question, then, is whether some definable security policy can be said to be generally expedient. Because the choice of goals is not a matter of expediency, it would seem to make no sense to ask whether it is expedient for nations to be concerned with the goal of security itself; only the means used to this end, so it would seem, can be judged as to their fitness—their instrumental rationality—to promote security. Yet, this is not so. Security, like other aims, may be an intermediate rather than an ultimate goal, in which case it can be judged as a means to these more ultimate ends.

Traditionally, the protection and preservation of national core values have been considered ends in themselves, at least by those who followed in the footsteps of Machiavelli or, for other reasons of political philosophy, placed the prince, state, or nation at the pinnacle of their hierarchy of values. Those who do so today will be shocked at the mere suggestion that national security should have to be justified in terms of higher values which it is expected to serve. But there is a large and perhaps growing current of opinion— influential as a matter of fact in this country for a long time—that holds to this idea. We condemn Nazis and Communists for defending their own totalitarian countries instead of helping to free their people from tyranny; we enlist support for armaments, here and in Allied countries, not so much on the ground that they will protect national security but that by enhancing such security they will serve to protect ultimate human values like individual liberty. Again, opposition in Europe and Asia to military security measures is based in part on the contention that it would help little to make national core values secure, if in the process the liberties and the social welfare of the people had to be sacrificed; the prevention of Russian conquest is useless, some insist, if in the course of a war of defense a large part of the people were to be exterminated and most cities destroyed.[11]

---

[11] Raymond Dennett goes further in making the generalization that "if economic pressures become great enough, almost any government, when put to the final test, will moderate or abandon a political association" (such as the alliance system of the United States with its usefulness to national security) "if only an alteration of policy seems to offer the possibility of maintaining or achieving living standards adequate enough to permit the regime to survive." "Danger Spots in the Pattern of American Security," *World Politics*, Vol. IV, No. 4 (July, 1952), p. 449.

While excellent arguments can be made to support the thesis that preservation of the national independence of this country is worth almost any price as long as no alternative community is available that could assure the same degree of order, justice, peace, or individual liberty, it becomes necessary to provide such arguments whenever national security as a value in itself is being questioned. The answer cannot be taken for granted.

But turning away now from the expediency of security as an intermediate goal we must ask whether, aside from any moral considerations which will be discussed later, a specific level of security and specific means of attaining it can claim to be generally expedient.

When one sets out to define in terms of expediency the level of security to which a nation should aspire, one might be tempted to assume that the sky is the limit. Is not insecurity of any kind an evil from which the rational policy-maker would want to rescue his country? There are obvious reasons why this is not so.

In the first place, every increment of security must be paid for by additional sacrifices of other values usually of a kind more exacting than the mere expenditure of precious time on the part of policy-makers. At a certain point, then, by something like the economic law of diminishing returns, the gain in security no longer compensates for the added costs of attaining it. As in the case of economic value comparisons and preferences, there is frequent disagreement among different layers of policy-makers as to where the line should be drawn. This is true particularly because absolute security is out of the question unless a country is capable of world domination, in which case, however, the insecurities and fears would be "internalized" and probably magnified. Because nations must to some extent "live dangerously," whatever they consent to do about it, then, a modicum of additional but only relative security may easily become unattractive to those who have to bear the chief burden. Nothing renders the task of statesmen in a democracy more difficult than the reluctance of the people to follow them very far along the road to high and costly security levels.

In the second place, national security policies when based on the accumulation of power have a way of defeating themselves if the target level is set too high because "power of resistance" cannot be unmistakably distinguished from "power of aggression." What a country does to bolster its own security through power can be interpreted by others, therefore, as a threat to their security. If this occurs, the vicious circle of what John Herz has described as the "security dilemma" sets in: the efforts of one side provoke counter-measures by the other which in turn tend to wipe out the gains of the first. Theoretically there seems to be no escape from this frustrating consequence; in practice, however, there are ways to convince those who might feel threatened that the accumulation of power is not intended and will never be used for attack.[12] The chief way is to keep the target level within moderate bounds and to avoid placing oneself in a position where the level has to be raised suddenly and drastically. The desire to escape from this vicious circle presupposes a security policy of much self-restraint and moderation, especially in the choice of the target level. It can never be expedient to pursue a security policy which by the fact of provocation or incentive to others fails to increase the nation's relative power position and capability of resistance.

The question of what means are expedient for the purpose of enhancing security raises even more thorny problems. Policy-makers must decide how to distribute their reliance on whatever means are available to them and, particularly, how far to push the accumulation of coercive power. No attempt can be made here to decide what the choice should be in order to be expedient. Obviously, there can be no general answer that would meet the requirements of every case. The answer depends on the circumstances. A weak country may have no better means at its disposal than to prove to stronger neighbors that its strict neutrality can be trusted. Potentially strong countries may have a chance to deter an aggressor by creating "positions of strength." In some instances they may have no other way of saving themselves, while in others even they may find it more expedient to supplement such a policy, if not to replace it, by a policy intended to negotiate their opponent out of his aggressive designs.

The reason why "power of resistance" is not the general panacea which some believe it to be lies in the nature of security itself. If security, in the objective sense of the term at least, rises and falls with the presence or absence of aggressive intentions on the part of others, the attitude and behavior of those from whom the threat emanates are of prime importance. Such attitude and behavior

[12] Not everyone agrees that this can be done. Jeremy Bentham wrote that "measures of mere self-defense are naturally taken for projects of aggression" with the result that "each makes haste to begin for fear of being forestalled." *Principles of International Law,* Essay IV.

need not be beyond the realm of influence by the country seeking to bolster its security. Whenever they do not lie beyond this realm the most effective and least costly security policy consists in inducing the opponent to give up his aggressive intentions.

While there is no easy way to determine when a nation can and should use means that are directed not at resistance but at the prevention of the desire of others to attack, it will clarify the issue to sketch the types of hypotheses that would link specific security policies, as expedient, to some of the most typical political constellations.

One can think of nations lined up between the two poles of maximum and minimum "attack propensity," with those unalterably committed to attack, provided it promises success, at one pole and those at the other, whom no amount of opportunity for successful attack could induce to undertake it. While security in respect to the first group can come exclusively as a result of "positions of strength" sufficient to deter or defeat attack, nothing could do more to undermine security in respect to the second group than to start accumulating power of a kind that would provoke fear and countermoves.

Unfortunately it can never be known with certainty, in practice, what position within the continuum one's opponent actually occupies. Statesmen cannot be blamed, moreover, if caution and suspicion lead them to assume a closer proximity to the first pole than hindsight proves to have been justified. We believe we have ample proof that the Soviet Union today is at or very close to the first pole, while Canadian policy-makers probably place the United States in its intentions toward Canada at the second pole.

It is fair to assume that, wherever the issue of security becomes a matter of serious concern, statesmen usually will be dealing with potential opponents who occupy a position somewhere between but much closer to the first of the two poles. This means, then, that an attack must be feared as a possibility, even though the intention to launch it cannot be considered to have crystallized to the point where nothing could change it. If this be true, a security policy in order to be expedient cannot avoid accumulating power of resistance and yet cannot let it go at that. Efforts have to be made simultaneously toward the goal of removing the incentives to attack. This is only another way of saying that security policy must seek to bring opponents to occupy a position as close to the second pole as conditions and capabilities permit.

Such a twofold policy presents the greatest dilemmas because efforts to change the intentions of an opponent may run counter to efforts to build up strength against him. The dangers of any policy of concessions, symbolized in contemporary thought by Munich, cannot be underestimated. The paradox of this situation must be faced, however, if security policy is to be expedient. It implies that national security policy, except when directed against a country un- alterably committed to attack, is the more rational the more it suc- ceeds in taking into consideration the interests, including the security interests, of the other side. Only in doing so can it hope to minimize the willingness of the other to resort to violence. Rather than to insist, then, that under all conditions security be sought by reliance on nothing but defensive power and be pushed in a spirit of national selfishness toward the highest targets, it should be stressed that in most instances efforts to satisfy legitimate demands of others are likely to promise better results in terms of security.[13] That is probably what George Kennan had in mind when he ad- vised policy-makers to use self-restraint in the pursuit of the national interest. While in the face of a would-be world conqueror who is beyond the pale of external influence it is dangerous to be diverted from the accumulation of sheer defensive power, any mis- take about his true state of mind or any neglect of opportunities to influence his design, where they have a chance of being successful, violates the rules of expediency. It should always be kept in mind that the ideal security policy is one that would lead to a distribu- tion of values so satisfactory to all nations that the intention to attack and with it the problem of security would be minimized. While this is a utopian goal, policy-makers and particularly peace- makers would do well to remember that there are occasions when greater approximation to such a goal can be effected.

We can now focus our attention on the moral issue, if such there be.[14] Those who advocate a policy devoted to national security are not always aware of the fact (if they do not explicitly deny it) that

[13] As A.D. Lindsay puts it, "The search for perfect security . . . defeats its own ends. Playing for safety is the most dangerous way to live." Introduction to Thomas Hobbes, *Leviathan* (J.M. Dent & Sons, London, 1914), p. xxii.

[14] On the moral problem in international relations, see Chapter 4, "States- manship and Moral Choice." In one of his statements on the subject, Reinhold Niebuhr (*The Irony of American History*, Charles Scribner's Sons, New York, 1952, p. 39), points specifically to the moral problem involved in security policy —"No imperiled nation," he writes, "is morally able to dispense with weapons which might insure its survival."

they are passing moral judgment when they advise a nation to pursue the goal of national security or when they insist that such means as the accumulation of coercive power—or its use—should be employed for this purpose.[15]

Nations like individuals or other groups may value things not because they consider them good or less evil than their alternative; they may value them because they satisfy their pride, heighten their sense of self-esteem, or reduce their fears. However, no policy, or human act in general, which calls for the sacrifice of other values, as any security policy is bound to do, can escape being made a subject of moral judgment—whether by the conscience of the actor himself or by others. Here it becomes a matter of comparing and weighing values in order to decide which of them are deemed sufficiently good to justify the evil of sacrificing others. If someone insists that his country should do more to build up its strength, he is implying, knowingly or not, that more security is sufficiently desirable to warrant such evils as the cut in much-needed social welfare benefits or as the extension of the period of military service.[16]

Many vivid examples of the moral dilemma are being supplied by current controversies concerning American security policy. Is a "deal with fascist Spain" morally justified, provided it adds an increment to our security, though principles valued highly by some are being sacrificed? Should we engage in subversive activities and risk the lives of our agents if additional security can be attained thereby? Should we perhaps go so far as (when ready) to start a preventive war, with its enormous evils, if we should become convinced that no adequate security can be obtained except by the defeat of the Soviet Union? In this last case, would not the exponents of amoralism have some moral qualms, at least to the point of rationalizing a decision favoring such a war by claiming that it

[15] It is not without irony that of the two authors who have recently come out for a policy of the national interest, the one, George F. Kennan, who calls for a policy of national self-restraint and humility, usually identified with morality, should deny "that state behavior is a fit subject for moral judgment" (*American Diplomacy, 1900-1950,* University of Chicago Press, Chicago, 1952, p. 100), while the other, Hans Morgenthau (*op. cit.*), calling for a policy of unadulterated national egotism, claims to speak in the name of morality.

[16] It would be unrealistic to assume that policy-makers divide their attention strictly between ends and means and only after having chosen a specific target level as being morally justified decide whether the means by which it can be attained are morally acceptable. Moral judgment is more likely to be passed on the totality of a course of action which embraces both the desired end and the means which lead to it.

would serve to satisfy not primarily an egotistical national demand for security but an altruistic desire to liberate enslaved peoples? It is easier to argue for the amorality of politics if one does not have to bear the responsibility of choice and decision!

Far be it from a political scientist to claim any particular competence in deciding what efforts for national security are or are not morally justified. What he can contribute here is to point to the ambiguities of any general normative demand that security be bought at whatever price it may cost. He may also be able to make it more difficult for advisers or executors of policy to hide from themselves or others the moral value judgments and preferences which underlie whatever security policy they choose to recommend or conduct.

The moral issue will be resolved in one of several ways depending on the ethical code upon which the decision is based. From one extreme point of view it is argued that every sacrifice, especially if imposed on other nations, is justified provided it contributes in any way to national security. Clearly this implies a position placing national security at the apex of the value pyramid and assuming it to constitute an absolute good to which all other values must be subordinated. Few will be found to take this position because if they subscribed to a nationalistic ethic of this extreme type they probably would go beyond security (the mere preservation of values) and insist that the nation is justified in conquering whatever it can use as *lebensraum* or otherwise. At the opposite extreme are the absolute pacifists who consider the use of coercive power an absolute evil and therefore condemn any security policy that places reliance on such power.

For anyone who does not share these extreme views the moral issue raised by the quest for national security is anything but clear-cut and simple. He may have no doubts about the right of a nation to protect and preserve values to which it has legitimate title or even about its moral duty to pursue a policy meant to serve such preservation. But he cannot consider security the supreme law as Machiavelli would have the statesman regard the *ragione di stato*. Somewhere is drawn a line, which in every instance he must seek to discover, that divides the realm of neglect, the "too-little," from the realm of excess, the "too-much."

Decision-makers are faced then, with the moral problem of choosing first the values that deserve protection, with national independence ranking high not merely for its own sake but for the guarantee it may offer to values like liberty, justice, and peace. They must further decide which level of security to make their target. This frequently will be the most difficult moral task although terms such as adequacy or fair share indicate the kind of standards that may serve as guides. Finally, they must choose the means and thus by scrupulous computation of values compare the sacrifices, which this choice of means implies, with the security they promise to provide.

It follows that policies of national security, far from being all good or all evil, may be morally praiseworthy or condemnable depending on their specific character and the particular circumstances of the case. They may be praised for their self-restraint and the consideration that this implies for values other than security; they may instead be condemned for being inadequate to protect national values. Again, they may be praised in one instance for the consideration given to the interests of others, particularly of weaker nations, or condemned in another because of the recklessness with which national values are risked in quest of some chimera. The target level falls under moral judgment for being too ambitious, egotistical, and provocative or for being inadequate; the means employed for being unnecessarily costly in other values or for being ineffective. This wide range of variety which arises out of the multitude of variables affecting the value computation would make it impossible, and in fact meaningless, to pass moral judgment, positive or negative, on "national security policy in general."

It is this lack of moral homogeneity that in matters of security policy justifies attacks on so-called moralism, although not on moral evaluation. The "moralistic approach" is taken to mean a wholesale condemnation either of any concern with national security—as being an expression of national egotism—or of a security policy relying on coercive and therefore evil power. The exponent of such "moralism" is assumed to believe that security for all peoples can be had today by the exclusive use of such "good" and altruistic means as model behavior and persuasion, a spirit of conciliation, international organization, or world government. If there are any utopians who cling to this notion, and have influence on policy, it makes sense to continue to disabuse them of what can surely be proved to be dangerous illusions.

It is worth emphasizing, however, that the opposite line of argument, which without regard for the special circumstances would praise everything done for national security or more particularly everything done for enhancement of the national power of resistance, is no less guilty of applying simple and abstract moral principles and of failing to judge each case realistically on its merits.

Normative admonitions to conduct a foreign policy guided by the national security interest are seen, then, to be ambiguous and misleading. In order to be meaningful such admonitions would have to specify the degree of security that a nation shall aspire to attain and the means by which it is to be attained in a given situation. It may be good advice in one instance to appeal for greater effort and more armaments; it may be no less expedient and morally advisable in another instance to call for moderation and for greater reliance on means other than coercive power. Because the pendulum of public opinion swings so easily from extreme complacency to extreme apprehension, from utopian reliance on "good will" to disillusioned faith in naked force only, it is particularly important to be wary of any simple guide, even one that parades in the realist garb of a policy directed solely by the national security interest.

Chapter Eleven

COLLECTIVE SECURITY
AND THE
WAR IN KOREA

THE ACTION TAKEN by the United Nations in 1950 to
halt the attack on South Korea has been heralded as the first experiment in collective security.[1] The implication is that a radical break
with the traditional foreign policy of nations has occurred; power
politics, we are told, has been replaced by police action of the
world community. Quite likely, many who suffered in the Korean
War on our side have been comforted by the thought that they
served the cause of law enforcement by community action, although
others who believe that no vital interests of their country were at
stake may have found the ordeal harder to bear. Whatever the
emotional reaction, it is necessary to investigate dispassionately
whether a turning point in world politics was reached when the
United Nations flag was unfurled in Korea. On the answer may
depend what future policy we and others are entitled to expect of
this country.

It may sound like quibbling to ask whether Korea was an example of "collective security." Obviously, the answer depends on
the definition of the term. If one chooses to make collective security include every collective action undertaken for defensive purposes by a group of nations, then the Korean intervention by the
United States and its associates falls under the term. As a matter
of fact, it has become the habit of official spokesmen of our government to use the term in this way. For instance, they speak of NATO
as a means of "collective security," although the treaty was legally

[1] This chapter is reprinted, with minor changes, from *The Yale Review*,
Vol. XLIII, No. 4 (June, 1954), by permission of the publisher.

justified by reference to Article 51 of the United Nations Charter, which explicitly permits "collective self-defense" in cases where the universal collective security provisions of the United Nations *fail* to protect a victim of aggression. But there is nothing new or revolutionary in nations' aligning themselves for purposes of defense against their common national foes. Except for countries that pursue a "going it alone" policy, such conduct has been traditional among the members of multistate systems. But what exponents of the principle of collective security have in mind is to urge nations to change the customary direction of their defense policy. They call upon them to go beyond aligning themselves with one another only to meet threats emanating from common national enemies and instead to embrace a policy of defense directed against aggression in general or, more precisely, against any aggressor anywhere. Having made arrangements to name the aggressor by community decision, nations—instead of reserving their power to defend or enforce their national interests—would be lined up like a police force to strike against any country, friend or foe, that had been declared an aggressor. Such a policy would constitute a radical break with tradition.

Since there are fundamental differences between these two types of collective action, with only one of them constituting a break from traditional national foreign policy, to avoid confusion and misunderstanding the two should be distinguished by the use of different labels. And since "collective security" has become the symbol for a break with power politics, it should be reserved for action that meets this test. It will be so used in this discussion, while other types of multilateral defensive action will be called "collective defense." Aside from semantics then, the problem is whether intervention in Korea represents a radical break with the traditional foreign policy of nation-states and, as a consequence, fulfills the expectations widely held for "collective security."

How serious a break with tradition the policy of collective security would be is evident when one considers what risks and sacrifices nations would incur in order to make such a policy effective and meaningful. Provisions and commitments for police action presumably would add nothing to the protection that victims of aggression have enjoyed under the old system unless such victims could now expect more military assistance than they would have received otherwise. The exponents of collective security have stressed this point, advocating a system under which, they assume, overwhelming force would be placed behind the law and at the disposal of a victim of attack. As in municipal affairs, the power of the police usually would suffice to deter any would-be attacker and thereby serve to maintain the peace rather than merely to punish the offender.

For collective security to add in this way to the strength of the defense and to the chances of deterrence, some nations, including one or more of the great powers, must be prepared to resort to force—that is, for all practical purposes, go to war—whereas if they had not been devoted to the principle of collective security, they would have remained neutral or fought on the side of the aggressor. Instead of being allowed to reserve their military strength for the exclusive task of balancing the power of countries considered a threat to themselves or their allies, nations committed to a policy of collective security must divert their strength to struggles in remote places or, worse still, take action against friends and allies on whom reliance had been placed for defense against common foes. In extreme cases, a nation might even be called upon to defend and strengthen a foe at the expense of a friend or ally, if this ally were condemned as an aggressor.

If these should seem to be farfetched contingencies, French experience, as well as possibilities now facing this country, prove them to be anything but theoretical. When Italy attacked Ethiopia the French were urged in the name of collective security to participate in sanctions and if need be military sanctions against Italy, a country which had just become a virtual ally against Germany (then considered France's number-one opponent); in the Korean War France came under pressure to divert more of her strength to the fight with the North Koreans and Chinese aggressors at a time when she already felt too weak at home even to dare consent to German rearmament.

To justify the assertion that collective security became a living reality in the Korean War, it is necessary to show that one or more countries proved ready to run the risks and consent to the sacrifices that this radical break with traditional defense policy presupposes. This means inquiring whether there is evidence that such a switch to defense against aggression *per se* was made by the United States and its associates. Before doing so, it may be worthwhile to ask whether it is possible to conceive of incentives that might be powerful enough to induce nations to change their habits in so radical a fashion.

Those who seek to make a case for collective security, either as having become a reality or as being a practical goal for the future, argue along two lines, one more idealistic, the other more realistic. Nations, it is said, might take up arms against any aggressor anywhere simply because the crime of aggression arouses their moral indignation. The existence of such indignation both here and abroad is not in doubt. The desire to see perpetrators of wanton attack stopped and punished is widespread in a world with so much experience of brutal attack on weak and peaceful peoples. Yet, it is one thing to be indignant; it is another to be prepared to plunge one's country into war (though it be called police action) especially in an age of increasing wartime horror and destruction. Even aside from narrow nationalist preoccupations which might lessen the ardor for punitive action on behalf of the world community, there is reason to doubt whether moral indignation alone can be relied upon to carry nations into military action when no vital national interests push them in the same direction. In order to have a chance, it seems that collective security itself would have to appeal to those interests traditionally considered vital to the nation.

According to the more realistic argument, such a vital interest is in fact at stake, although nations may often fail to realize it. The argument rests on what has been called the principle of "indivisible peace." If aggression is allowed to go unpunished anywhere, it is said, potential aggressors will be encouraged everywhere, and as a result no nation will be secure. Instead, if any aggressor anywhere is stopped or deterred by overwhelming police power, all other potential aggressors will understand the warning and cease to constitute a threat. Thus, by a kind of detour, nations which for reasons of collective security are forced to divert strength or to weaken alignments against specific opponents gain more security in the end, even against their national foes.

A discussion of Korea might appear necessarily to focus attention on the United Nations rather than on its members. In a sense this is true. Had no world organization such as the United Nations existed in 1950, there could have been no question of police action on behalf of the world community. Collective security presupposes that the aggressor be named and condemned by means of some recognized procedure; resort to violence in defense of the law against such an aggressor must be authorized by an organization which can claim to speak for the community. Yet no provisions, resolutions, commands, or recommendations of a world organization of sovereign nations can suffice to make collective security a reality. It can become real only by the employment of military power for police purposes; the decision rests with the members who possess such military power and can use it for collective security if they will. In regard to the United Nations, the question is merely whether it did its part in inducing members of the organization to take police action on its behalf and under its auspices.

This is not the place to investigate whether the Charter of the United Nations was aimed at collective security as defined here or whether it offered the best means of inducing countries to act in accordance with this principle. The veto provision certainly allowed members to assume that they never would be expected to participate in police action which would seriously antagonize one or more of the major powers. Furthermore, Article 43 left the implementation of any commitment to participate in such action to subsequent negotiations which have not taken place. However, when the members of the United Nations subscribed to the purpose of the organization as being "to take effective collective measures . . . for the suppression of acts of aggression," they accepted the principle of common defensive action against any aggressor anywhere. Their legal or at least moral obligation to do so whenever the competent organs of the United Nations order or recommend such action would seem to be beyond doubt, unless one were to assume that the "inherent right of self-defense" permits nations to beg out of any military action that would endanger their security. If one accepted this reservation, the Charter could not be said to create much legal embarrassment for members who wanted to avoid the risks of collective security.

The attack by the North Koreans occurred on June 25, 1950. On the same day, the Security Council in the absence of the Soviet delegate, determined that a breach of the peace had occurred. It called upon North Korea to withdraw its forces and proceeded to invite its members "to render every assistance to the United Nations in execution of this resolution." Some hours prior to the second meeting of the Council on June 27, the United States government announced that it had ordered American air and sea forces to go to the assistance of South Korea for the specific purpose of executing the June 25 resolution of the Security Council. If this were not enough to qualify American intervention as United Nations action, the Security Council identified itself with the action of the United States by voting on the same day that urgent military measures were required. The members were now called upon to furnish assistance of the kind necessary to repel the attack. From then on, the action of the United States and its associates was carried forward in the name of the United Nations, under the United Nations flag, and under a unified United Nations command set up by the United States in accordance with a resolution of the Security Council. Limited to recommendations, the United Nations continued to put what little pressure it could on its members to get them to participate or to make larger contributions; at the same time it sought to influence the United Nations command in the conduct and termination of the war, acting in this respect as a restraining factor.

Aside from this rather marginal though not unimportant role played by the United Nations itself, the character of the action in Korea must be judged by the decisions and acts of the United States and its associates. It would seem permissible, in fact, to concentrate on the conduct of the United States because the other nations which made contributions to the defense of South Korea might conceivably have done so as friends and allies of the United States, whether this country were acting traditionally in what it considered to be its national interest and that of its friends or were conducting police action on the principle of collective security.

It is not a simple matter to discover whether or not United States intervention in Korea qualifies as collective security in the restricted sense in which the term is used here. The motivations of the chief architects of the policy are not decisive. The devotion of men like Mr. Truman and Mr. Acheson to the idea of collective security as they conceived it is not in doubt, any more than their desire to prevent the United Nations from suffering the same dismal fate that befell the League of Nations at the time of Italy's aggression against Ethiopia.

What is being asked is whether the United States, even if it believed itself to be engaging in police action in conformity with the concept of collective security, did in fact break with traditional national defense policy by accepting the kind of risks that such a break presupposes. If the aggressor had been South Korea rather than North Korea, the answer could not be in doubt. To take up arms in that case against South Korea would have meant siding with this country's chief national enemy, the Soviet bloc, and strengthening the Communist countries at the expense of a country on which the United States could have relied as an ally in the cold war. No more striking proof could have been given of unqualified American support for police action against any aggressor anywhere. But, the aggressor was Communist North Korea backed by the Soviet Union. It becomes necessary therefore to investigate how intervention in these circumstances looked from the point of view of American security interests as interpreted in Washington at the time.

Speaking negatively first: the United States obviously was not taking up arms against a friend or ally. On the contrary, it was setting out to stop expansion by the Soviet bloc, thus serving what had long been proclaimed to be the major goal of American foreign policy. It might be argued, however, that in extending the "containment" policy to Korea the United States was diverting military power from Europe, which was considered the chief danger area. As the war proceeded, and American involvement exceeded all early expectations, much fear of such diversion was in fact expressed in Europe. But in this country, the opinion continued to prevail that in terms of the cold war it would have been even more dangerous for Europe if Communist aggression had gone unpunished in Asia. Moreover, powerful groups in Congress had long pressed for a stronger stand against Communism in Asia. Thus while the sacrifices in men and resources borne by the American people in the course of the Korean War were far in excess of even the most pessimistic initial expectations, they did not include the sacrifice or diversion of defensive military power from the tasks of the cold war. Instead, the rearmament effort provoked by Communist aggression in Korea led to a multiplication of this power.

The fact that no sacrifice in terms of national protection against a major enemy was involved is not enough, however, to explain why this country should have decided to resort to military force. Except for a radical break with tradition, nations are not expected to take up arms unless there are interests at stake that they consider vital. Accordingly, the apparent absence of any vital American interest in South Korea made it seem as if devotion to collective security alone could have induced the United States to intervene. It was known that our civilian and military leaders did not consider the defense of the Thirty-eighth Parallel or the preservation of a free South Korea a matter of vital strategic importance to this country, despite the fact that loss of the area to the Communists would have rendered Japan more vulnerable to attack.

The Joint Chiefs of Staff had reached this decision at the time American troops were withdrawn from the territory of the Republic of Korea, long before Secretary Acheson made his famous "perimeter" speech. It is also true that the United States was not bound by any treaty of alliance to go to the assistance of South Korea. However, this lack of what might be called a local strategic interest and the absence of any specific commitment to assist South Korea, other than that implied in the United Nations Charter, do not suffice to prove that vital interests of the United States were not at stake. Rather, one can discern a threefold American interest of exactly the kind that governments thinking along the line of traditional power politics would normally consider serious enough to justify military action if not to make it imperative.

In the first place, according to the views prevailing in both political parties at the time of the North Korean attack, any further expansion in any direction on the part of the Soviet bloc constituted a threat to American security. The "containment" policy was under attack not because it went too far in this respect but because it was thought too negative. As a matter of established policy, then, no area adjoining the Soviet Empire was held to be strategically nonvital; any addition to territory behind the Iron Curtain would threaten to upset an already precarious world balance of power.

In the second place, the United States was vitally interested in proving to its European allies that they could rely on American military assistance in case of a Soviet attack. NATO, this country's main bulwark against the threat from the East, was weakened by European fears of a resurgence of isolationism in this country. It was strongly felt, therefore, particularly by Secretary Acheson, that if South Korea were left at the mercy of the attacker, all of Russia's weak neighbors—and there were none but weak neighbors—would lose what confidence they gradually had gained that this country meant business when it promised to prevent further Soviet conquest.

As if this were not enough, there was a third reason for this country to be most seriously interested in not allowing a challenge by its number-one enemy to go without military response. The United States was engaged in a vast and strenuous effort to unite the entire free world in a common effort of defense against the Soviet and Communist menace. From most countries, particularly in Asia, it had not succeeded in obtaining commitments of mutual assistance of the kind customarily laid down in treaties of bilateral or multilateral alliance. Therefore, all other non-Communist countries were committed to common defense against Communist aggression only if they could be made to accept the United Nations Charter as such a commitment. From the point of view of American security policy, consequently, it was of paramount importance that the United Nations be made to serve as a substitute for a formal alliance of the free world. If there were any chance of achieving this result—and subsequent events showed how slim the chance was—it could only be done by demonstrating that under the Charter the United States considered itself committed to take up arms against the North Korean aggressor.

If it is correct, then, to assert that strong American national interests, beyond an interest in collective security, pointed in the direction of intervention in Korea, certain conclusions can be drawn concerning the character of this action. In order to avoid misconceptions, it is important to point out certain other conclusions which do not follow from what has been said.

In the first place, because the resort to force against North Korea served to maintain and even to strengthen this country's power position relative to its major national opponent, it cannot be considered the kind of break with tradition earlier defined as a prerequisite of effective collective security. However, this does not mean that the Korean action did not represent a drastic change—or call it a break—in United States policy. This country demonstrated its intent to stop Soviet and satellite aggression everywhere, thereby identifying its interests with those of the entire non-Communist world. This is a far cry from earlier isolationist policies which sought national security in withdrawal from areas of conflict. Moreover, the fact that American security interests were at stake does not prove that the Administration or the public would have considered them sufficiently vital to warrant a resort to force if defense of these interests had not coincided with the assertion of the principle of United Nations police action against aggression. Faith in this principle may at least help to explain the almost unanimous support Mr. Truman received at the start of the war.

In the second place, despite the popularity that collective security undoubtedly enjoyed in 1950, American military action against a member of the Soviet bloc cannot be taken as evidence that this country would be prepared to follow the same road in the case of an aggressor who was not a member of the Soviet bloc, or had attacked a member of that bloc. Here the national interest as traditionally understood and the interest in collective security would not coincide; instead, they might run directly counter to each other.[2]

Korea, then, has not established the practicability or reality of collective security in the sense the term is used here. Instead of being a case of nations' fighting "any aggressor anywhere" and for no other purpose than to punish aggression and deter potential aggressors, intervention in Korea was an act of collective military defense against the recognized number-one enemy of the United States and of all the countries that associated themselves with its action. If would-be aggressors have reached the same conclusion, they will not be deterred by the Korean War unless they belong to the Soviet bloc.

This is disheartening news to those who have placed their faith in deterrence through collective security, unless they believe that aggression by non-Communist countries is out of the question anyway. Disappointment of the high hopes placed on the "first experiment in collective security" should be weighed, however, against possible advantages accruing to this country for not having committed itself by precedent to fight all aggressors everywhere.

While it will always remain a matter of controversy whether a certain commitment or course of action is or is not in the national interest, one may assume wide agreement on the proposition that in the present circumstances this country cannot afford seriously to jeopardize its ability to balance the power of the Soviet bloc. If this is so, any military action against an aggressor would run counter to the elementary rules of prudence if it threatended to tip the balance in favor of the Soviets. It need not do so in the case of every non-Communist aggressor. One can imagine cases of aggression by a non-Communist country against another non-Communist country in which the United States would have more to lose from allowing such aggression to be successful than from weakening and antagonizing the aggressor and his friends. In some instances there might be grave danger in allowing violence to continue and spread. But it needs little imagination to see how rare the cases are likely to be in which military intervention against a non-Communist country would favor this country's security position in the cold war. One need think only of the disastrous consequences that might fol-

[2] The Suez crisis of 1956 during which Britain, France, and Israel attacked Egypt occurred after these lines were written. The American reaction and its bearing on the problem of collective security is discussed in Chapter 12, "Collective Defense versus Collective Security."

low from a resort to force against, say, one of the Arab countries, or against Yugoslavia, or against a member of NATO. These consequences would be particularly grave if a large part of American military strength had to be diverted to such an operation.

A commitment to intervene would be most serious if a non-Communist country launched an attack on a member of the Soviet bloc. While it is to be hoped that this will remain a theoretical contingency, it nevertheless must be taken into consideration. Police action in such instances necessarily would favor the Soviet bloc if not lead to Soviet expansion; it would be hard enough for the United States to remain on the sidelines while one of its erstwhile allies was being defeated by Communist "police" forces. In the present situation, when this country and the other members of the free world are having the greatest trouble mustering enough strength for their defense against the East, how could their statesmen risk destroying what non-Communist solidarity and common defense positions now exist, even if in doing so they were serving the cause of collective security and the deterrence of future aggression?

This does not answer the moral question. Some insist that it is the duty of nations to participate in police action because peace and the establishment of the rule of law in the world require that aggressors be stopped or punished. This means placing higher value on such punishment than on national self-defense whenever the two conflict. Against this view it can be argued on moral grounds that when as today everything the American people and most free peoples cherish, from independence to their way of life, is in grave danger of Soviet and Communist attack, precedence must be given to the defense of these values. After all, even staunch supporters of collective security are apt somewhere to draw a line beyond which nations cannot be expected to go in their devotion to the cause of police action; they will not expect governments to commit national suicide for the sake of observing the long-run interests of the world community.

But what about world public opinion? Will people abroad not be shocked to learn that the United States cannot be counted upon to use force against all aggressors, Communist or non-Communist, and will this not make enemies for this country? Where the public stands on this issue is a matter of conjecture. Experience during the Korean War may be revealing, however. This country was given almost unanimous and in most cases enthusiastic moral support by articulate opinion throughout the non-Communist world when it first took up arms to stop the North Koreans. Yet, when the question arose of taking more forceful action against Red China after that country had been declared an aggressor, condemnation of any such "adventurous" or "militaristic" move was hardly less widespread. Liberal opinion—always most keen to see collective security applied—was now most vigorously opposed to any extension of the war.

The reason for this apparent inconsistency is not hard to discover. Punishment of an aggressor is desired but not if it means plunging nations into major war, in this case a world war, and not even perhaps if it means gravely endangering the immediate security of nations. "Before the great powers can join in sacrifices of blood and treasure to keep the peace in regions where they have no real interest," as Samuel Flagg Bemis said, prior to the Korean War, "a great transformation of will must take place among the peoples of the nations." This would still seem to hold true, more particularly so, of course, where intervention runs directly counter to these "real interests." Thus, however tempting a system of collective security may appear in the abstract, its implementation in the case of aggressors of considerable military power runs into serious objections on the grounds of morality as well as of prudence.

If it is doubtful, to say the least, whether this country will intervene against any aggressor anywhere, serious disadvantages will accrue to it if the popular label of "collective security" is applied to United States foreign policy. There is first the danger of future disillusionment. There has been some already because Red China, found guilty of aggression by the United Nations, did not receive the same punishment as North Korea, the weaker country. If the expectation takes root that American military forces will be available against any aggressor anywhere and if in some future instance this expectation is disappointed, the bitterness of the victim of an attack and its friends might have embarrassing consequences.

A second disadvantage also has been borne out by the events. If the American people are made to believe that this country involved itself in a costly and in many ways inconclusive war for no other interest than to serve the cause of collective security, is it surprising that there is resentment against other members of the United Nations who failed to live up to a principle to which they were no less committed than the United States? Such criticism of our friends and allies may be silenced if it is understood that this country in fact did have what were then considered to be very pressing national interests in stopping the North Koreans. It will also be better appreciated that some of the other members of the United Nations, including India, went quite far in backing the United Nations when, in disregard of what they believed to be their interest in neutrality, they voted to authorize the actions of the United States and its associates and to condemn the North Koreans and Chinese as aggressors.

It may be objected that if Korea has not opened the way for a universal system of collective security against all aggression, then it has served merely to demonstrate once more the tragic hold that power politics has on the nations even of the free world. The United Nations as a security organization, it will be said, can have no place in such a world. Such conclusions are not warranted. The United States and its associates made good on a policy of "collective defense of the free world" carried out under the authority and control of the United Nations. While the control was weak, it nevertheless brought a restraining influence to bear on one of the world's greatest powers engaged in a bitter and costly defensive struggle. The one great contribution to the development of more lawful conditions in the world which this country can claim to have made in Korea consists therefore in its willingness to recognize the authority of the United Nations over actions that required sacrifices mainly from the American people. If some deplore the way in which the majority in the General Assembly exercised this control, believing that it would have been better for this country and the free world to have fought for victory at all costs, they give testimony thereby to the price countries may have to pay for the advantages of having collective defense operate according to the rules and with the approval of an international organization.

As to the United Nations itself, it gained stature because it proved useful to the free world in its defense against Communist aggression without having to give up its universal character and its mediatory potentialities. Obviously, its role has been a more modest one than that contemplated by the exponents of collective security. Instead of being able to order the bulk of its members to fight aggressors whatever their relations to the aggressor, all the United Nations could do was to name the aggressor, to authorize and recommend action by its members, to lend its name to their action, and to seek to exert influence on the way this action was carried out and terminated. If nations will resort to force only against national opponents when it accords with their national defense interests, as was true in Korea, the United Nations must limit itself to functions that are consistent with the needs of collective defense of like-minded countries. This has now been shown to be a practical and beneficial way of using an organization which, it should be added, has many important tasks to perform other than to stop or punish aggression.

Chapter Twelve   COLLECTIVE DEFENSE
VERSUS
COLLECTIVE SECURITY

THE RADICAL CHANGE that took place in American foreign policy at the close of World War II—when the United States shifted from a policy of "going it alone" to its new policy of "going it with others"—has been widely discussed, explained, and acclaimed and therefore may seem to require no further discussion.[1] Yet, attention here once more is to be directed toward the new policy not because the wisdom or necessity of the shift is to be questioned, but on the contrary because there may arise along the new path troubles that, not properly handled, might compel the United States to return to the old policy of isolation out of sheer desperation. There may seem to be no cause for worry. Rarely has a foreign policy enjoyed as much public support as the new policy of collaboration has. Hardly any isolationist rumblings have been heard despite many disappointments and many harsh words against the United States from most of the "others" with whom the United States set out to collaborate. If the present unqualified dedication to the new policy were to lead into serious dilemmas and provoke widespread disillusionment, a swing of the pendulum to the other extreme could not be ruled out. The following discussion does not cover all of the pitfalls on the road of collaboration with other nations; it is limited, instead, to those problems arising out of the collective security system of the United Nations, widely heralded as the chief instrument of an up-to-date policy of "going it with others."

[1] This chapter is reprinted, with minor changes, from *Alliance Policy in the Cold War*, ed. Arnold Wolfers (The Johns Hopkins Press, Baltimore, 1959), by permission of the publisher.

181

I

BEFORE ENTERING upon the particular case of the United States, I shall take up in a general or theoretical way the problems posed by a nonisolationist course of action under conditions as they exist in the contemporary world. Without seeking any precise definition of the terms (which will not prove necessary) I shall take an "isolationist" course to mean a policy of national security that neither relies on commitments by other nations to give assistance in defense nor involves the country in such commitments to others. The alternative, a policy of "collaboration," then is one in which promises of future assistance, usually mutual and military in character, form one of the cornerstones of national defense, second in importance only to national armaments.

Prior to the establishment of the League of Nations in 1919, nonisolationist countries—including most of the major powers—based their collaborationist policy on treaties of alliance and related pacts, also known under the name of pacts of mutual assistance. As I shall hope to show, such alliances and pacts continue to represent the chief instrument and an indispensable means of every policy of collaboration for defense. Starting with the League of Nations Covenant and revived after World War II under the Charter of the United Nations, however, a second and clearly distinguishable course of collaboration, operating through a different instrument, has come into existence side by side with the traditional alliance; it is known as "collective security" and is generally considered the chief function of the United Nations. The question is whether the two types of policy and instruments can be relied upon to work in constant harmony with each other, or whether there are possibilities of clashes between them that might seriously endanger the national security of countries caught between their conflicting demands.

There are some striking similarities in substance between these two types of collaborationist policy. They have recently acquired a similarity in name, too, which is confusing as we have seen because it tends to obscure their divergence. Both in the case of alliances, now usually called collective defense arrangements, and in the case of collective security under the United Nations, countries commit themselves to assist others against attack. In both instances, then, the victim of an attack expects his own defensive strength to be supplemented by the strength of other nations. And yet the two policies differ fundamentally in respect to both intent and modes of action, so that the cases in which they are complementary and helpful to each other are largely a matter of happy coincidence.

Nations enter into collective defense arrangements to ward off threats to their national security interests, as traditionally conceived, emanating from some specific country or group of countries regarded as the chief national enemy, actual or potential. The motive behind such arrangements is the conviction that the creation of military strength sufficient to ward off the specific threat would be beyond their national capacity or would prove excessively and unnecessarily costly in view of the opportunities for mutual support and common defense.

The peculiarity of collective defense arrangements exists, therefore, because they are directed against an opponent known to the partners of the pacts, although he may not be named in the pact for reasons of diplomatic caution. One further peculiarity following from the first is that the allies can define in geographical terms the danger they are seeking to thwart and are thus able to make their military preparations and work out their strategy in advance of any conflagration. For example, in the 1890's when France and Russia (later France and the Soviet Union) were parties to an alliance, they were promising to assist each other against Germany with armed forces suited to and deployed for the particular purpose. Similar pacts and arrangements—some bilateral like our pact with South Korea, some multilateral like NATO—are so familiar today that no further elaboration is necessary. It is obvious also that such collective defense arrangements against specific opponents, when entered into by countries devoid of offensive purposes, are aimed primarily at deterrence, i.e., deterrence of the country against which the common strength and determination of the allies are visibly pitted.

Collective security belongs to a different and presumably better world, as Woodrow Wilson once said, which explains why it is so dear to the idealist who wants nations to have at least a foothold in the better world right now. In contrast to alliances, it is not the goal of collective security arrangements to provide their members with strength either against their national enemies or for the defense of their national interests, unless one redefines the terms "national enemy" and "national interest" in accordance with the philosophy upon which collective security rests. Collective security is directed against any and every country anywhere that commits an act of aggression, allies and friends included. The theory holds that "any aggressor anywhere" is in fact the national enemy of every country because in violating the peace and law of the community of nations it endangers, if indirectly, the peace and security of every nation. It is further argued that every country, as a consequence, has a "national interest" in protecting every victim of aggression, even if in so doing it may have to turn its back on its immediate national opponent or antagonize a reliable ally.

Whatever the merits or demerits of such a system of all-round protection against aggression—about which more will be said later—there is one difference in the effects of collective action under the two systems that needs to be stressed. Few of even the most forceful exponents of collective security expect it to assure the deterrence of all aggressors at the outset. Instead, they place their hopes on the success of a kind of learning process in which the punishment of one or more actual aggressors will deter subsequent would-be aggressors from deeds that would provoke "police action" against them. By itself this delay in the immediate effectiveness of the collective security system rules out any prestabilized harmony between collective defense and collective security. After all, during the period of the learning process with its indefinite duration, nations may be attacked or annihilated by their chief national opponents because they have diverted their strength to a struggle with some other aggressor or have antagonized and weakened an indispensable ally. There are other types of clashes that may occur between the two lines of policy, but it is worthwhile at this point to inquire into the tendency, existing at least in Western countries, to regard collective security and collective defense as supplementary and as mere variations of one and the same policy.

This assumption of harmony has several roots. One is of a legal character. The United Nations Charter in Article 51 explicitly permits collective self-defense—or, briefly, collective defense—which it calls an inherent right of nations. In the Covenant of the League of Nations there was no such provision, a fact that caused a country like France embarrassment since she sought national security very largely through alliances. While she insisted that her alliances were merely "underpinning" the collective security system, others considered them incompatible with the League Covenant.[2] It was understandable, therefore, that France and the Soviet Union, allied

---

[2] See the discussion of the problem in Arnold Wolfers, *Britain and France Between Two Wars* (1st ed., Harcourt, Brace & Co., New York, 1940), pp. 167 ff.

once more against Germany, should have been particularly eager at San Francisco that the United Nations Charter legitimize alliances. The Charter does this under the name of "collective self-defense," a provision supported by the United States, although for different reasons.

A second factor tending to make the two lines of policy appear not only compatible but practically identical is of a semantic nature. If confusion were intended, nothing could promote it better than to describe alliances or coalitions as "collective defense arrangements," thereby joining them with collective security through the use of the same term "collective." It seems not unlikely that confusion was in fact intended, at least in some quarters. One can see why American statesmen should be particularly inclined to use the two terms as synonymous, often applying the term "collective security" to such collective defense arrangements as NATO and SEATO or even to such bilateral military pacts as the ones concluded with South Korea or Nationalist China. Consciously or unconsciously, they are seeking to make these arrangements more palatable to a people they believe to be adverse to alliances as the "power-political" instrument that Woodrow Wilson condemned as a chief cause of war. One would think, however, that the time has come to combat what popular prejudice against alliances may still exist. If a country's security is in serious danger and popular support for its defense measures is badly needed, the true value of alliances and related pacts of military assistance—all of which serve the same purpose as national armaments—should be widely recognized and accepted without moral qualms or inhibitions.

Finally, the self-deluding expectation in Western democratic countries that collective security and collective defense will regularly support each other grew out of the particular historical circumstances under which collective security was introduced and activated between 1919 and 1956. Collective security was first written into the law of nations at a time when aggression by the autocratic governments of the Central Powers was foremost in the minds of the peoples of the West. Later, when in the early thirties collective security became a live issue, it again was directed against nondemocratic countries: Fascist Italy, Nazi Germany, and autocratic Japan. Finally, when the United Nations acted under the Charter provisions on collective security, the aggressor was North Korea, a member of the totalitarian Communist bloc. Thus, all through the period from the establishment of the League to the war in Korea, it was natural for many people in Western democracies to assume that committing themselves to deter or punish "any aggressor anywhere" meant in fact committing themselves to oppose nondemocratic aggressors who were their national enemies anyway. As long as this coincidence lasted, collective security and collective defense were indeed directed against the same opponent, and the two concepts supplemented rather than contradicted each other.

For France, the happy dream of a kind of prestabilized harmony between the two policies came to an end as early as the Ethiopian War of 1935, which was the only occasion on which the provisions for collective security in the League Covenant were applied. On that occasion, France was called upon to participate in a leading capacity in collective action against Italy just after she had allied herself with Italy against her national enemy, Nazi Germany. Some might argue that France had only herself to blame for the dilemma, inasmuch as she had allied herself with a nondemocratic and therefore potentially aggressive country, but such an argument carries little weight today when a limitation of collective defense pacts to the few truly democratic countries would almost certainly spell defeat for the West. And other more recent events struck further blows at the illusion of harmony.

Soon after the Korean War had rekindled the hope that collective security under the United Nations would of necessity be directed against nondemocratic countries belonging to the Soviet bloc—the same countries, therefore, against which all Western collective defense arrangements were directed—the Suez crisis brought a rude awakening. The "aggressors" on this occasion were two of the leading democracies of Europe, and democratic Israel. The three countries resorted to war against Egypt in the very fashion that their own leaders and publicists, no less than those of other countries, had persistently labeled as "aggression" and condemned as a crime. No longer was there any necessity for proof that action against "any aggressor anywhere" might mean action against closest friends or allies even though they be democratic. Instead of supplementing each other, the two policies of collective defense and collective security crashed head-on as far as the West was concerned: countries committed to both had to choose between their conflicting commitments.

But the possible clashes between the two types of commitments to collective action are not limited to the kind of clash illustrated by the Suez or Abyssinian crises. Instead, there are three different kinds, all of which pose serious problems for countries caught in the dilemma.

So far, both under the League and under the United Nations, only the one kind of clash just mentioned actually has occurred: the case in which nations are called upon to participate in collective security action, even in the mild form of condemnation, against a friendly or allied country on whose support they depend for defense against a recognized national enemy. When faced with the choice of either losing the support of Italy or else defaulting on collective security, France chose the latter course. In the Suez crisis, the United States took the opposite line, upholding the principles of collective security despite the damage that might have resulted for two of her most essential alliances. Fortunately for the United States, the outcome was not calamitous because the three "aggressors" did the exceptional thing of restoring the *status quo ante* despite the absence of collective military sanctions. The members of the United Nations can hardly expect to resolve the dilemma as easily on every occasion.

A second type of clash may arise from the participation of a country's national enemy in collective security action against a third power. To take a fictitious example: if Greece were condemned for committing an act of aggression against Turkey and punitive action were recommended by the General Assembly of the United Nations, Bulgaria, as a member of the United Nations, would have the right to participate in "police action" against Greece and might do so with enthusiasm. In the course of such collective action, Bulgaria's troops might occupy Thrace, thereby upsetting the balance of power between East and West in the vital area of the eastern Mediterranean. Who would venture to predict that, once the United Nations decided to call a halt to collective action and invited its members to restore the *status quo ante,* the Bulgarians in such a case would withdraw from territory they had long coveted and now occupied? Instead, it would be in line with historical experience to expect the military situation at the close of hostilities to affect profoundly the territorial provisions of any subsequent settlement. The results of initiating collective security measures in this hypothetical case, therefore, would probably be favorable to Bulgarian interests and damaging to the West. This example illustrates one of the dangers a country might face at a time of serious tension if the universal collective security system led national opponents to take part in common military action against a third power.

The third type of clash will not appear serious to people who are confident that their own country never will commit an act many nations would condemn as aggression. Surely few American statesmen have been worried that they were restricting their own freedom to act in defense of American security either by their constant efforts to strengthen and broaden the scope of collective security under the United Nations or by their success in popularizing the idea of "police action" against every aggressor. Yet, as Britain—once an equally staunch proponent of collective security—discovered to her sorrow in 1956, a policy that emphasizes the principles of collective security can, under certain conditions, prove a dangerous trap. If what is condemned as "aggression" were necessarily an act similar to Hitler's military invasion of Poland in 1939 or even to Britain's initiation of war against Egypt in 1956, some countries might well feel satisfied that they would never commit such follies or crimes nor risk, therefore, being accused of aggression. But if earlier events under the League of Nations were not enough to prove that the definition of aggression and the identification of the aggressor are most difficult problems and may often become highly controversial political issues, recent developments under the United Nations should be driving the point home.

Even in the era in which a country's expansion would usually take the form of an armed attack across national boundaries, it was often uncertain which of the belligerents had first attacked or which could be held responsible for the hostilities. One can recall the heated and prolonged controversy after World War I on the "war guilt" question.

Since the dawn of the cold war, with conditions of revolutionary upheaval and ideological conflict, the issue of defining aggression has become a subject of new controversy. Now, countries like the Soviet Union or North Vietnam have been seeking to extend control beyond their national boundaries by methods that are more subtle than "armed attack." In response, an even more elusive concept, "indirect aggression," has been developed and come to be equated with the traditional type of aggression.

This extension of the meaning of aggression has had the unintended effect of leading to new and possibly more frequent situations in which the identification of the aggressor rests almost entirely on the sympathies, ideological predilections, fears, and alignments of the United Nations members who are called upon to vote on the issue. One might easily imagine a case in which a nation that has decided to send troops into another country to help it defend itself against "indirect aggression" arrives only to be faced with a government installed by rebellion. This new government might seek to resist with its own armed forces what it would call foreign military intervention, condemning it as an act of aggression. Especially at a time when it is not rare for two governments to exist side by side, both claiming to represent the same country and each, moreover, recognized by large groups of nations as the legitimate government, it is no longer possible to predict on which side the General Assembly might place the blame for aggression: on the side responsible for "indirect aggression" or on the side responsible for "military intervention." This uncertainty is greatly enhanced by the fact that "outside support" or "instigation" of a rebellion, as well as "military intervention" for its suppression, are terms referring to a wide variety of actions which lend themselves to an equally wide variety of judgments or rationalizations regarding their relative "aggressiveness."

Therefore, whether a country powerful enough to undertake military action is vulnerable to condemnation for aggression depends not simply on the danger that mad or vicious men will take over the reins of policy. Its vulnerability will depend no less on what collective defense measures it may feel compelled to take for its security. Here lies another source, then, of possible conflict between collective security and collective defense.

Despite the possibilities of such clashes between the policies of collective defense and collective security, it cannot be concluded, as a general proposition, that nations would do well to give up their commitments to one or both of these policies. Many states cannot forego collective defense because they lack the power of defending themselves without outside assistance; many may find that withdrawal from the collective security system in order to avoid the possible future embarrassment of conflicting commitments would cause them losses they dare not take. Because there is not likely to be any general answer that would fit the best interests of all countries, the possible solutions to the problem will be discussed in relation to the particular situation of the United States.

II

Once the outstanding exponent of an isolationist foreign policy, the United States has become involved in collaboration with other states on a scale and with a thoroughness unprecedented in history. As a consequence, the vexing problems that can arise from the contradictions between the two different collaborative policies may bear down on the United States with particular weight.

In the closing phases of World War II—when the Roosevelt Administration decided that the United States should break away from its isolationist past, a move that gained broad public support—neither the Administration nor the public had any intention of involving the country in a system of alliances or what today are called collective defense arrangements. Instead, isolation was to give way to "collective security." Any policies smacking of old-time alliances would have found little favor at that time. A few advocates of the United Nations may have seen in a collective security system a kind of continuing alliance of the victors of World War II by which to deter and hold down the onetime Axis powers, or an alliance of the great powers that would enable them to control small mischief-makers. But, despite the veto provisions of the Charter which excluded collective security action against the great powers and their clients, the general view was that the United States was committing itself to a policy designed to prevent or to fight aggression anywhere.

Even at San Francisco, where the United States joined with the Soviet Union and France in their demand for collective defense to be explicitly sanctioned by the Charter—as it was by the inclusion of Article 51—the United States was not contemplating entering into the traditional type of military alliance. The United States, it is true, had signed the Act of Chapultepec in the spring of 1945. This act prepared the ground, however, not for an alliance but for a regionally circumscribed system of collective security for the Americas, directed against any country, inside or outside the group of signatories, that was deemed to have attacked any state in the Western Hemisphere. However, the Act of Chapultepec shared with the Franco-Soviet concept of alliances one essential feature: its signatories, like allied nations, insisted on the right to take common military action against a country they considered an aggressor without waiting for the Security Council to identify the aggressor or to decide on the action that should be taken against him. Thus, by a happy coincidence, the United States helped make compatible with the United Nations collective security system the concept of collective defense on which its own subsequent alliance policy was based.

The American position, and with it the American policy of "going it with others," underwent a second and highly consequential change when involvement in a life and death struggle with the Soviet bloc became a recognized fact. Now the danger was no longer the abstract "aggressor anywhere," but the very concrete potential aggressor beyond the Iron Curtain who was soon to require the concentration of almost the total power of the United States together with the power of a large array of allies. From then on—except for a continuing reluctance to call alliances by their traditional name—the old American aversion to alliances evaporated. In fact, the United States now became the architect and leader of the most widespread and intricate system of alliances any country has found it necessary to establish in peacetime.

As a further consequence, the United States now became engaged in a double-track course, committing itself simultaneously to collective security under the United Nations and to numerous collective defense arrangements that were not subject to United Nations authority. It became vulnerable, thereby, to the adverse effects of any clashes that might arise between its two policies of collective action—particularly vulnerable, in fact, since it had become more deeply involved along both lines of policy than had any other country.

Before considering ways and means of eliminating or minimizing the adverse effects of such clashes, it is necessary to gain some idea of the relative importance of collective defense arrangements, on the one hand, and of collective security, on the other, as instruments toward the attainment of American foreign policy goals. It stands to reason that if one track is less important than the other, it will have to bear the brunt of any concessions necessary to free United States policy from the consequences of dangerous contradictions.

If one considers the position of the United States in the world today, the paramountcy of collective defense should hardly be open to question. The task of balancing the power of the Soviet bloc, as a minimum and necessary goal of American foreign policy, is a formidable one. Its successful accomplishment would probably transcend the power of the United States acting alone, even if the American people were prepared to make unlimited sacrifices. It is certainly a task that no country would voluntarily consent to undertake alone as long as other states were ready and able to share it. For this reason, pacts with other countries intended to assure the United States of allied support in the struggle with the Soviet bloc are, taken together, one of the two pillars on which American national security presently is based, the other being the American national military establishment.

The character and significance of the support the United States can expect to receive from its partners in collective defense arrangements are not readily recognizable in every instance. Although far from negligible, the military forces that other states are maintaining at their own expense for defense against the Soviets are on the whole disappointing. But there are other contributions, besides military assistance in the literal sense of the term, that other countries are able and willing to make for the cause of Western security. In its remoteness from the confines of the Soviet bloc, the United States continues to be dependent on its ability to operate from territory beyond the seas. Many countries are making heavy sacrifices in terms of national pride, sovereignty, and safety against nuclear attack by placing their territory at the disposal of the United States, whether for the deployment of troops or for the establishment of air bases and missile-launching sites. Even when a country merely decides to place itself under American protection, accepting the United States as the guarantor of its security, it may thereby contribute to the purposes of the alliance system by making itself accessible to the military forces of the West while denying itself and its resources to the Soviet camp.

In speaking of mutual military assistance, one is moving within the realm of the classical alliance, or what may be called "collective defense" in the narrow sense of the term. Mutual military assistance forms the core but not the whole of the American system of pacts and agreements. It alone can serve to block Soviet military expansion. Despite its continued importance, however, military assistance is not enough. Even from the point of view of American and Western defense, agreements with other nations that contain no military provisions have become necessary. The Soviet bloc has not been slow to discover—in the absence of opportunities for military expansion or in addition to them—other methods of gaining control over foreign governments and countries and thus of upsetting the world balance of power. The Communist drive for economic, ideological, and eventually political control over other states is hardly more easily contained than a Soviet military drive. Here, too, the support of other nations against the Communist threat is essential. In fact, if these "others," who are the direct targets of such nonmilitary expansion, refused to co-operate in warding off attacks on their independence, there is little the United States could do to meet the attacks. It was logical, therefore, that after realizing the new dimensions of the struggle, the United States should have extended the scope of its pacts and agreements with other states beyond the confines of a traditional alliance system. It is more accurate to speak of an American "alignment system" when discussing the United States collective defense effort.

There is no need to discuss in detail the kinds of arrangements that fall under the heading of alignments and do not constitute pacts of mutual assistance. The many agreements between the United States and other countries for economic and military aid and for support against subversion are well known. But it is worth pointing out that even "uncommitted" countries—which by definition are unwilling to enter into formal pacts of any sort—can be drawn into the alignment system by what might be called a tacit agreement that they will remain genuinely neutral and will not grant special favors to the Soviet Union.[3]

Ties with uncommitted countries are bound to remain extremely tenuous, however. It has become customary in the West to speak of the free world as if all of the non-Communist nations were aligned with one another in a common cause. Actually the term is the symbol of an aspiration rather than of a reality. Ever since the cold war started, one of its chief features has been a bitter East-West struggle for the "in-between" world. Early hopes have long been dashed that a policy of military containment would not merely arrest the tide of Soviet military expansion at the Iron and Bamboo Curtains, but also prevent the spread of Soviet influence to new areas. In many parts of Asia and Africa, a Soviet alignment system is in competition with the American system. The result so far has been to leave some non-Communist countries leaning toward the Soviet bloc, others vacillating between the two sides, still others re-

[3] The aftermath of the Eisenhower Doctrine demonstrated how difficult and politically inexpedient it may be for some governments to enter into formal pacts with the United States that would tie them to one of the "military blocs." Although the doctrine was nothing but a unilateral American declaration, any Arab government that expressed approval of the doctrine was open to attack at home for "allying" its country with the United States.

maining strictly uncommitted and, finally, others favoring loose ties
with the West. Under these circumstances, the United States as the
leader of the West has particularly cogent reasons to fear any situation in which it is compelled to antagonize non-Communist countries, as may happen if collective security commitments are invoked
against one of them.

There is a certain irony in the way in which the process of antagonizing friends or allies tends to work. At times, the United States
has more reason to worry about actions that antagonize a doubtful
friend than about those that hurt a trusted ally. The "friend" may
have more opportunity or more inclination to change over to the
Soviet camp, or, by threatening to do so, may be in a better position
to blackmail the United States. However, alliances—even with nations that depend heavily on American protection—are also vulnerable to the divisive effects of unwelcome American participation
in collective security action. Unlike some of the uncommitted nations, such as Egypt or Yugoslavia, France would hardly think of
accepting Soviet military aid, not to speak of switching camps, if
antagonized or humiliated by the kind of action under collective
security that the United States took at the time of Suez. Yet, her
government might not be able to assure continued French solidarity
with the West if large sectors of the French public, out of resentment, were to join the ranks of those Frenchmen who already prefer
nonresistance to the Soviets to the horrors of war.

It can be said, therefore, that American participation in United
Nations collective security action against any one of its many
partners—allies, friends, and neutrals—might lead any one of them
to beg out of the alignment system or at least to become an unreliable, worthless, or even dangerous member of it. Whether there is
any way in which the United States can protect itself against the
possibility of arousing the sensitivity of its friends and allies to
moves they consider inimical will be discussed later. Attention must
first be directed to the American collective security commitments
under the United Nations Charter.

If the collective defense system has become a chief mainstay of
American national security, for the foreseeable future at least, its
survival is worth any price in risks and sacrifices lower than the
price of "going it alone." This being so, it will not be easy to find
arguments justifying commitments under collective security that,
potentially, have a disruptive influence on American collective de-

fense arrangements.[4] However, the services the United States may expect from its participation in the United Nations collective security system need to be given careful consideration before we turn to a discussion of methods for preventing serious clashes between the two collective policies pursued by the United States.

There are cases in which collective security can serve as a valuable supplement to the American collective defense arrangements. Occasionally, it is the only available instrument with which to draw some uncommitted or neutral countries toward an attitude of partisanship and moral support for the United States and its allies and in favor of their actions of collective defense. Korea is a case in point. Since American intervention on behalf of South Korea was widely interpreted as representing police action for the world community and was placed under the auspices of the United Nations, it was easier for countries like India to side with the United States on the issue of North Korean aggression and to sympathize with its intervention in the war. Some countries were even willing to go beyond the mere condemnation of North Korea because in their opinion the war constituted United Nations police action. Here, the United Nations played the role of a kind of loose free-world alliance in accordance with the expectation mentioned earlier: that collective security and collective defense would be in harmony with each other.

The Korean case may repeat itself in the case of other satellite attacks on non-Communist countries. In the event of aggression by the Soviet Union itself, however, the situation in all probability would be different. Even if the countries that created the United Nations at San Francisco had not been assured—thanks to the great-power veto in the Security Council—that they would never be called upon to take action against a major power, it is hard to

---

[4] Readers may suspect that the present author will find such justification particularly difficult if they know that he has taken a dim view of collective security ever since its inception under the League of Nations. See Chapter 11, "Collective Security and the War in Korea," and Chapter 16, "Policies of Peace and Security after World War I." For a thorough and critical analysis of collective security by other authors, see Kenneth W. Thompson, "Collective Security Re-examined," *American Political Science Review*, XLVII, No. 3 (1953), 753-72; Howard C. Johnson and Gerhart Niemeyer, "Collective Security—The Validity of an Ideal," *International Organization*, VIII, No. 1 (1954), 19-35; Ernst B. Haas, "Types of Collective Security: An Examination of Operational Concepts," *American Political Science Review*, XLIX, No. 1 (1955), 40-67; also George Liska, *International Equilibrium* (Harvard University Press, Cambridge, Mass., 1957), pp. 81-118.

imagine them, merely because they were partners in the United Nations collective security system, daring to assume the risk of condemning the Soviet Union as an aggressor or recommending its punishment. As a matter of fact, the conduct of most of the members of the United Nations at the time of Red China's intervention in the Korean War speaks for itself in this respect. Their readiness to take sides against the North Korean attacker did not reappear in the face of the danger that action against Red China might set off a major conflagration.

Collective security, then, may be useful to the United States and its allies in deterring or stopping Soviet satellite countries, but obviously it would be folly to rely on collective security as a means of arresting the Soviet Union itself. Even in respect to the former case, it would be well to reckon with the possibility that events since Korea—the rise of Soviet and Red Chinese power and the new danger of two-way nuclear war—may have dampened the inclination of many countries to take hostile steps even against relatively weak members or associates of the Soviet bloc. It is necessary, therefore, to search for other advantages to be derived from commitment to United Nations collective security less far-reaching than the gain of additional allies in a war.

Because the American policy of alignment requires dozens of countries to remain on good terms not only with the United States but also with one another, the pacification of the entire non-Communist world has come to be a goal of American foreign policy, second in importance only to the containment of the Soviet bloc itself. Therefore, to the extent that the threat of sanctions under United Nations collective security provisions serves to deter non-Communist countries from undertaking aggressive action against one another, the United States stands to gain from the restraints thus imposed on its friends and allies. The importance of this service is hard to estimate. It is impossible to say how effective such deterrence has been or is likely to prove in the future, because there is no way of telling what wars would have occurred in the absence of these provisions. Fear of provoking the United States by flagrant violation of the peace quite likely acts as the main deterrent and would operate even if the United States were not committed under the Charter to take part in collective action against aggressors.

There is another line along which the collective security system may affect the United States, but here only hindsight will tell whether its impact is helpful or harmful on the whole to the United

States. The fear of being accused of aggression in the United Nations General Assembly, even by a minority of its members, may place restraints on the United States itself. Whether this has actually happened in the past is hard to judge. If such restraints were operative at the time of the Lebanese crisis in 1958, preventing a "march on Baghdad," they probably were imposed more by the fear of Soviet reactions than of any displeasure of the United Nations. For better or for worse, however, defensive action, particularly against what the United States regards as "indirect aggression," is rendered more difficult by the fact that "world opinion," being opposed to any steps involving the risk of war, may in the name of collective security be turned against the United States.

The services discussed so far that collective security can render to the United States can hardly compensate for the danger and losses that may arise from clashes between this collective security and American collective defense. Therefore, if continued participation is justified, or even indispensable, the reason must lie elsewhere. Promotion of the idea of collective security has created a psychological situation in which the United States cannot turn its back on the concept, not because of what collective security can accomplish and actually has accomplished, but because of what millions of people inside and outside the United States believe it may accomplish in time. Collective security has come to be the chief symbol of hope that someday international relations will be brought under the rule of law and that a community of nations will develop in which there will be no more war. A reputation for dedication to such a system of collective security and for leadership in its operation has become an asset that the United States could forego only at a high cost in terms of appeal to foreign peoples and also in terms of public support for its foreign policy at home.

Thus, by a kind of irony, a collective security system that may seriously interfere with the alignment system has become an important ingredient of the latter because of the place it holds in the minds of people throughout the world. With suspicion of American intentions rife as it is throughout the non-Communist world, withdrawal from the collective security system, however carefully explained, would be interpreted in many places as a move dictated by American aggressive or imperialist aims. Many friends would be lost and much antagonism aroused if it could be said—and made a topic of Soviet propaganda—that the United States was betraying man's hopes for peace and lawfulness.

III

FROM WHAT has been said about the two lines of collective policy, then, it seems that the United States must remain on its double-track course, with simultaneous commitments to collective defense and collective security. While a collapse of the collective defense system would be a calamity of the first magnitude and would allow no alternative except return to a highly hazardous and extremely costly policy of "going it alone," withdrawal from collective security commitments and exclusive reliance on collective defense would also be imprudent methods of escaping the dilemmas of the double-track policy.

How serious are these dilemmas likely to be in the particular case of the United States? There is no doubt that a direct conflict between the American commitment under the United Nations Charter and its commitment to allies and friends under the alignment system can become a reality. Yet if attention were limited to the Suez experience, one might be inclined to minimize the potentialities for serious trouble. While one could not imagine a more severe blow to the American collective defense effort than would have resulted from an actual break with Great Britain, America's most important ally, and with France, such a break did not in fact occur. However, there are a number of reasons, which may never be duplicated, why the break was avoided in this particular instance. Britain, France, and Israel gave in to the demand for re-establishing the *status quo ante* before any more compelling action than condemnation was recommended or taken. One need only imagine the gravity of America's dilemma if Britain and France—or even Israel alone—had persisted in military efforts and if the United States had been unable to prevent a United Nations vote recommending coercive measures against the "aggressor" or "aggressors." Moreover, in the Suez case, the American decision to favor its collective security commitments and to join in condemning the "aggressors" did not antagonize the entire British and French peoples, large sectors of which were no less hostile to the invasion than was the American government. Many realized, too, that the United States had pulled the rug out from under Soviet intervention and, for the time being at least, had prevented a radical shift of the Arab countries in the direction of the Soviet camp.

It is easier to imagine situations that would lack these redeeming features. To take a fictitious illustration: if France were to be condemned for launching a military attack on Tunisia and if she persisted in her action as constituting defense of her own territory, another American decision in favor of collective security might leave France with no alternative but to get out of NATO. Here, then, would be a case in which the collective security commitment would lead to an almost irreparable disruption of the American alliance system in Europe and thus of the Western policy of collective defense against the East.

The potential threat to American security from the second type of clash—that is, the dangers posed by the participation of its national enemy in "police action" of the United Nations—follows from what has been said earlier. Whether or not the United States decided to join in supporting action recommended by the United Nations, the existence of the collective security system would open the door to Soviet military action beyond its borders. If Britain, France, and Israel in 1956 had not complied in time with the recommendations of the United Nations General Assembly, there was nothing to prevent the Soviet Union from taking the lead in military sanctions, arrogating to its armed forces the title and function of a "police force of the community of nations." The collective security provisions of the Charter would legalize such Soviet military action, which might completely upset the world balance of power. One cannot help pointing to the grotesque contradiction between a collective defense system directed against a national opponent and a collective security system that may call for military action by that same opponent against an indispensable ally in the collective defense effort.

Finally, one cannot rule out the possibility that the United States could become involved in the third type of clash: that is, American collective defense action opposed by other nations in the name of collective security. Restraints imposed upon the United States in its efforts to stop or defeat what it considers "indirect aggression" were mentioned earlier. Under the Truman Doctrine—although not under the Eisenhower Doctrine, which speaks only of "overt armed aggression"—the United States proclaimed its intention of supporting "free peoples who are resisting attempted subjugation by armed minorities or by outside pressures," whether by "direct or indirect aggression." The United States confirmed this intention by its action in Lebanon. If American military assistance for this purpose reaches a threatened country before its government has been overthrown, as was the case in Lebanon, there can be no question

either of American aggression or of American initiation of international hostilities.

But it takes little imagination to visualize a situation in which
the dispatch of military forces would coincide with the overthrow
of the native government and lead to hostilities with the armed
forces at the disposal of the new rebel government. In such a case,
there can be no assurance that a majority of the United Nations
members would see eye to eye with the United States in deciding
which of the two belligerents was to blame for the hostilities or for
their continuation. Even if no formal condemnation of the United
States occurred, the American position might be gravely damaged
by the present world-wide inclination to pin the label of aggressor
on one party to every military encounter, an inclination that has
been fostered by years of collective security propaganda. The
choice might be between losing a friend or an area deemed vital to
American security and arousing the opposition, if not open hostility, of large numbers of nations belonging to the American alignment system. The dilemma would be particularly serious for an
American government that had sought to present the United States
as the chief champion of collective security.

IV

IF IT IS TRUE, then, that serious embarrassments are in store for the
United States on its double-track course of "going it with others,"
the question of how to meet the problem is of immediate importance.

One way out is usually open: a course of action known as "mud-
dling through," which means trusting one's ability to avoid major
damage by *ad hoc* maneuvers taken on the spur of the moment.
Sometimes there is no better solution, but it is useful even then to
anticipate the kind of difficulties that may lie ahead so that improvisation or *ad hoc* adjustments will not aggravate rather than
remedy a distressing situation. It need not be left entirely to instinct, for example, to decide whether it is wiser to antagonize ally
X, at the risk of losing him, than to run counter to the views of a
large body of opinion in the General Assembly. A continuous and
careful check on the value of ally X to American defense policy and
an equally careful scrutiny of the respect and authority enjoyed by
changing majorities in the General Assembly may prove helpful to
future decisions.

There is no need, however, to resign ourselves to the hazardous game of improvisation. Even though continuing along the course of both collective security and collective defense, the United States can modify the execution of its two policies of collective action in a way conducive to greater harmony between them.

The necessity of preserving the alignment system—in fact, continuously and substantially strengthening it—does not imply that every member of the system is essential to American security and no member can be antagonized. Even if there were no collective security system, the United States could not always escape the necessity of choosing among its friends and allies. At one time, for example, it looked as if the Cyprus crisis might create the need for such a choice irrespective of whether questions of aggression and collective security were to arise. If the United States wants to be in a position to participate on occasion in the condemnation or even punishment of a non-Communist country, it must be prepared to get along without that particular country.

While not every ally is dispensable—if France turned her back on NATO, the chance of defending Europe, slim enough as it is, might disappear completely—the United States might compensate in some cases for the loss of a weak, half-hearted, or unreliable member of the alignment system by increasing its own armaments or its economic and military aid to the remaining members. Excessive fear of losing friends opens the door to blackmail. Moreover, such fear may be predicated only on an unwillingness, often allegedly dictated by limitations on American solvency but in fact stemming only from limitations on our readiness to raise and pay higher taxes. The United States cannot afford to tell every blackmailing country to go over to the Communists if it pleases, as has sometimes been proposed, since the support of some nations is strategically indispensable. Nevertheless the present boundary line separating East and West is largely accidental, after all, and therefore allows for some flexibility. If the United States was able to survive the loss of Czechoslovakia and of continental China, it would be sad indeed if it had now become so vulnerable to defections and loss of prestige that it could not make up for the loss of less important countries, particularly if the loss consisted merely in their shift from alliance to neutrality.

Flexibility may help in yet another direction without requiring sacrifices at the expense of collective defense. The United States will not always lose a friend or ally if, in pursuit of collective security action, it antagonizes a non-Communist government. The government in question and its policy may be so unpopular with its own people that American opposition to its policy—even action against it—will win more reliable support for the United States in the long run than could be obtained by surrender to its demands. However, the narrow limitations on this type of flexibility need to be stressed. Only too frequently the choice today is between a government that is unpopular at home but strongly pro-Western and one that gains most of its popularity by its hostility toward the United States or even by its pronounced partisanship for the Soviet Union.

All in all, only a minimal alleviation of the dilemmas discussed here seems possible through modifications of the American policy of collective defense and alignment. It becomes all the more important, therefore, to look for practical changes in the American policy toward collective security that may offer a solution. Fortunately, there is more room for modification in this area.

Since American security is dependent upon the continuation of her alignment system, the United States has a major interest in avoiding situations where it has to take sides against any member of this system, whether to condemn, stop, or punish it. Under these circumstances, it should be the objective of American policy within the United Nations to discourage rather than promote a policy of labeling as the aggressor one of the parties to every violent international conflict. Some of the weaker would-be aggressors may be deterred by fear of condemnation or punishment, but the price of this deterrence is high. If it fails, and if the "police force" is called into action, all of the dangerous consequences discussed earlier threaten to unroll themselves: an essential ally may be antagonized beyond repair; hostilities may spread far beyond the confines of the original theater of conflict; the Soviet bloc may be given an opportunity to take "police action" beyond its borders; the United States itself may be accused of initiating the trouble. It is suggested, therefore, that American efforts to turn the United Nations into a "strong reed"—efforts to which the other members of the United Nations have given lip service at best—may backfire. There is no doubt that the United States has engaged in such efforts. American initiative has been directed, for example, toward a reinterpretation of the Charter which would permit the veto-free General Assembly to recommend police action and make such recommendations binding upon United Nations members. The United States has even insisted that it has the right and the intention to enforce the principles of the Charter against an aggressor in cases where neither the Security Council nor the General Assembly is prepared to recommend police action.

The possibility of dangerous clashes between collective defense and collective security commitments can be minimized by a reversal of the present trend of American policy, namely by an effort to push into the background rather than to emphasize the concepts of "enforcement of the peace" and "police action." These concepts should better be reserved for cases of unmistakable and flagrant initiation of war across recognized national boundaries and be considered the *ultima ratio* of American and United Nations peace strategy.

If taken alone, modifications in the tenor of United States collective security policy along the lines suggested might be mistaken as a sign of a general decline of American confidence in the United Nations as an instrument for the prevention of war. Such a view would be based, however, on an excessively narrow conception of the ways in which the United Nations can help promote peace, a misconception fostered over the years by official and unofficial American pronouncements. Because the major emphasis has been placed on the collective security or "enforcement of the peace" functions of the United Nations, the role the world organization can play as a mediator and conciliator on the road to compromise and peaceful settlement—as well as the importance of such mediation—has received scant attention and credit. In practice, the chief services the United Nations has been able to render to the peace of the world have been in this noncoercive field and specifically in its efforts to bring the parties to a dispute to some form of accommodation or truce. These efforts include the dispatch of observation teams and the policing of borders or strips of territory undertaken in agreement with both parties. Therefore, if the value of the United Nations to the cause of world peace is not to be jeopardized, and if the intentions of the United States are not to be misunderstood, it is imperative that any reduction in American zeal for the identification, condemnation, or punishment of aggressors be accompanied by conspicuous efforts both to strengthen the role of the United Nations as mediator and conciliator and to convince world opinion that the best services the United Nations can render in the field of pacification lie in the pursuit of such a role.

The United States has a special stake in elevating respect for United Nations mediation above that for "enforcement." It has little need, if any, for the assistance of collective security in its great struggle with the Soviet bloc; in its national armaments and collective defense arrangements, it has more reliable means of deterrence and defense than anything collective security could provide. In addition, the reliability of these arrangements will suffer if collective security is not prevented from throwing roadblocks in their path. And within the non-Communist world, all the way from North Africa through the Middle East to Southeast Asia and the Far East, where impassioned antagonism and violence are erupting again and again, mediation by the United Nations offers the most promise of preventing a split or breakdown of the American alignment system. Not that mediation is a panacea: it has failed conspicuously on more than one occasion, whether undertaken by the United Nations or by the United States itself. Also, it may hurt American interests if the majority of the members of the United Nations, fearful of war, expect the United States to make most of the concessions. But collective security may fail, too, even when it enjoys the complete support of the United States. It failed as a deterrent prior to the Korean War and to the Suez adventure; and, when put into practice, it means war rather than peace, though such war be called "police action." The United States will have done all it can both for its own protection and for that of its friends and allies if it succeeds in maintaining a reliable collective defense network backed by adequate national armaments and if, in addition, it gives strong support to United Nations mediatory and conciliatory efforts within the non-Soviet world while preserving United Nations collective security as a last resort.

Chapter Thirteen STRESSES AND
STRAINS IN
"GOING IT
WITH OTHERS"

EVEN BEFORE World War II came to an end, there were unmistakable indications that a radical shift was going to take place in American peacetime foreign policy.[1] The traditional policy of "going it alone" was to be replaced by a policy of "going it with others." This change did not reflect any expectation that a new threat to American security would follow upon the defeat of the Axis coalition and make the United States dependent on the military support of others. It was assumed, on the contrary, that after the war the United States could look forward to a period of friendly relations with all of the remaining major powers. Nevertheless considerations of national security did affect American thinking and were a dominant motive behind the break with tradition. Isolationist sentiments had vanished as a result of the bitter experiences of two world wars, which it was believed, could have been avoided if the United States had collaborated with others prior to the outbreak of hostilities. What appeared to be needed, then, was American participation in an international organization devoted to the preservation of peace and the punishment of aggression. Only later, when the Soviet threat to American security materialized, did the new policy take on the form of an alliance policy directed against a specific country or group of countries.

[1] This chapter appeared originally as the introduction to *Alliance Policy in the Cold War,* ed. Arnold Wolfers, (The Johns Hopkins Press, Baltimore, 1959); it is reprinted here, with minor changes, by permission of the publisher.

The American response to the threat of Soviet or Sino-Soviet expansion is too narrowly described as an alliance policy if the term "alliance" is used in the customary sense to mean a pact of mutual military assistance. For brevity's sake, however, "alliance policy" is employed to cover all efforts to prevent other countries from siding with the camp of the Soviet opponent. As used here, the term suggests an American cold war policy directed toward the development of an extensive system of alignments in which actual military alliances form the iron core.

The scope of American foreign policy is not, of course, exhausted by efforts to defend the non-Communist world against the economic, political, or ideological expansion of Soviet control. There continue to be other objectives of American policy, purely economic and humanitarian objectives, as well as the original purpose of preventing aggression from any quarter. These have not been wholly sacrificed to the necessities of the cold war. As Sino-Soviet power has grown, however, and as the threats to the United States and other non-Communist nations have become more fully appreciated, alliance or alignment policy for purposes of defense has come to dominate the scene and must do so as long as the East-West struggle continues unabated.

That the relations between the United States and its mighty Communist opponents should have become the focus of interest and attention both to policy-makers and to students of international relations is not surprising. By comparison, the relationships within the non-Communist world have seemed much less important and receive, therefore, much less attention. Moreover, interallied relationships in view of their great diversity appear to elude treatment as a phenomenon with characteristics of its own. On closer examination, however, one can detect—apart from some more positive aspects—a series of disruptive or erosive forces operating within the entire American alignment system; they are forces that make their imprint on the relationships between the non-Communist countries and especially on the relations between the United States, leader of the coalition, and the rest of its members. The present chapter seeks to throw light on these relations.[2]

[2] After this was written, George Liska completed his book *Nations in Alliance,* the first elaborate and sophisticated study of policies of alignment and nonalignment. This is to be published by The Johns Hopkins Press in the summer of 1962.

Because analysts are likely to concentrate on defects rather than on achievements, a distorted picture of the alliance system might be created if no mention were made here of the evidence of solidarity within the non-Communist world and of common resistance to Soviet blandishments and threats.

Again and again, conflicts either between the United States and other free countries (as in the Suez case) or between friends of the United States (as in the case of Cyprus) have threatened to defeat attempts at building up a comprehensive network of alignments. On other occasions, the attitudes of uncommitted countries have become a cause of alarm. At one moment it looked as if Nasser were ready to cross over to the Soviet camp and to take other Arab countries with him; at another, Tito's defection to the East was confidently predicted. Yet in spite of all the crises, rifts, and erosive forces besetting the free world, none of its members—the "uncommitted" countries included—so far have voluntarily joined the Soviet bloc, and none of the countries allied with the United States in postwar collective defense arrangements have allowed resentment, fear, or a change of government to lead them into a policy of neutrality, although Iraq deserted its alliance with Great Britain. Quite generally, whenever the danger signals have been unmistakable, there has been a tendency to rally around the United States rather than to defect. Therefore, while complacency might well prove disastrous in view of the many centrifugal pulls to which the non-Communist world is exposed, it would be misleading to suggest that the future offers only the prospect of continuous and irreparable disintegration.

With these qualifications in mind, however, it seems proper to focus attention on the sources of serious tension between nations and groups of nations on whose solidarity the future independence and security of all the non-Communist countries may depend. Only if the stresses and strains are carefully identified and understood is there hope of discovering appropriate ways of overcoming or reducing their harmful impact.

It might be argued that solidarity, even among close allies, has usually proved a perishable asset. Wartime coalitions rarely have long survived the termination of the war for which they were formed. The present danger is not the dissolution of a wartime coalition, however, but the dissolution of an alignment intended to prevent a war that has not yet occurred. Therefore, if the present coalition were to start breaking up before the threat that brought it into being had disappeared, it would fall far short of its original purpose. The return of the United States to a policy of "going it alone" might then become a desperate but inescapable alternative. Should the cold war come to an end or fade into the background, conceivably the United States could afford to withdraw from military alliances while continuing its policy of "going it with others" in nonmilitary areas of co-operation and within the United Nations.

An inquiry into the chief causes of the many irritating conflicts that characterize relations with and among our friends and allies must take into consideration the numerous psychological features and motivations of the human actors in whose hands the conduct of alliance policy lies. The personalities and idiosyncrasies of leading statesmen, the preconceptions and biases of influential groups, and the emotions, resentments, fixed ideas, or peculiar anxieties of whole peoples can all become divisive forces. Since the success of a policy of alignment depends on the creation and maintenance of a sense of common interest, of mutual confidence among governments, and of solidarity among entire nations, these psychological factors can exert a decisive influence on the course of events. This is particularly true in an era when leaders of unusual authority—like Adenauer, de Gaulle, or Nehru—carry so much responsibility that their personal approaches to problems or to one another may make or break alliances. Moreover, where so many peoples of widely divergent cultural backgrounds and ideologies are simultaneously involved in the process of hammering out common policies, national peculiarities like Indian pacifism or American moralism may become serious psychological handicaps, while such typical national attitudes as Arab fanaticism or the complacency of democracies may create almost insuperable obstacles to concerted action.

While the human factors go far in determining the way in which alignments consolidate or dissolve, many of the psychological elements of stress and strain that make themselves so painfully felt in the present American alignments with others can best be understood as reactions to particular aspects of the environment in which the coalition operates. In fact, one does injustice to the responsible governments if one fails to recognize the vexing external conditions —some of them unique—that tend to render collaboration among the non-Communist countries an extraordinarily delicate problem.

The geopolitical approach to international relations is not popular today, perhaps because of excessive claims made by its enthusiastic exponents. It makes sense, however, in this instance to stress the very marked geographical hurdles that lie in the path of American collective defense efforts. They represent such serious handicaps to the common pursuit of security *vis-à-vis* the Sino-Soviet bloc that they could prove fatal to the alignment system if nothing were done to counter their effects.

Soon after the fall of the Axis coalition, it became evident to those responsible for American foreign policy that the Soviet Union, occupying the area Mackinder called the "heartland" of Eurasia, had emerged from the war as an expanionist power of great military and industrial potential and extraordinary dynamism. Already it had extended its control far beyond the old borders of its predecessor, the Czarist Empire. More ominous was the fact that the rising giant was surrounded by a virtual power vacuum along its entire periphery, from Scandinavia and the British Isles, along the rimlands of Eurasia, to Japan and Korea.

Clearly, the non-Communist countries on the Eurasian mainland and adjoining islands would not be able to generate enough strength or unity within the foreseeable future to contain the Communist bloc, should it attempt to take advantage of the weakness of its neighbors as was to be expected. If there were to be established and maintained any reasonable balance of power that would give assurance of continued freedom from Soviet control to countries interested in maintaining their independence, only one nation was strong enough to provide that balance, and this nation was located on the other side of the globe. Perhaps more by instinct than by premeditated design, the United States took upon itself the task of building an alliance system that would wield the necessary counterpower.

As the potential strength of the Sino-Soviet bloc matured, the United States gradually began to realize how ambitious was its project of spanning the oceans with a defensive coalition whose holdings on the shore of the Eurasian land mass were, for the most part, easily accessible from the heartland but thousands of miles from insular America.

Under these circumstances, promises of United States assistance to countries across the oceans were not credible without additional evidence of American intentions. The only hope of effective deterrence and defense lay—and still lies today—in a projection of American power across the water barriers: the establishment and maintenance of a substantial American military presence in or close to the chief Eurasian danger areas.

Although it was an unavoidable consequence of geographical circumstances, the need for the projection of American power far beyond the confines of the United States almost inevitably places a heavy psychological mortgage on the alliance system. This deployment of forces is an easy target for hostile Soviet propaganda, which plays on such themes as "American occupation of sovereign countries" and "provocative American encirclement" of the Russian homeland. In the non-Communist countries that permitted or invited American forces to be stationed within their territories, those who for whatever reason are opposed to the alignment of their country with the United States condemn the American presence as an abnormal situation and a threat to national independence. The fact, in light of historical experience, is that it would have been more abnormal for the United States to have allowed a power vacuum to persist in areas adjoining a state whose leaders frequently had proclaimed it their duty to exploit the weaknesses of the "capitalist" enemy. Moreover, at the same time that it projected its own power across the oceans, the United States, at great financial sacrifice though with only moderate success, has sought to fill the vacuum with indigenous military and economic power; this, it was hoped, would eventually render superfluous American overseas deployment.

Whether normal or abnormal, the presence of American forces on the territory of its friends and allies places on their relations with the United States strains that were absent in former peacetime coalitions. Demands for "disengagement" or insistence that the "amis go home," voiced strongly in some quarters abroad, are symptomatic of a psychological reaction that can weaken allied solidarity. One may wonder, in fact, why this reaction has not been more widespread and why it has not evoked from Americans a response of "bring the boys home," considering that, until very recently, the United States has been so strongly isolationist.

These problems of distance between members of the alliance are compounded by yet another geographical handicap. If one visualizes the alliance system in the form of a wheel, one may say that the friends and allies of the United States are spread out along its rim, each occupying the end of a spoke, while the United States is located at the hub of the wheel. Danger to any allied country—to the end of a spoke representing the Formosa Straits, or the territories south of Soviet Turkestan, or those on the Iron Curtain in Central Europe—is communicated to the United States at the hub as a threat to the entire wheel and it therefore elicits a correspondingly strong defensive reaction. No similar reaction can be expected, however, from countries located on opposite spokes or on remote sections of the rim. Instead, any American military action or exercise of "brinkmanship" on behalf of an ally in immediate danger tends to strike other more remote allies not only as a diversion of American attention and strength to tasks of minor importance, but as a risky maneuver that may involve them all in conflicts incapable of being localized. This attitude may appear parochial, but it is not dissimilar to the reaction of a military theater commander who would like all support channeled to his particular section of the front, despite the necessities of an over-all strategy that is hard for him to comprehend since he did not share in its formulation.

Illustrations of this attitude are numerous. Just after West German newspapers had deplored American inflexibility in defense of Quemoy, the Berlin crisis turned the Adenauer government into the chief exponent of Western policies of unwavering firmness. On this occasion, in turn, some Asian allies of the West may well have feared threats to their security from excessive American concentration on the problems of Western Europe. Inevitably, then, the coalition leader whose strategy must be guided by global considerations will find it difficult to satisfy both the ally who, in a particular case, is on the firing line and those allies who happen to be remote from it.

The image of the wheel helps also to explain another and seemingly paradoxical aspect of the difficulties encountered by the leader of the coalition. In contrast to normal expectations, many of the nations, especially in Europe, that are directly exposed to Soviet encroachment have consistently shown less apprehension at Soviet intentions than the United States, which, until recently, was relatively safe from foreign attack. Often Americans have been chided for their hysteria or suspected of exaggerating the Soviet menace in order to push their allies into more vigorous armament efforts. However, one must think in terms of the position of the "hub power" and its sensitivity to threats against any point on the wheel's rim. Such a power of necessity must be particularly aware of the constant pressures exerted by the Soviets, first in one area, then in another. In a sense Turkey is closer to the United States than to Denmark, and Taiwan is closer to the United States than to Pakistan.

Another hindrance to allied solidarity lies in the fact that the American alignment system is plagued by an unusually drastic discrepancy between the strength and prosperity of the United States and its allies. This is a source of tension, whether the issue be the distribution of collective defense burdens, the relative influence of the allies on the policies of the system, or American interference (however subtle) in the internal affairs of allied countries. This situation is especially delicate because, among the friends and allies of the United States in need of assistance and protection, there happen today to be so many who are exceptionally sensitive to foreign encroachments on their national independence. In the case of the new states recently emancipated from Western colonial rule, this sensitivity is a natural result of their pride in an independence won after long and bitter struggles. Some of these states refuse even to accept economic aid, generously offered with no strings attached, because they regard it as a new form of "economic imperialism." Some of the larger countries that not long ago enjoyed the prestige and benefits of empire and world-wide influence are sensitive because dependence on another power is hard for them to accept. On the whole, the graceful adjustment of the former great powers to the *capitis diminutio* that has been their fate is worthy of admiration.

The United States itself must be given credit, too, for the relative lack of serious tensions within an alignment system where inequalities are so great. Rather than showing much disregard for the sovereignty, self-respect, and wishes of its allies, the United States has erred more perhaps in allowing itself to be blackmailed by some of even its weakest friends. Certainly Soviet allegations that the allies of the United States have been turned into satellites and used as unwilling tools of egotistical imperial ambition are not borne out by the facts. Nevertheless, whenever any of America's allies feel that they are not consulted sufficiently on policy or not given sufficient support for their views, resentments are provoked and constitute another source of stress and strain.

Aggravating this source of tension within the alignment system is the new dimension to the power discrepancy that has been added by the nuclear age. There exists today within the coalition a sharp division between the nuclear "haves" and the nuclear "have-nots." Practically all of America's friends and allies currently belong to the second category; even Britain and France, who are acquiring some nuclear capacity, must remain so far behind the United States in independent strategic nuclear striking power that a more than quantitative gulf will separate them from the United States for the foreseeable future.

In its early phase, the introduction of nuclear weapons did not place strains upon relations between the United States and its European allies; on the contrary, it helped tighten the bonds between them. During its short-lived monopoly of atomic power, the United States was able—or was believed able—to spread a protective nuclear umbrella over what was to become the NATO area and to offer Western Europe a reliable guarantee against Soviet attack. In fact, reliance on SAC became so deeply ingrained in the minds of those people in Western Europe who gave any thought at all to the Soviet danger or to the possibility of future war that it outlasted by years the period of the American nuclear monopoly.

Only after the successful launching of the first Soviet sputnik in 1957 did Europeans in growing numbers awaken to the disturbing fact of United States vulnerability to nuclear attack and thus to the possibility—or probability—that Soviet and American strategic nuclear power might neutralize each other. For the Europeans, this would mean that the alliance with the United States had been deprived of what they considered its major value. Gone was the assurance that the grand deterrent of American nuclear power made Europe safe from any major attack or that a minor attack on Europe, if it occurred nonetheless, would automatically trigger an American blow at the Soviet homeland.

American nuclear capabilities have also placed a peculiar strain on United States relations with Asian countries. Even though race had nothing to do with the 1945 choice of atomic targets, Asians have not forgotten that the only atomic bombs ever used in war were dropped on a non-Caucasian people. As a result, there is some fear in Asia that the United States might be less inhibited in employing nuclear weapons on battlefields outside the North Atlantic area. Whether such considerations strengthen Asian neutralism is difficult to estimate since another factor, which we must examine, explains why so many countries today are pursuing policies of neutrality.

An American policy seeking to embrace most of the non-Communist world in a network of military alliances was almost certain to run up against the insuperable obstacle of neutrality. After opposing "entangling alliances" and insisting on a policy of neutrality for their own country for more than a century, Americans should hardly be surprised by this particular obstacle, unless they assume that *quod licet Jovi non licet bovi*. At all times, weak and vulnerable countries have sought refuge in neutrality and found it a source of protection, as long as their stronger neighbors held each other in check. For the non-Communist countries today, many of whom are weak and vulnerable, neutrality again appears as the most prudent policy. The more American and Soviet power have come to balance each other, the greater the premium on neutrality. Moreover, under conditions of a reasonably stable world balance of power, a policy of neutrality or of noncommitment to either of the opposing blocs offers advantages transcending mere immunity from attack. If free from ideological or moral inhibitions, a noncommitted country can swing toward one camp or toward the other as it sees fit and can hope thereby to elicit concessions from both. Leaders of relatively minor countries—a Mossadegh or a Nasser— are well aware of the influence they can exert by taking advantage of the opportunities open to noncommitted countries.

The United States has endeavored to make the best of a world in which neutrality has so many attractions. Realizing the impossibility of convincing even a bare majority of the non-Communist countries that their best interests would be served by joining with America in pacts of mutual military assistance, the United States has come to accept genuine neutrality as the maximum degree of "collaboration" that is possible with many of the non-Communist nations of the world. Certainly, neutrality is a far lesser evil than a swing of the uncommitted countries toward the Soviet camp. The more this has been recognized in the United States, the easier it has become for Americans to accept as valuable supplements to the Western alliance system such open or tacit assurances of friendship by the uncommitted states as may be attainable. For this reason, one may consider as partners in the American alignment system all countries neither giving preferential treatment to the Sino-Soviet bloc nor entering into anti-Western agreements with members of the bloc. The governments of the uncommitted countries probably would refuse to be so listed for fear of being labeled pro-American or pro-Western and of provoking hostility at home and abroad as a consequence. Inevitably, relations with the uncommitted "third force" represent a particularly delicate aspect of American alignment policy.

A further source of interallied tension deserves attention: the discrepancy between the United States and other non-Communist countries in the variety of external conflicts with which they are faced. Whereas the security of the United States is directly endangered today only by the Sino-Soviet bloc, many of its friends and allies are absorbed by other dangers as well, by threats to their national interests from non-Soviet quarters that often seem to them more immediate and real than the Communist threat. The Algerian rebellion struck more deeply into the hearts of Frenchmen than any hypothetical threat to France's security emanating from beyond the Iron Curtain. Pakistanis are more inclined to turn their guns in the direction of eastern Kashmir than toward the Khyber Pass.

Meanwhile, for American policy-makers who are able to concentrate American efforts exclusively on counterbalancing the Sino-Soviet bloc, it is a source of concern and often irritation that the same primary focus on the Sino-Soviet danger does not prevail among all non-Communist nations. Clearly, disputes between members of the alignment system are disruptive of over-all non-Communist solidarity and they run counter to American interests.

As a consequence the preservation and, when necessary, restoration of the peace within the free world has become almost as much of a concern to American policy-makers as the conduct of the cold war itself. While there is bound to be pressure on the United States to take sides against the "aggressor" in any dispute that erupts into armed conflict between its friends and allies, it is also clear that American partisanship endangers the likelihood that the accused "aggressor" country would later participate willingly as an active member of the alignment system. Therefore, the general tendency has been for the leader of the coalition to serve as a neutral mediator who seeks to mend the fences of the alignment system by promoting a peaceful settlement between the disputants. Even if successful, however, such mediation usually becomes a source of dissatisfaction with American behavior. While the compromises of a peaceful settlement will leave fewer wounds than collective security measures against a friendly country, both sides are inclined to feel that greater American backing of their positions would have resulted in a settlement more favorable to their interests. Neither the colonial nor anticolonial powers, for instance, and neither the Israelis nor the Arab states have spared the United States from harsh criticism for not giving them full support. The damage to the American alliance policy is obvious, though inescapable.

While the nuclear age has raised the strains of power inequalities to a new level of seriousness, the "revolutionary age" in turn has aggravated and increased the possibilities of internecine strife within the non-Communist world. Two forces are operating concurrently to keep the free world in turmoil. One is the Communist ideological and propagandist onslaught on the tenets and institutions of the West; the other is the nationalist struggle against Western colonial rule and against any remnants of that rule which keep alive the bitter memories of colonialism. Both Communists and the vanguards of colonial emancipation, who are no less fanatically dedicated to their goal, make life difficult for any government seeking to co-operate with a United States depicted as the mainstay of the hated *status quo*. Because American policy has been forced by the circumstances of the cold war to place more emphasis than is popular on military defense and the preservation of order, the United States is falsely identified in many quarters with social reaction and militarism, a fact not conducive to the smooth operation of collaborative policies that depend on broad public support. Under such circumstances, an effort to create a favorable image of the United States in the minds of other peoples is not a negligible part of a policy of "going it with others."

That makers of American alliance policy are faced with an impressive set of adverse circumstances does not mean that they are relieved of the responsibility for success or failure. Stormy weather and treacherous currents are no excuse for shipwrecks that able navigation could have avoided. Even if the stresses and strains imposed by conditions beyond the control of the United States are inescapable, there is still enough leeway for different courses of action to justify the contention that the final outcome will depend substantially on the wisdom of the actual policy choices and of the attitudes on which these choices rest.

Chapter Fourteen

ALLIES, NEUTRALS,
AND NEUTRALISTS IN
THE CONTEXT OF
UNITED STATES
DEFENSE POLICY

IT IS FREQUENTLY said that Soviet conduct in international
affairs has undergone a radical change since Stalin's death.[1] Allegedly, the Soviet leaders have transferred the struggle with the
West from the military to the economic and ideological sphere. If
this is true, such a change in Soviet policy would relieve the United
States of much of its concern about its military position and permit
it to concentrate on competition with the Soviets for the support of
the uncommitted countries. It would be a comforting thought if a
bid for the friendship of the world's less favored peoples could be
substituted for the distasteful preoccupation with military power
and policy.

I shall not attempt to judge how much of a shift has taken place
in Soviet foreign policy. The apparent recognition by Soviet leaders
that a nuclear war would destroy not merely the "capitalist" nations
but the "socialist" countries as well makes plausible the belief that
they would prefer, more than ever, to attain their objectives without
resorting to military force. In any case, they seem to attach great
importance to the success they expect to gain by nonmilitary means,
particularly in the areas presently neutral or neutralist. What
matters here is that such success, even if attained by economic,
propagandistic, or subversive means, might have a very serious im-

---

[1] Reprinted from the symposium, *Neutralism* (Washington Center of Foreign
Policy Research, Washington, D.C., 1961).

217

pact on the world balance of military power and it may, in fact, be directed toward this end. If that were the case, "peaceful competition" would make the military task incumbent upon the United States and its allies more burdensome, rather than less.

It is easy to see how the Western defense position could be weakened, nibbled away, or undermined, by means short of military force. A switch of any one of America's major European allies from alliance to neutrality might make NATO untenable. Therefore, if the Soviets should ever succeed—for instance by propaganda pointed at the dangers of nuclear armaments and alignment with the United States—in bringing about such a switch, they could achieve thereby a major military victory without firing a shot. Similar success might result for them if they induced uncommitted countries to align themselves with the Soviet bloc. One can hardly assume that the Soviet leaders are unaware of such potentialities inherent in what they label peaceful competition.

The divergent attitudes of three categories of nations lying between the United States and the Soviet bloc, and changes in attitude peculiar to each of them, deserve attention here because of the impact they can have on the United States defense position. The first category comprises the allies of the United States, countries committed to support the American collective defense effort; second are the genuinely neutral countries which give no support to the United States but, simultaneously, withhold it from the other camp; and, finally, there are the "neutralists" whose more or less marked partiality against the West tends to interfere with United States defense policies. In terms of changes of attitude, the Soviets stand to profit from any transfer of United States allies to the category of neutrals, of neutrals to the category of neutralists, of neutralists to the category of allies or satellites of the Soviet Union or of Red China. Whatever the Soviets can do to encourage and promote such transfers serves their interests and might at any point tip the world balance of military power in their favor.

It would be a distortion of the facts to assert that over the last fifteen years the trend has been consistently away from positions relatively more favorable to the United States. No country, except Cuba and Iraq—the latter never directly allied with the United States—has deliberately switched from alliance to either neutrality or neutralism. Large areas of the world, however, which formerly were allied territory, having freed themselves from Western rule are now inside the neutralist camp. The countries that chose to remain neutral from the start have adhered to this position. Of the new neutralist states, with the exception of Cuba, it is still an open question whether any can properly be said to have joined the Soviet bloc.

Although it would be defeatist to create an image of a definite trend against the United States in the positions of "in-between" countries, deterioration has taken place in the United States defense position compared with what it was or was expected to become at the close of World War II and even later. At the end of the war it was anticipated that a concert of the major powers, victors in the war, would police the world in the name of the United Nations. Since this meant enforcing the peace merely against the then disarmed Axis powers and against minor members of the world community if they turned aggressors, there was no reason why the United States as one member of the powerful "policing group" would have to meet heavy defense requirements.

Conditions underwent a radical change when, roughly after two years, the "one world" concept had to give way to the "two world" realities of the cold war. The United States found itself burdened now with the chief responsibility for establishing and maintaining a reasonable balance of power between two hostile camps if it wished to protect itself and the rest of the world against further Communist expansion. In view of the actual or potential military power of the opponent, and the military weakness of most of the non-Communist world, the defense requirements of the United States were bound to increase greatly.

Yet even this was not the end of the process of deterioration. The outbreak of the Korean War revealed the extent of United States military responsibilities. At the beginning it also served to reinforce the comforting illusion that the world had in fact split into two parts only, and that one of them properly could be conceived as the "free world," a community prepared to defend itself collectively against Communist aggression. The United for Peace resolution expressed the view that the United Nations could be made to serve as a kind of general alliance among all the members of the free world, committing them to any collective defense action recommended by the General Assembly. Before the war was over, however, the free world community proved itself a myth. The world had been divided not into two but into three parts, one of which consisted of nations determined to remain uncommitted to either of what they called the military blocs and to take no share, therefore, in the United States collective defense effort. The additional difficulties for the United States caused by such "noncommitment" will be discussed later.

Soon after the United States had accepted the fact that the world was divided into three groups, another vexing problem presented itself. Not all of the noncommitted nations turned out to be neutrals in the traditional sense of the term. Instead, many of the new states in Asia and Africa which called themselves "neutralists" showed a more or less pronounced partiality if not against the United States itself then at least against some of the basic tenets of United States defense strategy. As a result, their attitude and behavior—which might be termed "unneutral neutrality"—placed further strains on this strategy. Obviously, if a country goes further and accepts Soviet assistance against "United States aggression," as Cuba has done, or permits its territory to become a staging area for Soviet military operations, as it once appeared that Syria might do, then neutralism has ceased and gives way to alignment with the Soviets with serious consequences for the United States defense position. So far, however, earlier expectations that some neutralists such as Egypt, Indonesia, and Iraq would in time join the Soviet camp have not materialized.

It is not always appreciated abroad why the United States set out to establish a widespread alliance system and why it stands to suffer if additional areas of the world come under neutral rather than allied control. It is rightly pointed out that few countries are less in need of allies for the defense of their own territory than the United States. When NATO was established the danger of a direct attack on the United States did not exist at all, because the Soviets did not have the means at that time to strike at the American homeland. By the time they did acquire this capacity, the United States strategy of nuclear deterrence, which was the only means of countering the threat, was soon to become virtually independent of overseas bases and did not have to rely on allied military contributions. Yet, allies continued to be indispensable to the United States if the Soviet bloc was to be prevented from gaining a dominant position in the world, for should this occur it would in time threaten the survival of the United States as a free and independent nation.

In order to be able to contain the Sino-Soviet bloc inside the Eurasian land mass, as was discussed earlier, the United States must be able to project its military power across the great oceans. It can do so only if given adequate opportunity for the deployment of

American forces and facilities overseas and if assured of military co-operation by local allied forces stationed in the Eurasian danger zones. Thanks to its geographic location, the Soviet Union has no similar need—whether for its own protection or for that of its allies—of engaging in peacetime deployment of forces beyond the borders of the bloc. This asymmetry in the geographic positions of the two great powers gives the Soviet Union a marked propagandistic advantage. It has nothing to fear and much to gain from arousing hostility against "military blocs" and the stationing of troops on foreign soil.

From what has just been said about the need of having allies, it should not be inferred that the United States would profit if all non-Communist nations were prepared to join its alliance system. Even some of the present members may be a military liability rather than an asset. If a country has little to offer, militarily, and is so exposed that an effort to protect it exceeds United States capabilities, there is danger that failure to live up to a commitment to defend it may have the much-feared "domino effect" of driving other allies into the arms of the Soviets. Moreover, efforts to protect such a country may be so costly or provocative that the United States is worse off as a result of the alignment than if the country in question had remained uncommitted.

Any appeal of nonalignment or neutrality to peoples within allied countries is a threat to the United States collective defense system. Unfortunately there are forces at work, quite aside from Soviet propaganda, that tend to enhance this appeal. The realization that a strategic nuclear stalemate is in the making, if it does not already exist, undermines allied confidence in American military protection which for years has rested on faith in the deterrent power of the United States strategic force. At the same time growing public awareness of the potential destructiveness of war in the nuclear age is increasing the fear of involvement in such a war and playing into the hands of those who proclaim neutrality as the safest means of avoiding such involvement.

Whether the United States approves of neutrality or not, it has little choice but to resign itself to it where it is espoused by other nations. No nation can be forced into becoming an ally, least of all a reliable ally. But it should also be stressed that, from an American point of view, genuine neutrality is the least disadvantageous choice that countries can make if they decide to remain outside of the United States collective defense system. This was not realized when Secretary Dulles branded neutrality as downright immoral. At that time, the illusion prevailed of a kind of predestined solidarity among all free nations. In the case of the new states today the alternative to neutrality is either some degree of "neutralist unneutrality" or outright alignment with the Soviet bloc. It remains true, however, that every increase in the area outside of the alliance system narrows the opportunities for United States military deployment overseas. The liquidation of European colonial empires already has cut deeply into the territory once available for American and allied overseas bases and staging areas, which are indispensable for effective local deterrence and limited war. A point might be reached at which American support for limited war operations, particularly on the fringes of Red China, would be rendered almost impossible—with consequences easily to be imagined.

The refusal of neutral countries to offer military support and opportunities for deployment thus tends to hurt the defense effort of a country that has to rely on the co-operation of others. Yet the attitude and behavior of countries adhering to the traditional rules of neutrality compare very favorably with those of neutralist countries, not to speak of countries aligned with the Sino-Soviet bloc. The chief concern of the old-time neutrals is to avoid involvement in any future hot wars of other nations. They hope to achieve this goal by maintaining strict impartiality in peacetime. By persuading future belligerents that they will play no favorites, they expect that their neutrality will be respected by both sides in time of war; it often has been in the past. The desire to arouse no suspicion of partiality—and to have no occasion for being partial—leads them to exercise the utmost restraint in their external dealings. Any activity in international politics, even in the relatively harmless form of taking sides in the voting process at the UN, may arouse doubts about their impartiality. Therefore, the traditionally neutral policy is one of passivity and abstention.

This policy is in sharp contrast to that of the neutralists. The behavior of the noncommitted states in Asia and Africa, or at least the behavior of their more radical leaders, deviates drastically from passivity and restraint. They themselves insist that their "neutralism" is "active" or "positive." They obviously seek to play a role in world affairs. Such departure from the age-old rules of neutral behavior calls for an explanation. When it occurs it presents new problems to United States defense policy and justifies the distinction between neutralism and traditional neutrality.

Before identifying typical traits of neutralist behavior, it must be stressed that wide divergencies exist in the attitudes of the new Afro-Asian states. Attitudes range from a marked benevolence toward the French community, to outspoken partisanship for the Sino-Soviet bloc (as in the case of Guinea or Mali where it becomes extremely difficult to decide at which point neutralism ends and alignment with the Sino-Soviet bloc begins). The difficulty encountered by neutralist leaders who would like to form a neutralist "third force" stems to a considerable extent from their differences concerning the attitude to be taken toward the East and the West. It also reflects direct conflict or tension between the new states themselves. If one of them infringes upon the interests of another, it may drive the other into closer alignment with the West or the East, depending on the circumstances. More important, if the Soviet Union oversteps its bounds by imposing controls overtly on one of the neutralists, it may drive others into closer ties with the West. In view of these divergencies, and the fluidity of the attitudes involved, neutralism must be understood not as conformity with a fixed pattern of behavior but rather as a current tendency toward a pattern peculiar to the states involved and one that may be weakened or reversed in time.

The new neutralism stems from circumstances and motivations substantially different from those underlying traditional neutrality and its quest for respect of neutral rights by belligerent powers. This is not to say that the neutralists are not concerned, too, with preventing involvement of their countries in the wars of others. But even when it comes to protecting themselves against such involvement they will be shown to rely upon means different from those employed by neutrals of the traditional type. What chiefly distinguishes neutralists from neutrals, however, is the primary concern of the former not with future war but with objectives to be pursued under present cold war conditions. The old-time neutrals are *status quo* powers which have no urgent demands to make on others. By contrast, the new states—and especially those that are under radical or revolutionary leadership—have their eyes fixed on peacetime opportunities and dangers that call for action in the name of both nationalist and universalist objectives, two sets of objectives not always compatible with each other.

Their nationalist objective is the attainment, or the consolidation, of sovereign national independence. Once emancipation from colonial rule (or what is considered its equivalent) has been achieved, consolidation becomes the dominant nationalist concern. There are two facets to the process of consolidation, both of which affect the attitude of the neutralists toward international affairs; one concerns the position of the new states in the world community, the other the position of the new leaders and elites within the national community.

In order to gain stability the new states need as much international respect for their sovereign independence as they can obtain. They seek, therefore, to bolster their international prestige. Passivity of the kind practiced by traditional neutrals is not the road to such prestige. Instead the neutralists try to make themselves heard and to play a role among the nations of the world. In addition, the more dynamic members seek to mold the group into a united "third force." On occasion they will even attempt to demonstrate their ability to influence the policy of the two superpowers as they did when they called on President Eisenhower and Prime Minister Khrushchev to meet and settle their differences. The United Nations has provided an ideal forum for weak nations in search of international prominence; it permits them to compete in the battle of words and votes at a time when they lack the means for other more demanding forms of competition.

But consolidation of independence in the eyes of the world goes hand in hand with efforts of nationalist leaders and ruling elites to consolidate their position on the home front. A reputation for being important in the world arena may spell victory in the fierce struggle with domestic rivals, particularly with indigenous Communist factions. Here, again, only an activist foreign policy can promise rewards. What matters most in this connection is to be courted by the two major powers and, possibly, by playing them off against each other, to receive support and economic aid from both of them.

The United States has little reason to be disturbed about the passion for independence which possesses all neutralist countries. The trouble is that so few neutralist leaders seem to recognize that adequate American counterpower to Soviet power is the best safeguard of their country's independence. If they do recognize this, they dare not say so publicly. As a consequence, there is little to check them from condemning measures of United States defense policy such as the deployment of forces overseas which, as a matter of fact, by serving to maintain the world balance of power, offers protection to the independence of weak countries. Such independence might also be lost if a neutralist country like Guinea came to lean so heavily on Soviet support that, inadvertently perhaps, it might find itself subjected to Soviet control. Leaders of neutralist countries whose nationalism is sincere are obviously far more sensitive to this danger than their domestic Communist rivals who prefer the unity of world Communism to national independence even if it means subservience to Moscow or Peiping; the latter cannot be expected to be deterred from their quest for Sino-Soviet support merely at the sight of some other neutralist country's being sucked from the neutralist camp into the Sino-Soviet orbit.

The nationalist craving for self-determination and sovereign independence continues, then, to be a powerful force even in those postcolonial areas where liberation has already occurred; it may burst into flames if provoked by any act that can be interpreted as outside interference or infringement of sovereign rights. Yet a second objective, universalist in character, competes with nationalism for the prime allegiance of the neutralist leaders and peoples. It is well to remember that most of these peoples become nations in any meaningful sense of the term only after emancipation from colonial rule is accomplished and the beginnings have been made of independent statehood. Prior to that, what prods them toward their goal of liberation and carries the battle cry of liberation across Asia, Africa, and into the Western Hemisphere, is a revolutionary ideology and movement that transcends parochial nationalist interests and, by its universal claims, appeals to all "victims of Western colonialism and imperialism." It has been the tragic fate of the West that all of the new states and would-be nations that presently are capable of affecting the course of world events happen to recognize out of experience none but Western colonialism and imperialism, just as the followers of Marx and Lenin see economic exploitation and social injustice only where it can be labeled as capitalist. As a result, present-day neutralist ideology has a kind of built-in anti-Western bias particularly marked where anticolonial zeal goes hand in hand with strong socialist aversion against the capitalist system of free enterprise.

Because of their anti-imperialist ideology the more radical leaders in neutralist countries consider it their mission, even after their own countries have attained independence, to continue the fight against all remnants of European colonialism as well as against all forms of what they conceive to be American imperialism. So popular is this cause that statesmen in the neutralist world who appreciate the dangers to national independence arising from an acute anti-Western attitude frequently dare not oppose it; there are enough domestic aspirants to power to take advantage of any lack of zeal for the revolutionary cause.

Unless more resistance develops among moderate neutralist leaders against the extremists who see their countries virtually at war with the Western "imperialist cliques" and their "stooges," the prospects for neutral impartiality on the part of the bulk of the presently neutralist states must remain dim. This means that on many vital issues the United States and its allies have to contend with a marked degree of ideological affinity and solidarity between the Communist camp and the partisan or "unneutral neutralists" within the camp of the uncommitted states. This solidarity shows itself on issues such as disarmament, the dismantling of foreign bases, and the relaxation of tension through East-West negotiations.

Disarmament offers a good illustration of how the neutralist ideology may, intentionally or unintentionally, lead to a position unfavorable to the West. It was mentioned earlier that the neutralists share the desire of the neutrals to stay out of future wars that might arise from the East-West struggle. According to their spokesmen they also wish to keep out of the cold war, although it cannot escape them that they have everything to gain from the competition between East and West for their benevolence. What distinguishes the neutralists from the traditional neutrals with respect to war is that the neutralists seek to escape it not through impartiality and abstention in foreign affairs but through active promotion of specific peace strategies to which they are ideologically committed and which in their opinion will lead to enduring peace in the world.

One such strategy, according to them, is a strategy of total disarmament, starting with the withdrawal of all military forces and facilities from foreign soil and including the abolition of nuclear weapons. Because these also are the measures advocated by the Soviets, the United States and its allies are placed at a grave disadvantage. They seem to be hedging when they insist on careful inspection schemes as part of any disarmament agreement although inspection is indispensable to them in view of the closed character of Soviet society. America and her allies also appear to reflect bad faith when they oppose the liquidation of all American military positions overseas even though their liquidation might tip the world balance of power irreparably to the Soviet side. As mentioned earlier, lack of concern for the balance of power characterizes many neutralist ideological predilections and attitudes. Promotion of peace through a relaxation of tensions brought about by East-West negotiations is a case in point. The tendency among the neutralists has been to regard any compromise arising from such negotiations as a gain for peace, irrespective of whether it shall be reached by means of a genuine "give and take" or result, instead, from unilateral Western concessions involving a loss in relative Western strength and counterpower.

Obviously, ideological partiality for the Soviets expressed merely through verbal pressures on the West is not the most virulent form of "neutralist unneutrality" though it may affect the American defense position adversely. Much more serious in their effects if they occur are discriminations in favor of Soviet military assistance; they could reach a point where the Soviets would gain a military foothold in the country receiving aid and turn it into a Soviet ally or staging area. Some of the more revolutionary nationalist leaders may not be aware of the dangers to their country's independence that could arise from a lack of restraint in ideological fervor or they may not be able to recognize in advance precisely at what point they risk forfeiting their country's independence. It would be ironical, however, if any of the new states, out of resentment against even mild forms of Western "imperialist" control, were led into new captivity, and a captivity more painful than that which they have suffered in the past. In any case, while the United States can afford to be tolerant about many neutralist moves and attitudes with which it disagrees, it could not afford to remain passive if incursions of hostile military power into positions vital to its defense were to result either from partiality of neutralist governments toward the Soviet bloc or from neutralist indifference to the prerequisites of international equilibrium.

The preceding discussion has dealt with the impact on the American defense position of the respective attitudes and policies of allied, neutral, and neutralist members of the non-Communist world. Each of the three groups was found to present the makers of American foreign and defense policies with peculiar problems. These problems are rendered more delicate by the fact that policies directed at any one of the three groups necessarily affects the two others. A policy modeled exclusively with a view to improving relations with allies, for instance, may greatly increase the diffi-culties encountered in dealing with neutralists, as the United States has experienced again and again when faced with the struggle be-tween colonialist allies and anticolonialist neutralists. Because each of the three groups may be led, under grave provocation, to switch to a group less favorable to vital American defense interests, the United States cannot afford to ignore the reactions to its policies of any of the three groups even though at times it may have to choose between them or place priorities on its concern for their respective allegiance.

The neutrals, one might presume, raise no particular problems. The United States has ceased to condemn them for their refusal to participate in collective defense efforts, and profits from the role genuinely neutral countries play as international mediators and conciliators. Moreover, expressions of American benevolence to-ward nations that maintain a position of strict impartiality, and American respect for their right to act independently, may help attract neutralist countries toward a position of traditional neutral-ity. However, favors extended to neutral nations may adversely affect United States relations with its allies, either by increasing the appeal of neutrality to their peoples or by causing resentment of the favorable treatment accorded countries that bear no share of the burden of collective defense. Thus the United States must avoid adding to the lures of neutrality, while at the same time rewarding it where it replaces "neutralist unneutrality."

The allies of the United States rank second only to the American armed forces as pillars of American security. It might be tempting to conclude, therefore, that when the three groups of countries are seen from the point of view of American defense interests, the allied group would always merit priority over the others. In many in-stances this is the case. If a choice had to be made between a move to keep France in NATO and a move that would prevent one or more neutralist countries from becoming hostile to the United States, it is hard to imagine circumstances under which the preserva-tion of NATO would not have a primary claim on American policy. But not all cases fall into this extreme category. The way in which allies or neutralists react to similar moves by the United States may vary widely and the weight to be accorded a specific ally or neutral-ist group is not the same in every instance. What matters most is to minimize the chances of having to make the kind of invidious choices here illustrated. In view of the prevailing concern about the attitude of the new states and their revolutionary leaders it is necessary, however, to remind oneself of the indispensable contributions to the common defense effort that only allied countries are ready to make.

Fortunately, their own self-interest will usually suffice to hold allied countries in the alliance provided faith in the protective value of alignment with the United States is made to rest on strong foundations. Similarly, national self-interest, if recognized by the leaders of neutralist states, will tend to restrain them from allowing antagonism against the United States to carry them beyond a point at which they might lose the benefits they derive from being able to choose between two camps and to obtain support from both of them.

The danger remains that some ally or some neutralist country may be blinded to its own best interests by fear or resentment and turn its back on the United States and the West generally. But if such cases can be kept at a minimum, the United States should be capable of taking the loss if it occurs and of compensating for it elsewhere. Whereas it would be folly to ignore the value of allied solidarity and the usefulness of neutralist benevolence, it is defeatist —and exposes the United States to dangerous blackmail besides—to assume that the American defense position is dependent on a favorable attitude on the part of each and every American ally or of each and every group of neutralist states. Moreover, only when vital United States defense positions are endangered by inimical behavior of countries unmistakably allied with the Sino-Soviet bloc should it be necessary to contemplate direct interference and, possibly, to take military action.

III.

Annexes

Chapter Fifteen

POLITICAL THEORY
AND INTERNATIONAL
RELATIONS

NOWHERE IN English-speaking countries would the study of
government and politics be considered complete if it did not include
political theory; in fact, at many universities theory is regarded as
the very foundation on which all other aspects of the subject should
be made to rest.[1] This does not hold true, however, for the study
of international politics. What a student of international relations
may happen to learn about political thinkers of earlier centuries
usually comes to him from outside the program of his specialty,
and if he takes a course in political theory he is not likely to hear
much about earlier thought on foreign policy.[2]

A cleavage exists between international relations and political
theory, and it is a two-way affair. If specialists in international
politics with rare exceptions have neglected political theory, the
political theorists in turn, departing from older tradition, have paid
little attention to what the thinkers of the past—Machiavelli not
always excepted—have had to say on international relations. From
reading the current histories of political doctrine, particularly as
they deal with the political and moral philosophers representing

[1] This chapter was published originally as the introduction to *The Anglo-American Tradition in Foreign Affairs,* ed. Arnold Wolfers and Laurence W. Martin (Yale University Press, New Haven, 1956); it is reprinted here, with minor changes, by permission of the publisher.

[2] As far as the literature on international relations is concerned—and the same is true for the teaching in the field—there are exceptions to this rule of silence on political theory. There is Frank M. Russell, *Theories of International Relations* (D. Appleton-Century, New York, 1936) and notably the more recent book of readings by Hans J. Morgenthau and Kenneth W. Thompson, *Principles and Problems of International Politics* (Alfred A. Knopf, New York, 1950).

the Anglo-American tradition, one might be led to believe that these thinkers had been interested in domestic problems exclusively.

Such mutual neglect, if that is what it should be called, is not a matter of accident. It has deep roots in the political experience of England and the United States and in the way this experience has been intellectually absorbed. The question today, however, is whether the reasons that explain this divorce between the two fields also justify its continuation; if they do not, early "remarriage" may commend itself to both parties.

As is well known, international relations as a special field of study made its appearance on the academic scene only after the close of World War I. It came as a fruit of Wilsonian idealism and the founding of the League of Nations. On the grounds that a "new era" had been ushered in and that the League if properly used and implemented would mark the end of European power politics, the study of international relations was meant to promote the cause of peace and international co-operation by showing how the new peace machinery should be used and developed. It was centered, therefore, on the "ought" of a better future order rather than on the "is" and "was" of the sorry conditions to which policy-makers and their advisors had traditionally addressed themselves. Under these circumstances only those earlier thinkers deserved to be studied who, like Sully, Kant, Penn, or Bentham, had proposed schemes of international organization for peace and could thus qualify as precursors of the new prophets.

When in the 1930's disillusionment and a sharp reaction against this Wilsonian approach set in, the new realist school of thought, dominant today in academic circles, had reasons of a different kind for paying no attention to the doctrines of the past. The effort was now directed toward building up an empirical or causal science of international politics. Because its subject was now to be the "is" and "was" rather than the "ought" of external state behavior, the new program left even less incentive for concern with what was believed to be the exclusively normative outlook of political and moral philosophers of the past, Machiavelli alone being placed in a different category. Even if it had been realized that past thinkers on the subject had been anything but inarticulate about what they considered to be the actual workings of the state system, their observations and generalizations on this aspect of the subject probably would have been discounted because of their lack of scientific methodology.

As in the 1930's the climate of thought is undergoing another important change today, this time in a direction that may prove far more favorable to the study of political doctrine. It is no longer so confidently expected that an empirical science of international politics can meet all our needs; with new and growing interest in the theoretical bases of scientific work in this field, attention is being drawn to normative thought and philosophical speculation. Moreover, doubts have arisen whether new methods of investigation really allow the political scientist of today to dispense with such traditional tools as impressionistic observation, historical analogy, and common sense judgment, on which through the ages his predecessors relied for the validation of their assertions. Thus the road is being opened for a new appreciation of earlier contributions to the knowledge of international affairs.

The nonnormative aspects of earlier thinking on the subject deserve to be emphasized first because they are less obvious. Much of the time the political philosophers of the past were preoccupied with the way statesmen and nations should behave toward each other. Yet they could not have felt justified in offering advice on rules to be followed had they not believed that they possessed knowledge of what would happen if their advice were accepted. This means, then, that some causal theorizing, however inadequate, was at least implicit in much of their normative effort. Thus Godwin states views about the way nations actually behave by declaring it "an improbable supposition" to conceive of a nation's being attacked "so long as its own conduct is sober, acceptable and moderate." Hamilton's admonition not to continue wars to the point of the enemy's surrender if compromise should be possible, advice that deserves to be taken seriously in our time, rests on the explicit assertion that such surrender will cause the subsequent peace to be less secure. Some theorists will be found to have made explicit propositions concerning some such cause and effect relationships; others have made them by implication. Hume's chapter on the balance of power offers a good illustration of a study directed primarily at empirical rather than normative theory. While Hume can be said to imply that governments should aim at balanced power in the world, his reasoning is based on generalizations concerning the way states as a rule have behaved in the past and are likely to behave in the future, the emphasis being on factors that induce them to push beyond the point of equilibrium. The bulk of the discussion of international relations by both Hobbes and

Locke is of a similar kind. Because it serves them merely as an illustration of the state of nature, it is clearly directed toward a generalized description of what to them seemed to be the way sovereigns behave toward each other in fact; it was not intended as advice in matters of foreign policy.

Without any doubt, most of the sweeping generalizations running through the writings of the political philosophers of the past are open to severe criticism. They are often crude, in many cases patently prejudiced, and as a rule presented without even the claim of meticulous verification. Hobbes "proves" to his own satisfaction that war coalitions cannot last beyond victory—a shrewd and prophetic hunch—by deducing his conclusion from premises he can hardly be said to have substantiated. Neither he nor others have been able to prove that men and nations are by nature enemies of one another and can therefore co-operate only as long as they are threatened by a common foe. Also from a scientific point of view, there is not one theorist or philosopher who cannot be blamed for a lack of clearly stated hypotheses and for failure to validate them by means less open to prejudice than mere random experience and arbitrary choice of historical illustrations.

Yet before turning away contemptuously from the inadequate work of his predecessors, the social scientist of today who is struggling with the problems of international relations should ask himself how much better he is able to validate the hunches on which he is forced to base himself. He would have to remain within a narrow circle of rather marginal problems if he excluded all but scientifically unimpeachable investigations, particularly of the controlled experiment or quantitative kind. For example, significant scientific work has been undertaken by psychologists and sociologists in recent years on the effects of insecurity and frustration on human behavior, some of it applicable to the behavior of nations. However, a political scientist called upon to evaluate the effects on foreign policy of frustration suffered by a nation in the wake of a punitive peace settlement, or of feelings of insecurity arising out of recollections of past invasions, while he would hardly refuse to express a scholarly opinion on the ground that there is no way open to him to "prove" his contentions, would have to rely heavily on personal experience and observations to supplement and qualify his tenuous scientific insight. Like the political philosophers before him, then, he would find himself mustering all the evidence that history, personal experience, introspection, common sense, and the gift of logical reasoning put at his disposal.

If there is any difference between today's political scientist and his predecessors—who, like himself, were confronted with such problems as alliance policy, the balancing of power, intervention in the affairs of other countries, and the pursuit of ideological goals—one would hope it might lie in a keener realization of the controversial and tentative nature of his reply, in a greater effort to consider alternative answers, and in a more conscious attempt to remain dispassionate and objective. Sometimes the scientifically minded scholar of today may turn out merely to be more pedantic in his formulations and less afraid of belaboring the obvious. In any case, analyses of national conduct undertaken by men of keen insight into human behavior and wide experience in the affairs of the political world cannot fail to be valuable to anyone seeking to understand what makes the clock tick in international relations. The reflections of the thinkers of the past—on such matters as the advantages and weaknesses of the balance of power, the peculiarities of insular location, and the dangers of preventive war—are far removed from amateurish guesswork; the arguments as well as the evidence offered to sustain them are, in kind at least, the same as those used today in even the most scholarly debates on the same subjects.

Whether the political philosophers of the past have contributed much or little to empirical theory, the main test of their importance to the student of international relations today must rest on the continued value of their normative thought, which was undoubtedly their chief concern. They were seeking to decide when it is right or wrong for a nation to participate in "other peoples' wars," to interfere in the domestic affairs of others, to keep faith with allies, or to expand into new territory. They were also concerned with what they called the prudence of certain types of action, prudence meaning expedience guided and moderated by morality and wise judgment. To a considerable extent they were expressing value preferences—often couched in the form of "laws of nature"—and inquiring into the consequences that follow when nations fail to act in conformity with these preferences.

More and more it is coming to be appreciated that such moral preferences as well as broad assumptions about man and his motives are an inescapable starting point for even the most strictly empirical enterprise in matters of national behavior. Attempts to escape from this scientific dilemma merely lead to a lack of awareness of one's own presuppositions or to a failure to make them explicit. The very words that are used—self-preservation, aggression, imperialism, national interest—are loaded with emotional connotations, moral judgment, and prescientific assumptions. There might never have been any study of how to outlaw and prevent "aggressive" war had it not been for the tacit assumption that any *status quo* is morally preferable to a resort to international violence. It would make no sense to say or assume that nations must seek power adequate for survival if high value were not placed on the existence of independent nations. No expectations regarding the conduct of nations can be formulated that are not affected by either the optimistic hunch of a Locke, who entertained the belief that "calm reason and conscience" would guide the behavior of most men, or the pessimistic hunch of a Hobbes, to whom man appeared obsessed by fear and greediness. While the pessimist is likely to expect that peace will be maintained only if the power of all nations is held in check by a balance of their respective power, the optimist fears war only at times when the exceptional aggressor nations are not met with the unchallengeable predominance and solidarity of the great majority of peace-loving peoples. In this sense, all students in the field, consciously or unconsciously, belong to schools of moral and philosophical thought.

If this be so, the normative and speculative ideas of the great thinkers of the past are worthy of even more attention than are their clearly impressionistic insights into the realities and laws that explain the actual behavior of nations. Here is a wealth of explicit formulations and judgments concerning most of the problems of moral choice and prudence that plague the thinkers and practitioners of our time. Today there is still heated discussion about the respective value of the general human interest and the particular national interest, as Burke called them, and of the line to be drawn between justifiable and unjustifiable resistance to the demands of others. What this indicates is a search for standards, rational and moral, by which to judge policy—one's own and that of others—and by which to be guided in reaching decisions.

Although it is regrettable that value judgments in the past, as in the present, are often presented with assertions of fact as if there were no fundamental difference between them, the theorists left no doubt that most of the time they were seeking to guide statesmen and nations in choosing their ends and means with a view to maximizing desirable values or minimizing their sacrifice. If this meant treating the subject of values extensively, as in discussions about justice, weighing values against one another, and bringing them into conscious and discriminating perspective, it was an exercise that no policy science can avoid if it is to be useful.

While the student of international politics has every reason, then, to bridge the gulf that has separated him from political theory, it remains to be asked—remarriage requiring the consent of both sides—whether contemporary teachers of theory or of the history of doctrine may not have equally good reasons to break the silence they have maintained in respect to political matters transcending national boundaries.

Three factors may account for the lack of interest that political theorists are currently showing for anything but domestic government and politics: the first is the persistent impact of what until quite recently could be called the strategic insularity of both the British Isles and the American continent; the second is the striking contrast that exists for both countries between the internal and the external political scene; the third is a difference in the degree of moral opportunity offered by the domestic and the foreign fields of political activity.

As long as the relative insular security of Great Britain and the United States lasted—or was thought to exist—it was possible to conceive of the development of institutions at home as being entirely separate from and independent of the events occurring beyond the frontiers of the nation. Where propinquity rather than isolation was characteristic of the relations between states, as on the continent of Europe, domestic affairs could hardly be conceived of except in interdependence with foreign affairs. In fact, the main emphasis was on the so-called primacy of foreign policy. In sharp contrast to this attitude the insular political theorists could choose to concentrate on internal politics, overlooking or leaving to the tender mercy of others the unsavory problems of international power politics and anarchy. Now that insular security has gone, this justification for aloofness from external problems has vanished too.

The second factor is also a phenomenon peculiar to Britain, the United States, and in this instance, a few democracies in Western Europe. In these countries domestic political conditions stand in striking contrast to the conditions these nations face in their external relations: the domestic conditions are characterized by order, lawfulness, and peace arising from a popular consensus on principles, so marked that some believe coercion has practically ceased to play a role; but the external relations continue to be full of bitter struggle, violence, and Machiavellian practices. Obviously, no such contrast is experienced by peoples whose country is the frequent scene of revolution and domestic violence or suffers the cruel terrors of tyranny; to them "civil society," or "order under government," if it is experienced at all, possesses most of the objectionable features we attribute to international anarchy. The sharper the contrast between the domestic and the international scenes, the greater will be the inclination, then, to treat the two fields of political activity separately and to overlook the traits they have in common. It is not a happy sign that much of what has been occurring in this century militates against the continued separation of the two fields. For the difference between them has been reduced, even to the observer in countries of democratic orderliness, not primarily because the international arena has taken on new and striking traits of lawfulness and order under government but because tyrannical suppression and persecution as well as revolutionary strife have come to be the order of the day in wide areas of the world. Thus government no longer appears as the safe panacea against the evils of Machiavellian practice or violence that set domestic affairs in sharp and unmistakable contrast to international anarchy. Working to lessen the contrast, but from the opposite side, has been the experience that the lack of supranational government, for example in the case of the British Commonwealth, has not prevented close and friendly co-operation within this "anarchical" partnership. It would therefore seem that the two poles of the political continuum, civil society and international anarchy or power politics, are not as far apart in reality as they appeared at times, which suggests that a comprehensive theory of politics, including both foreign and domestic affairs, would make good sense.

This leads to the third, though closely related, factor: the difference in "moral opportunity." During the modern age England and the United States, together with a few Western countries, managed to put their sovereign control of internal affairs to excellent use for the progressive development of institutions of lawful government and civil liberty. This occurred in the course of the same four centuries during which the very existence of national sovereignty produced externally a multistate system with all the conflict, struggle, and war that this implies. Therefore, for political and

moral philosophers the internal scene with its opportunity to promote the good life under civil government was as encouraging as
the external scene was frustrating. One can hardly wonder that
teachers of political theory, in the end, should have come to be
interested far more in the way the theorists of the past had helped
to solve the problems of government at home than in what they
had to say about the comparatively barren and stagnant power politics of the multistate system. The more clearly normative their
concern with politics, the more incentive they had to concentrate
on the field in which sovereign control gave each people and government, individually, a high degree of power and opportunity to
conduct itself according to its own moral precepts. There cannot
fail to be a difference in moral opportunity between a realm in
which every nation is at the mercy of the acts of others and one
in which the course of events is predominantly shaped by its own
decision. If there is to be less separation in the treatment of the
two realms, the change must come from a growing realization that,
after all, the single mind and will of the nation even at home is
more fictitious than real and that moral opportunity is not so
radically lacking in external politics as some impatient perfectionists of our time, impressed by the horrors of two world wars, are
inclined to maintain.

If one may look forward, then, to a growing readiness to draw
international relations and political theory closely together—as
moral and political philosophers in past centuries were accustomed
to do—the question is whether the student of international relations awakened to this need, would do well to focus his attention,
first on the political thought of men with a particular national
background and of a particular historical period.

Theory pertaining to foreign policy is not an invention of the
modern age. For obvious reasons the topic became a matter of
live interest whenever the political arena was occupied by more
than one sovereign political unit, thereby giving rise to interunit
relations and foreign policies clearly distinct from the domestic
affairs within these units. This situation did not exist at all times,
however. There was little occasion for theoretical thought on foreign policy in the days of the Roman Empire once it had disposed
of all of its serious competitors. There is no medieval theory on
the subject of international relations properly speaking, because
under what has been called the theory of universal community,
political activity within European Christendom was not conceived

in terms of a dichotomy between domestic and foreign policy; theoretically, relations between pope and emperor and between feudal kings were expected to follow the same rules and moral principles as those between kings and subordinate feudal lords, or between kings and their subjects. If in fact conduct deviated, often radically, from these precepts, it did so no less in internal than in external relations.

All of this means, then, that political theorists writing in periods of multiple sovereignty are of major if not exclusive interest to the study of international relations; and among them preference will go necessarily to those who since the age of Machiavelli and More were dealing with the behavior of political units similar in most respects to the nation-states of our own day.

This of course does not preclude the possibility that at some future time speculations and observations of medieval thinkers like Saint Augustine, Thomas Aquinas, or Dante will become relevant again in matters of world politics. Even today it is not fantastic to speak of recent changes within the international arena as pointing toward a kind of "new medievalism." The trend would seem to be toward complexities that blur the dividing lines between domestic and foreign policy. We are faced once again with double loyalties and overlapping realms of power—international Communism versus nation-state, transnational affinity versus nationalism—as well as with wars like those recently fought in Korea and Southeast Asia that partake of the character of international and civil war simultaneously. Yet despite these novel developments, which deserve theoretical as well as practical attention, the traditional problems of interstate or intersovereign relations, predominant over the last four centuries, continue to occupy the center of the political stage whenever relations transcending national boundaries come into play. From this it follows that the theories dealing with interstate relations are most pertinent at the present time.

If drastic change has occurred in recent times, it has not taken the form of bringing to a close the modern era of interstate power politics, as many had hoped; it has merely brought to an end the "European Age" of such politics. The character of international relations has not been revolutionized, rendering obsolete earlier thought on these relations. The entry of the United States and other non-European countries as actors into the company of the world's leading powers has merely made past theory of international politics directly relevant to the United States, as it was all along to the European nations to whom it was originally addressed. Thomas More wrote at the time when, with the discovery of America, the great powers of Europe were starting on their course of world predominance; Woodrow Wilson spoke at the close of World War I when, partly because of him, American leadership in world affairs was asserting itself for the first time. Since then, any theory of international politics, though dealing with the same set of problems, must be concerned with the global multistate system that has taken the place of its European predecessor.

While it makes sense, therefore, to draw insight primarily from those who have lived to see the modern multistate system at work, the question remains whether English and American thinkers deserve special attention. Obviously, theoretical discussion of international politics has not been the preserve of the English-speaking peoples. In fact, in matters of international relations the works of Continental authors such as Machiavelli, Grotius, Spinoza, and Kant have received much more attention than those of their Anglo-Saxon contemporaries. But the very silence that surrounds the latter provides one good reason for paying special attention to them.

There are other, still more cogent reasons for giving attention to the English and American thinkers. If it can be shown that their response to the challenging issues raised by the multistate system differs from that of the Continentals, knowledge of their views should serve at least two important purposes: it should help explain some of the peculiarities of the contemporary British and American approach to world affairs, which often puzzle the foreign observer and lead him either to praise the special virtues of Anglo-Saxon policy or condemn what he considers its hypocritical wrappings; it should also help to promote critical self-understanding within the English-speaking world, making for more awareness of its moral presuppositions and of the deeply ingrained traditional habits of thought that inevitably color conduct in a field where emotion and value judgment play an important role. These are the chief reasons why an attempt is made here to arouse special interest in the Anglo-American tradition of thought. It might be added that by paying respect to an impressive intellectual ancestry, contemporary Anglo-American study in the field of international relations should also gain in philosophical depth, historical perspective and academic respectability.

If insular security has been responsible, at least in part, for the divorce between political theory and international relations, it has had yet another and more important effect, this one bearing on the substance of the theory itself. It may be dangerous to lump together into two distinct categories all Anglo-American theorists on the one hand and all Continental theorists on the other, as if agreement within each camp had been the rule. On most points it has not. Yet in one vital respect it would seem permissible to so generalize about the two groups, even at the risk of doing injustice to exceptions.

It would be grossly misleading to suggest that all Continental thought in matters of international politics has been Machiavellian; passionate opposition to the views expressed in Machiavelli's *Prince* was voiced throughout the centuries that followed its publication. Friedrich Meinecke in his book on Staatsräson[3] has given a brilliant account of the Continental debate between Machiavellians and anti-Machiavellians. Yet his discussion of Continental thought on foreign policy justifies the contention that Continental theory centered around the idea of the "necessity of state," which was the core of Machiavelli's argument. As the Continental political philosophers saw it, the main problem presented by conditions of multiple sovereignty was that of a deep conflict between morality and *raison d'état.* This was in line with the experience common to all Continental countries which in the face of constant external threats to their national existence believed themselves exposed to the compelling impact of forces beyond their control. The main question as they saw it was whether statesmen and nations were under moral obligation to put up resistance against these "compelling" demands of state necessity. While not all were ready, fatalistically or cynically, to advocate sheer resignation, there was ever present a feeling that nations were puppets in the hands of demonic forces, with little leeway if any to rescue moral values from a sea of tragic necessity.

English and American thought, as well as experience, traveled a different road. Even the concepts of necessity of state and reason of state remained foreign to the political philosophers of the English-speaking world. While the Continentals were arguing about the dilemma of statesmen faced by the irreconcilable demands of necessity and morality, English and American thinkers in turn were engaged in a debate about the best way of applying accepted principles of morality to the field of foreign policy. Here the assumption was

---

[3] *Die Idee der Staatsräson* (Munich and Berlin, 1925).

that statesmen and nations enjoyed considerable freedom to choose the right path in their external conduct as they did in their internal policies. If there was any question about the compatibility of service to the national interest on the one hand and the avoidance of evil on the other, there was surely room, it was held, to decide for the good ends and to pursue them with the least evil of the available means.

This was a philosophy of choice, then, which was bound to be ethical, over against a philosophy of necessity, in which forces beyond moral control were believed to prevail. Choice presupposes freedom to decide what goals to pursue and what means to use in accordance with one's desires and convictions. Not to follow the dictates of moral conviction becomes a matter of guilt, subject to moral judgment. Thus from Thomas More to Woodrow Wilson the recurrent topics of concern and debate were questions such as the right of self-defense and its limits, the right and duty to intervene or not to intervene in the affairs of others, or the extent to which colonial rule and territorial expansion were justified under given circumstances.

Whereas the philosophy of necessity tends to lead to resignation, irresponsibility or even the glorification of amorality, the philosophy of choice lends itself to excessive moralism and self-righteousness as if the leeway for choice were unlimited and of the same dimension for all. What saved most of the theorists of England and America from the pitfalls of such excesses was the care with which they defined to themselves the limitations that the need for national self-preservation—or the duty of self-defense as they might call it—sets on the freedom of choice. Nations were not being advised to sacrifice themselves on the altar of humanity or human liberty nor to set the general interest above the national interest of self-preservation. There was no inclination to forget the rules of prudence for the rules of morality, and prudence taught men to use common sense and wise judgment in deciding where the duty of self-defense deserved primacy over other duties. Prudence also meant husbanding one's means and staying within these means even in the pursuit of good causes.

There was room for hypocrisy in this argument. If there is a place for moral choice only within the limits set by a prudent concern for self-preservation, it becomes tempting to interpret and thus to justify, as a means of sheer self-preservation, almost anything seemingly reprehensible that one's own country might undertake in foreign affairs. Moreover, if in order to receive moral approbation every resort to violence must be strictly a matter of self-defense, there is much incentive to accuse others of evil aggression when they use force, while justifying one's own acts as purely defensive. On the whole, however, the moral philosophers here in question, rather than posing as apologists of their nation, placed themselves in the creditable role of serving as the conscience of the nation, reminding statesmen of the dictates of justice and reason.

Also, English and American theorists were not blind to the exceptional freedom of choice that insularity gave to their respective countries. Long before there was any science of geopolitics, More, Bolingbroke, Jefferson, and others praised the privileges offered their countries by the fact of insular location. The advantage, it was suggested, lay in the freedom to remain aloof from many international struggles without a sacrifice of national security, and thus in the chance of keeping one's hands clean of many of the morally more obnoxious vicissitudes of power politics to which others were subjected.

There may be some question whether all the English and American thinkers whose work fell within these four centuries—the period running roughly from the beginning of the sixteenth to the early part of the twentieth—can be said to belong to the school of thought described here as typically Anglo-American. About a Locke, Godwin, Jefferson, or Wilson there can be little doubt. They were not merely urging nations to apply the Golden Rule in the conduct of their foreign policy to the maximum compatible with a moderate, prudent policy of self-preservation; they were confident that this was the road to peace and human happiness. But what about men like Hobbes, Bacon, Bolingbroke, Hamilton, or Mahan, usually characterized as conservatives, realists, and pessimists? In many respects they will be found to have stood closer to Machiavelli than to the moralists of their own countries, and to have concurred with views of their Continental contemporaries. Bacon speaks of wars—although of just and honorable wars—as being the "true exercise to a kingdom or sovereignty"; Hobbes sees nations "in the position of gladiators one against the others"; to Bolingbroke, self-love is the determining principle in international relations; and Hamilton declares harmony to be impossible "among unconnected sovereignties." The conclusions to which these men are led are not made to please those who expect "good" nations to be capable in time of eliminating the use of force from international politics except as it

might be needed to stop and punish the exceptional criminal dis-
turber of the peace.

Yet even among these representative exponents of what is now
often referred to as the power-political school of thought, we find
Bacon asserting that he would "never set politics against ethics,"
Hobbes maintaining that the state of nature when applied to sovereign nations allows for moderation in war and for self-restraint,
Bolingbroke advising against acquisition of territory, and Hamilton
agreeing with Locke that even the state of nature is "governed by
moral law perceivable by reason" and advocating a foreign policy
of moderation and vigilance in the exclusive service of self-preservation. Hume deserves to be mentioned as representing a middle
road. He maintains that the "obligation to justice is less strong
among nations than among individuals," thus suggesting a double
standard of morality, one for individuals, the other for nations; but
he leaves no doubt that his support of the balance of power, for
example, is based on moral considerations as offering the best chance
for "moderation and the preservation of the liberties of mankind."

Thus pessimists and optimists, realists and idealists, emphasize
the moral aspects of political choice. While all of them take the
right of national self-defense for granted, nowhere do they suggest
that competition for power, conflict, struggle, or war could be regarded as signs of national health or heroism. If there is any awareness of a moral dilemma arising out of the conflicting demands of
self-preservation on the one hand and the obedience to moral principle on the other, it is resolved, without apparent strain on the
conscience, by reference to the analogous case of the individual who
is considered morally justified in defending himself by force against
external attack. This analogy is the weakest point in the argument.
It fails to take into account how far more extensive and arbitrary
than in the case of individuals are the claims that nations can label
as self-defense. The emphasis on moderation and self-restraint indicates some awareness of this moral pitfall.

Moreover, for the two "island" countries external attack and invasion were unlikely contingencies most of the time, so that self-
preservation in a strict sense of the term rarely came to place re-
strictions on the leeway they enjoyed in respect to other policy
objectives. In matters of colonial expansion, for example, or the
spread of ideologies by means of intervention—often even by efforts
to influence the outcome of other peoples' wars—there was much
freedom to choose the road that appeared most consistent with one's

scale of values. Here the door was wide open for soul-searching
as well as for the exercise of wise judgment. Political theory in the
Anglo-American tradition was full of such soul-searching, though
the enjoyment of relative national security and an abiding confidence in reasonableness and common sense took out much of the
sting.

It can be argued that however lofty the ideas and however noble
the advice proffered to their governments by these philosophers,
much of it in sharp contrast to what Machiavelli laid down in the
admonitions to his Prince, they may have been deluding themselves
about their chances of being heard or about the true motives by
which statesmen of their countries actually were guided. Thomas
More faced up to this problem at the very start of the modern era
and appears to have reached the conclusion that while sovereigns
cannot be swayed by counsels of perfection, "indirect" advice by
philosophers may induce them to take the path of lesser evil. His
successors, at least the more realistic among them, may well have
concurred with this view. After all, most of them at least held
responsible public office themselves, if they were not leading statesmen at some period of their lives. Unless they had sensed the need
for guiding principles in reaching decisions and believed moral
guidance no less important than advice on expediency, they would
hardly have wasted so much of their energies figuring out what was
right and wrong in foreign policy. In any case, their mode of
approach so molded the outlook and expectations of the peoples
of the two countries that it has become in itself a powerful factor
in world affairs.

Inasmuch as the English and American theorists of the past applied a philosophy of choice to both internal and external politics,
they had every reason to devote attention to both and to consider
them closely related. Yet the two fields of policy differ in one
important respect, with a cleavage within the theory of politics
remaining to be noted. Since the dawn of the modern nation-state,
domestic politics, particularly in the English-speaking world, constituted a gradual and progressive evolution from absolutism to
constitutional government and democracy. Theory addressed itself
here to a series of problems that came up consecutively in the
course of this historical process, and it found a solution as time
went on. The theory that dealt with issues such as the relative place
of church and state, the separation of powers, or the rights of the
individual, all-important at some period, is on the whole a matter

of historical and philosophical rather than of contemporary political interest, although it may again become pertinent in the latter sense within some new context. This accounts for the practice of treating the theory of internal politics as a history of political thought with emphasis on the interdependence between specific theories and the specific conditions prevailing at successive historical periods.

No similar evolution has taken place in international politics during the same four centuries in which the nation-state underwent its internal transformation. The essential features of the multistate system and of the conduct of its members had changed little by the time Woodrow Wilson made his speeches from what they were when Thomas More wrote his *Utopia* in 1516. As a consequence, theorists contemplating the international scene have been responding throughout this long period to one and the same pattern of events and addressing themselves on the whole to the same set of problems.

Because of this lack of evolutionary development there would seem to be no need to study the views of past theorists on international politics in the historical manner that is customary in matters of domestic politics. So far as international politics are concerned, theory is related not to a particular period of the multistate system but to a single persistent historical situation now extending back over more than four centuries. In this sense the theorists of this entire period must be considered contemporaries. The problems of self-preservation in the light of external danger, of expansion into new territories or of contraction, of intervention in the affairs of others, of alliances, peacemaking, and the conduct of wars are as much matters of concern and controversy today as they were when a More, Hume, or Bentham put his mind to them.

This contemporaneousness has its positive as well as its negative side. To start with the latter, the inability of nations to fashion the world according to their wishes and thus to dispose of worrisome problems once and for all has meant that the theorists cannot generally be said to have moved step by step to the discovery of solutions of ever greater perfection. There is little reason to expect here the kind of accumulation of knowledge or increasing depth of insight that characterizes other parts of political theory. Had Hume written his classic chapter on the balance of power two centuries later, it is not likely that his treatment would have appeared outdated any more than Woodrow Wilson's argument in favor of a peace without victory would have seemed strange if stated a few centuries earlier.

For the student of international politics there is a great advantage, however, in what from other angles may seem to represent sheer stagnation and a source of frustration. Even if his interests were focused exclusively on the contemporary scene and the policy problems that statesmen of his own age are facing, he could still turn with profit to the discussions of theorists of the past. Except for one significant change in external conditions which will be discussed in a moment, and with one qualification necessitated by this change, the theorists of the last four centuries looked out on the same kind of world that today's theorist does and were seeking answers to the same questions that occupy his mind today. In this sense they are his contemporaries, too. To study their views is not a diversion satisfying a purely historical or what some might consider antiquarian interest. Any reader will find himself on familiar ground in most of the texts if only he is prepared to take a few semantic and stylistic hurdles, like translating "kings and subjects" into "decision-makers and the public," and to recognize that if, for example, the old colonialism is coming to an end, territorial expansion of control continues to present a serious problem today.

But there is one qualification to this statement which needs to be emphasized and put in the form of a warning. If it was correct to relate the peculiar outlook of the English-speaking theorists— their philosophy of moral choice—to the insular security that their countries enjoyed, the disappearance of this security in our time, now an acknowledged fact, may call for a significant modification of the traditional philosophy. The leeway for choice which the two countries enjoyed in the past has been gravely curtailed. For all practical purposes, Great Britain and the United States have become "Continental" in terms of the dangers and compulsions pressing upon them from the outside. While the multistate system has remained what it was before, their place in it has radically changed. The question is how they will and should adapt to this new situation not only their foreign policy but their way of thinking.

There are two extreme ways open to them, both tempting, both dangerous. One consists in swinging over to the Continental philosophy in its most extreme form, meaning the acceptance without qualification of a philosophy of necessity. All major decisions in foreign policy would then be conceived of as dictated by external circumstances beyond human control, statesmen and people alike being absolved as a consequence from all moral responsibility. With resignation, anger, or glee the old quest for moral guidance would be laid aside to give free play to expediency and the concern for power. In this case the ideas of the old theorists would come to appear no less obsolete than the former insular policies with which they coincided; they would be condemned as naive and moralistic.

The other departure from tradition, more subtle than the first, would consist in closing one's eyes to the diminution of leeway that has taken place and to pretend that in doing under strong compulsion what was considered evil when undertaken by others was no longer evil when done by oneself. Thus if it became necessary to participate in wars in remote places, to threaten the use of force, or to build up military alliances in peacetime, theory would provide the suitable moral labels, catering thereby to the sense of self-righteousness.

The lesson that can be learned from the theorists of the Anglo-American tradition points toward neither such cynicism nor such hypocrisy. As mentioned earlier, it was never suggested that national self-preservation itself should be sacrificed to moral principle. Instead, statesmen were urged to combine two basic goals: one, the primary though prudently conceived objective of self-preservation—call it the vital national security interest; the other, implied in such prudence, a fulfillment of the moral law to the maximum compatible with the primary duty of defense. If national security has come to occupy a much larger place in the policy of the two countries which have lost the advantages of insular remoteness, a break with tradition need not follow. Even now survival is not always at stake. Even now there is freedom of choice between more or less moderation, more or less concern for the interests of others, more or less effort to preserve the peace, more or less respect for justice, more or less of a sense of responsibility for the whole of mankind. In other words, there may be plenty of opportunity even now to justify the belief that a wise interpretation and responsible pursuit of the national interest will be found to conform with the principles of morality, reasonably applied, and to the broader interests of mankind. If by the study of the theorists of the past the spirit which they expressed in happier days continues to influence Anglo-American thinking, it may prevent the adjustment which is imperative from leading to extremist theories; it may even help to keep the ship of English and American statecraft on an even keel.

Chapter Sixteen

POLICIES OF PEACE
                     AND SECURITY
                     AFTER WORLD WAR I

THE FOLLOWING five pieces are reprinted from *Britain and France Between Two Wars* which the author published in 1940.[1] The text has been considerably abbreviated here to cover only those events concerning the League of Nations and the attitudes of Britain and France toward the League that suggest striking parallels with issues now pertinent to the United Nations. This material is presented not as an excursion into history but to lend perspective to the continuing problems of peace strategy, accommodation, and collective security discussed earlier in this volume.

A. On France

I. Guarantees of Security

THE FRENCH quest for "security" had an amazingly broad scope in that it took into account the whole scale of threats to which France believed herself to be exposed.

She very naturally feared above all else lest she become the victim of another invasion, the battleground of another war. Her arguments at Versailles stressed the fact that German armies had crossed into France four times in a hundred years. (She glossed over the

---

[1] The sections in this chapter are abridged from Chapters 2, 10, 13, 20, and 21 of *Britain and France Between Two Wars* (1st ed. Harcourt, Brace & Co., New York, 1940) and are reprinted here, with minor changes, by permission of the publisher.

possibility that her own statesmen might have had some part in bringing about these invasions, three of which were directed against the Napoleons.) It was not astonishing that France should seek to avoid a repetition of what had been for her the greatest disaster of the World War.[2] There was sympathy, therefore, in many quarters for her desire to ward off the danger of a new invasion, that was referred to as direct attack or *agression directe*.

But France was not content with guarantees against direct attack, however elaborate they might be. She felt that such guarantees would not stand the test if Germany were allowed to gain mastery over Central and Eastern Europe. There existed, therefore, a second type of threat that was called indirect attack or *agression indirecte;* it would consist of an attack by Germany on one or more of her eastern or southeastern neighbors. Preventive measures had to be taken against this contingency. Indirect aggression covered a wide realm of possibilities, which France had little desire to define or delimit with precision. By a slight stretch of the imagination, indeed, any effort to change the new *status quo* in the east or southeast could be said to render France less secure or even to threaten her indirectly with invasion in the more or less remote future. The more unlikely it seemed that Germany would be capable or desirous of attacking France on the Rhine, the more decisive a role did *agression indirecte* come to play in European affairs, involving the whole controversial issue of the territorial, economic, and national problems of Central and Eastern Europe. The entanglement of France in the conflicts of that part of Europe became a matter of grave concern to the British.

France pushed her claims still further. It was not enough to set up barriers around Germany which would keep her from sending troops across her borders. Who could hope to stop Germany on those borders, particularly in the east and southeast where her neighbors were relatively weak and unconsolidated, if she were free to develop the strength of which she was capable and attain a political position that would allow her to risk such an attack? Precautionary measures of security would therefore have to reach back into what might be called the preliminary stages of German aggression. It was necessary to prevent the Germans from preparing an attack. Her armaments had to be kept at a low level, her troops prohibited from approaching the French border (occupation or

---

[2] All references to the World War indicate World War I.

demilitarization of the Rhineland). It has even been suggested that reparations were used to reduce Germany's economic *potentiel de guerre.*

In a country where statesmen were turning their attention almost exclusively to the problem of security, there was bound to be a display of ingenuity in the discovery of means to guarantee this security. In fact, the French developed a most elaborate theory of guarantees. A distinction was drawn between *"garanties physiques"* and the other types of guarantees, mainly contractual in nature, which were spoken of as *"garanties supplémentaires."*

The purpose of all of the guarantees was to add to the strength of French national armaments, her first line of defense. The *garanties supplémentaires* consisted in bringing the armies of other nations to the support of France in case she should become involved in another war with Germany. They were secondary lines of defense and part of a comprehensive system of security that could be measured in quantitative terms by being compared with the number of French army corps to which it was equivalent in the opinion of the general staff. To perform this function the guarantee had to consist either of a reliable promise of military assistance or, if that could not be obtained, of promises of such economic or financial aid as would help the French to win a war. Greater importance was attached, naturally, to promises of military assistance. If reliable, such promises might decrease the strain on the first line of defense, the national armaments, but they could be counted as substitutes only if they implied immediate and automatic assistance based on prearranged military plans providing for prompt technical execution.

The simplest form of promise of military assistance was the old-fashioned alliance, and it was hardly surprising, therefore, that France should set out to build up a whole system of such alliances and pacts of mutual assistance. A large part of her foreign policy centered around the negotiation of such agreements. Indeed, they provided the key to her relations with most countries. But these pacts were frowned upon in some circles because they conflicted with the new theories of international diplomacy which had spread from the Anglo-Saxon countries to the Continent. While France did not on this account abandon her alliance policy, she did attempt to give it a new form and to supplement the alliances by "international guarantees" or collective agreements. The League of Nations naturally presented itself as the most important and most

promising guarantee of this nature. Even French statesmen who
were skeptical about the League in the beginning supported it
when it was recognized as possibly offering an additional international guarantee which in the case of German attack might develop into a general alliance providing for reliable assistance to
France by all the members of the League. Since the League was too
cumbersome to offer aid rapidly and could not save France from
invasion, it was classified as a "guarantee of victory" rather than as
a "guarantee against invasion." Its function would in any case be
that of a last line of defense in a whole hierarchy of defense measures called *"l'organisation de la paix,"* ranging from national armaments through alliances and multilateral agreements to general
pacts and covenants.

France was often criticized, particularly in the days of Poincaré,
for being overpedantic about the legal aspects of international
affairs and for insisting with such vehemence on the sanctity of the
peace treaties. Actually, her attitude was a natural consequence of
her policy of security. Even the so-called physical guarantees depended for their success to some extent upon the fulfillment of
legal obligations and the acknowledgment of legal rights. Of what
use was the Rhine as a barrier unless France had the right to station
her troops on the bridges and could depend on being assisted in
the defense of her rights? The nonphysical guarantees were based
even more conspicuously on legal grounds. Since they consisted in
promises of assistance, their reliability depended entirely on the
way in which nations would live up to their legal obligations, and
on the interpretation they would give to the law by which they were
committed. Therefore, to uphold the principle of the sanctity of
treaties meant, above all, being sure that her allies as well as the
other members of the League would honor their signatures.

A similar legalistic attitude was adopted toward Germany. By
treaty after treaty, by signature after signature, France sought to
chain Germany to the *status quo* and to make any move of liberation by which she might seek to free herself of the *liens dans
lesquels on a essayé de l'enfermer* not merely illegal, but a breach of
promise to a large group of nations. The more France could rely
on public opinion throughout the world to react vigorously against
violations of the law, the more she could hope for action against a
lawbreaker. In a world of sovereign states every country is concerned with safeguarding itself from external attack. There is nothing unusual, therefore, in a policy whose objective is to obtain

greater security. The exceptional character of France's policy lay in a difference of degree rather than of direction.

II. "L'Organization de la Paix"

The League of Nations: "Garantie Internationale"

SO FAR, WE HAVE been treating French foreign policy as if it were restricted to national armaments, to alliances and other bilateral agreements. The League of Nations and the other "peace machinery" have been mentioned only incidentally. The time has come to analyze the Geneva institution as it fitted into French policy.

The League of Nations was not a French conception. The original plans were American and British. It was Woodrow Wilson who had insisted that the Covenant be incorporated into the peace treaty. Since the French were obsessed at Versailles by a desire for effective guarantees of security both against another invasion by Germany and against any future German breaking of the treaty, they were interested in the proposed League only so far as it would serve as an additional guarantee against the German menace. The British conception of a League as a kind of new concert of powers primarily for consultative and conciliatory purposes did not suit the French at all. To their way of thinking, the usefulness of a League for security depended on its means of coercion and not on provisions for conciliation likely to lead to a policy of concessions and compromise. The American proposal appeared far more promising. Wilson stressed the importance of guaranteeing the territorial integrity of the member states against external aggression; this was later incorporated in Article 10 of the Covenant. Here was a commitment in defense of the new *status quo* which needed only a gendarme capable of applying the sanctions with which to enforce it. From being the most skeptical participant in the negotiations, the French became the most fervent advocates of a powerful and coercive League and wished to equip it immediately with an international police force. The League, not the individual members, was to be the gendarme. This would have given the League much of the character of a superstate.

Although a League such as the French proposed would have been the most powerful collective guarantee of the established order that had ever existed, France, it should be emphasized, never showed the least intention of relinquishing her other guarantees of security, such as armaments and alliances, and accepting the League as a substitute. She had perfectly logical arguments with which to justify this attitude. First, even the most strongly worded Covenant might not prove workable and dependable. Second, a League with practically universal membership would be cumbersome and slow in its processes, however well organized, and therefore could never be expected to provide security against a sudden attack or invasion. The emphasis from the time of Versailles on, therefore, was on such guarantees as the strategic frontier on the Rhine, superiority in arms, and bilateral pacts or guarantees of military assistance.

Since the League was to be merely a *garantie supplémentaire* of French security and an integral part of a whole system of defenses, its purpose, as far as France was concerned, was obviously the same as that of her armaments and alliances. It was regarded as another instrument to keep Germany in her place and to deter or defeat *une agression de l'Allemagne*. But this meant that France was seeking to build up the League against a specific country, not against an unspecified potential aggressor. France's moves at Geneva become meaningful and logical if this is remembered. Her intentions became particularly clear whenever there was any question of punitive measures against any country other than Germany. On every such occasion her usual eagerness for League sanctions became lukewarm or ceased to exist. This was often a cause of conflict with other members. Britain and the so-called neutral countries had no intention of allowing the League to be directed specifically against Germany or against any one country. The main value and advantage of the League, as compared to the old-time alliances, in their opinion, lay in the fact that it could not be regarded as provocative by any country.

If the League was to be an alliance, was it an effective and hence a valuable one, or were its deficiencies too great to make it worth while for France to shape her policy in accord with its requirements? The answer the rightist parties gave was not complimentary to the League. The pledges of the Covenant were couched in terms that left room for evasion. The definition of the *casus foederis* was vague and too narrowly restricted. The operation of common action was left unprepared and would therefore lack the necessary military precision. If France could induce her fellow members to transform the League into a genuine coalition, the situation would be different; but the rightists doubted her ability to do so. If she failed, the League might become an obstacle rather than an effective supplement to France's other lines of defense. Would not some countries, notably Great Britain, refuse to enter any new bilateral defensive alliances on the ground that they were sufficiently committed by the Covenant? Would not objections be raised to French armaments and to alliances with other countries as injurious to the new peace machinery at Geneva or to the spirit of the League? The French themselves might be lulled into a false sense of security and put undue faith in the League, meanwhile neglecting more reliable defenses. The efforts devoted to the work at Geneva would in any case detract dangerously from the energy with which the government pursued more important tasks.

Notwithstanding her repeated failures to make the other members accept her proposals, membership in the League promised advantages to France that encouraged her to support the Geneva institution longer than the other great powers. In the first place, it was hoped that a large number of countries that never would have been willing to enter into an alliance with France would feel committed by the Covenant to assist her if she were attacked. While promises of assistance under the Covenant, in its existing form, might remain weak, they were not on this account to be regarded as negligible. In her struggle to make her system of defenses as comprehensive as possible, France was ready to incorporate into her organization of peace even weaker pledges than those contained in the Covenant if by so doing she could persuade still more countries to assure her of some kind of support. According to the Herriot plan of 1932, for instance, the "outer ring," composed of the non-European states including the United States, was not asked to pledge itself even to economic sanctions. Many efforts were made to bring these countries, and the United States in particular, into the organization of peace and of French security. The only effort that met with any success was Briand's proposal for outlawing war between France and the United States. It resulted in the Kellogg Pact.

The French, after all, fully realized that even from their fellow members in the League they might receive no more than economic and financial assistance. All the discussions on collective action at Geneva centered around economic rather than military sanctions. But while the French never shared the view, so widespread in Britain, that a country like Germany could be held in check by the mere threat or even actual use of no more than economic sanctions, they keenly appreciated the value of economic measures as a supplement to military action. The effectiveness of the British blockade during the World War had not been forgotten.

The universal character of the League offered a second advantage. The pledges of assistance under the Covenant were given not only to France, who might well have been able to find sufficient allies without the League, but also to weaker countries like her Central European allies, for whom it was difficult to acquire promises of assistance. Proof of this was Britain's reluctance to commit herself on the Danube. As long as the assistance to be given in case of aggression was available for some countries and not for others, the potential aggressor would be able to strike at the weak spots and hope that the conflict would be localized.

It may sound cynical to interpret the French conception of the League and of *l'organisation de la paix* as in effect the establishment of a new World War coalition. But from the French point of view, there was nothing objectionable in such an interpretation. The lessons of the World War had not been lost. It had taken months, if not years, to organize efficient common action by the Allied and Associated Powers. Bitter controversies had preceded the setting up of a unified high command. Long delays had ensued before the Supreme Council was properly established. It therefore behooved the peace-loving nations, warned by 1914, to provide in advance for a coalition that would at any moment be prepared, strong, and unified. It was firmly believed that so powerful a coalition would deter Germany from aggression. The old adage, *si vis pacem para bellum,* had been amended to read, "If you want peace, prepare sanctions against the country most likely to become an aggressor." The more nearly perfect the preparation, the most chance there would be of deterring the potential aggressor, who would shape his course according to his appraisal of the war coalition that he would have to face.

General Treaties and Special Accords

WHATEVER RELIABILITY the French might attribute to the League as an operating center for collective action of an economic or even military nature, there still remained advantages of a different and more important kind that could be gained only from alliances or from pacts of mutual assistance closely resembling alliances. Under the existing psychological circumstances—that is, in view of the dislike and distrust that Britain and other countries evinced for military alliances—it required a great deal of ingenuity and diplomatic skill to fit anything resembling alliances into an active League policy. Had not the League been set up primarily for the purpose of preventing a return to the prewar European system, with its antagonistic military alliances? While Wilson had in mind "that henceforth alliance must not be set up against alliance, understanding against understanding, but that there must be a common agreement for a common object," the French sought to have both alliances and the League. But was it not true that a "collective system and special alliances belong to different worlds"?

As early as 1922, when France and her Central European friends held a dominant position in the League, the French succeeded in getting the League Assembly to vote a resolution that accepted the French thesis regarding the relationship between the League and pacts of mutual assistance among League members. During the ensuing years this resolution came to serve as an entering wedge by which pacts having all the features that made alliances valuable to France could be interpreted as being part of the League system. The resolution stipulated that where "for historical, geographical, or other reasons, a country is in special danger of attack," it could enter into "detailed arrangements" with other countries, providing for "immediate and effective assistance in accordance with a prearranged plan." In accepting this principle, the League drew a distinction between two different groups of countries. One group, being in special danger of attack, *exposées aux "risques géographiques,"* not only was to be permitted to have "partial treaties" or "special accords," as they were later called, but was declared to be actually in need of such accords. The significance of this becomes clear when one remembers the military alliances that France already had concluded with Poland and Belgium. If they could now be interpreted as the detailed arrangements described in this resolution, they would be not only tolerated by the League but even sanctified and transformed into a part of the organization of peace.

Once it was conceded that there was need for special accords, the Covenant became merely a general treaty supplementing, as far as this particular group of countries was concerned, the far more solid foundation of security which these countries were laying down for themselves by stringent and reliable special agreements.

The inadequacy of the League to those who wanted immediate assistance becomes clear when it is compared with the typical bilateral military pact of mutual assistance. The outstanding difference between the League and the old-time alliances was that the former was not directed against any specific country. The potential aggressor was entirely anonymous. That left quite uncertain in what direction coercive action might someday have to be taken. But, said a report of the Permanent Advisory Commission, "immediate, pre-arranged and unlimited assistance . . . capable of providing guarantees which can be accurately measured," which was what France wanted, required an unequivocal definition of the *casus foederis*. This, it was said, would be easy to do in the partial treaty, since the case of aggression against which the treaty was directed would be expressly described within the treaty. It is hard to see what this could have meant except the inclusion by name of the country regarded as the potential aggressor against whose possible attack defensive measures were being prepared.

Such specific mention of the opponent was also necessary for another reason. Military assistance, as the French pointed out, was possible only if based on prearranged military plans. But since nobody ever seriously suggested that military plans could be worked out by the general staffs except for a given military situation and therefore against a specific opponent, the opponent would have to be known in advance.

B. On Britain

III. Schools of Thought in British Foreign Policy: Traditionalists and Collectivists

EVEN MORE THAN in the case of France, it is necessary to warn the reader against expecting an exposition of some consistent and unified policy that every British government and statesman accepted and pursued. A French minister, indeed, was once quoted in the House of Lords as having said, "It is better to have five Governments and one policy, like France, than to have one Government and five policies, like England." While this is an exaggeration, we shall find two profoundly different schools of thought struggling for control over Britain's foreign policy, producing conflicts in outlook and principle, sometimes within the same cabinet. One we shall call the "traditionalist" school. The opposing group we shall refer to as the "collectivist" school. The use of new labels when so many already exist calls for justification. Why not simply use the terms Conservative, Liberal, and Laborite? The reason is that the two outstanding ideological camps in Britain did not coincide accurately with old party lines. The collectivists found adherents not only among the left-wing parties. While the members of the Labor party and most of the Liberals were to be found among them, the collectivists were represented forcefully by such groups as the non-partisan League of Nations Union that numbered several outstanding Conservatives in its ranks. The name "collectivist" is chosen because this school came to lay emphasis mainly on collective security. Their opponents, who included only a few leftists, were characterized by their desire to conduct foreign affairs on traditional lines, hence the name "traditionalist." While this latter school tended to consider any policy that followed established tradition to be good policy, the collectivists were prone to discard anything reminiscent of prewar methods or objectives as outdated and reactionary.

To those statesmen in Britain who claimed that they conducted their foreign policy by sheer instinct and without principles, it must be distasteful to think of classifying the British into schools of thought or schools of political philosophy. But men who take this view are expressing traditionalist tenets. This school is characterized among other things by its skepticism in regard to general principles as a basis for conducting foreign affairs. The collectivists, on the contrary, took particular pride in having at last set out to make British policy conform with general rules and high moral principles. They criticized their opponents for having no other guide but opportunism. The issue, said Harold Nicolson, is "whether our foreign policy is to be conducted on a basis of expediency or on a basis of principle."

In trying to outline the course of Britain's policy since the World War, it must be remembered that during the period under consideration British foreign policy was conducted almost exclusively by Conservative or National governments. For only two short periods did Britain have a Labor government. The prime ministers of all these Conservative or National governments, as well as most of the members of their cabinets, belonged to the traditionalist school. While Conservative governments did yield occasionally, and on some very important occasions, to the pressure of a collectivist opposition outside and inside Conservative ranks, most of their foreign policy was conducted on traditionalist lines. The pressure of collectivist public opinion did not necessarily compel the traditionalists to take actions distasteful to them or to compromise, but very frequently it led them to make their policies appear to be in line with the collectivist doctrines.

When the collectivists are discussed, it is necessary to outline their doctrines in detail; about the traditionalist ideas in general, much less explanation needs to be offered. They have few theories, and since in every country they are the predominant group and cling to traditional concepts, their main beliefs are familiar. The starting point of the traditional approach to foreign policy is the national interest. (For the collectivists, as we shall see, it was the interest of an international community.) The term "national interest" covers a long list of specific interests, some vital, others of less importance. When a confirmed traditionalist raises general issues, moral or ideological (when for instance he proclaims that England's duty is to enforce world peace, democracy, or the rule of law), either he sincerely believes that Britain's vital interests run parallel to the need for defending these wider issues, or he may be pretending hypocritically that such general issues are involved, when actually some particular British interest is at stake. The traditionalists like to think of themselves as realists. This realism is not necessarily indifference to a better world and to high moral principles, or an approval of aggression and the use of force. It rather confirms the conviction that no nation or group of nations can, without embroiling the world in greater and more disastrous troubles and unhappiness, afford "to take on the risks of other countries and become policemen of the world," or to force high moral standards and respect for the law upon nations involved in age-old and often insoluble conflicts and struggles. This is a pessimistic point of view, since it assumes that man is incapable in the present state of world society of forcing his ideals or utopias upon other nations, and must therefore accept the tragedy of international conflict as something beyond the power of nations to terminate.

It is not difficult to distinguish between traditionalists and collectivists. Only the former are concerned with geographic areas and geographic necessity, with regional interest and discrimination between vital and secondary interests. They discuss foreign affairs not in general and abstract terms, but with concrete allusions to this or that country. The collectivists, on the other hand, speak of security in general, or of disarmament and of arbitration. They avoid mention of specific countries and use the terms "victim of aggression" and "potential aggressor."

IV. The League of Nations: Instrument of National Policy

THE LEAGUE PLAYED a significant role in Britain's policy even when the traditionalists were firmly established in power and had no reason, therefore, to make concessions to an opposition that adhered to the collectivist school of thought. Even though the League aspects of British policy were much more in evidence when the leftists were in office, the remarkable amount of time that was given to debates on the theory and practice of collective security, both in the House of Commons and in the House of Lords, gives an indication of how much political importance was generally attached to the issue. In no country was the government under such severe and relentless pressure to bring the foreign policy of the nation into line with the new League concepts. The traditionalists fought back, not by discrediting the League, but by interpreting it their own way. While the struggle often seemed to bear mainly on terms and definitions, the passions aroused were enough to show that the basic issue was more than a theoretical controversy on doctrine.

The collectivists wished to make the League the heart or center of world affairs; in the traditionalist scheme it was considered only as one instrument of national policy among others, which, if not necessary, could nevertheless be very useful to supplement the traditional methods of diplomacy.

It is hard to distinguish between what was mere lip service to the League, intended to satisfy a League-minded populace, and what was a realistic appreciation of the usefulness of the Geneva institution in terms of British national interests. Professions of faith in the League became so much a matter of routine that in most cases it is difficult to discover whether there was any intention behind them serious enough to affect Britain's policy in actual practice.

It is to be assumed that support of the League resulted from a mixture of motives, some nationalistic and realistic, others genuinely idealistic. That the majority of the British people, whether they adhered to the left or the right, hoped for progress toward a world of lawfulness and peace and welcomed the League as the most promising means to this end need not be doubted. Although some thoroughgoing die-hards openly derided the whole idea, calling the League a "mutual admiration society manned by well-meaning busybodies," most of the traditionalists merely expressed skepticism as to how much progress could be realistically expected. They emphasized the fact that the League would "serve you well if you do not overload it," that it was in its infancy and should, therefore, be kept "within the limits of what is possible at the present moment." Development, they said, should be slow and steady, as with the British Commonwealth. Hence there was little hesitation in pushing the League into the background whenever it threatened to interfere with urgent needs. When at last it came to be a real obstacle to policies that the traditionalists believed necessary—for instance, negotiation with the Fascist powers—opposition to further support of the League became strong. But the attitude of the British Conservative governments toward the League was not as negative as would appear from the debates in which the "splendid ideals" of the collectivist opposition were being rejected. From the point of view of British national interest and traditional principles there was much to recommend an institution like the League provided it did not involve Britain, by an unwarranted emphasis on positive commitments, in conflicts that were outside the realm of her own interests.

Everybody in Britain agreed that the preservation of peace was the essential purpose of the League. But peace could be sought in two different ways, the one generally spoken of as "conciliation," the other as "coercion." In the early days of the League, British opinion was unanimous in placing the emphasis on conciliation. The provisions for sanctions and for the organization of collective force were minimized or passed over in silence. If there had to be any use of sanctions, it would be the moral sanction of world opinion. With the negotiation of the Geneva Protocol in 1924, the collectivists went their separate way and became staunch supporters of a "League with teeth." The traditionalists persisted in the earlier attitude. The League, they affirmed, was to be "a great co-operative commonwealth," not an "armed guarantee of peace" nor an instrument of "international saber-rattling." Although they could not deny, of course, that the Covenant contained provisions both for coercion and for conciliation, it made all the difference in practice which of the provisions were to be stressed and what interpretation they were to receive. What the British traditionalists were aiming at resembled very closely the old Concert of Europe. Without some such institution the world would break up into separate groups and perhaps hostile camps. There was nothing the British feared more than that. It was in the true spirit of British tradition to wish that nations might join in conference and consultation with one another. The collectivists, for their part, had nothing but scorn for this conception of the League as a "mere debating chamber."

It seems paradoxical that Conservatives and even die-hard imperialists should be found in the camp of conciliation, while Liberals and Laborites, among whose ranks were so many pacifists, should have come to back coercion. The reason most frequently given by the traditionalists for their hostility to League sanctions was that the League was not universal, as had been originally expected, and was therefore incapable of fulfilling its coercive duties. What they meant when they spoke of the disappointed hope for universality was that the United States had remained outside the League. This was supposed to have changed fundamentally the conditions under which the Geneva institution originally was designed to operate and therefore to justify British reluctance toward a policy of sanctions. While it often is said that it is a convenient habit of the British to provide an alibi for themselves by laying the blame for their own failings on the United States, it was not merely an excuse in this case. The absence of the United States made it more difficult for the British to participate in collective action by the League. In the first place, without the help of the United States, economic sanctions had little chance of being effective and, secondly, naval action on the part of the British might lead to conflict with the United States over the freedom of the seas. If both great Anglo-Saxon naval powers had become members of the League, the idea of policing the world together with the other members might have appealed to the traditionalists.

The British traditionalists were opposed to a sanctionist League for a number of reasons that were firmly rooted in their philosophy of international affairs. They were opposed to the obligations it involved for Britain, who would be called upon to police the world for the benefit of others and would incur grave risks for quarrels that were not hers. They also refused to believe that Britain could count upon the support of others even if she decided to act on behalf of the League. Finally, collective security, as it came to be called, meant committing Britain to the enforcement of the *status quo* even where she had no vital interest in its preservation and no faith in its wisdom.

the traditionalists favored. Mediation, conciliation, and the redress of grievances were not to be excluded from the international peace machinery, but they were thought of as coming after the enforcement of the law. They are not the means by which a law-abiding community deals with its criminals.

Several perplexing aspects of the theory call for closer analysis. One is its hypothetical character. When an adherent of collectivism speaks of a community of nations or of a spirit of solidarity among the peoples of the world, it is difficult to discover whether he is speaking of a world as he imagines it actually to exist, or whether he is referring to a world that he believes should be established in the future. If it were the latter only, the hopes of these men for a better world and their appeal to men of all countries to bring it to pass would not have met with great political opposition in Britain. But when Henderson, speaking for the Labour party, for instance, said that "the security of each nation shall be the concern of every other nation," or when Attlee proclaimed that "you have to put loyalty to the League of Nations above loyalty to your country," they were demanding from the British government that it proceed *as if* the concern and the loyalty were already in existence and could be counted upon. The assumption apparently was that if a government, particularly the British government, would only take the lead in an act of international solidarity and call for collective action against an aggressor, the rest of the world would follow. The world would thus be made over into what it should be, if it were not already so.

Through all the discussions of collective security there was evident an almost religious faith that the mass of common people were intensely international-minded and only waiting for courageous leadership to throw off the restraining influence of reactionary nationalistic governments and vested interests. The sincerity of the adherents of this school of thought cannot be questioned. It can be seen in their missionary zeal, as well as in their willingness to have their governments take risks that might involve the country in heavy sacrifices.

There was a sharp line of demarcation between those who were willing to commit Britain only within the limits of her traditional national interest and believed that other nations would act in a similar manner, and the collectivist school. The latter regarded the willingness of the peace-loving nations of the world to defend the law and fight the aggressor as an overwhelmingly powerful though dormant force which could be awakened and brought into action if only the League were not left "in the hands of people who do not want to work it." What the collectivists regarded as reactionary and nationalistic relics of prewar days that could be swept aside, the traditionalists regarded as still the most real, stable, and potent world factors that should, therefore, be given first consideration. These included, for instance, the desire of the United States to keep out of foreign entanglements, the conviction of the French that collective action should be reserved to deal with Germany, the hesitation of many small countries to give up their neutrality, the aversion of the bourgeois classes to co-operation with the Soviet Union, or the refusal of the average citizen to fight except in defense of his country's vital interests.

The abstract type of reasoning that characterized every collectivist debate at Geneva and elsewhere is also worth considering more closely. In theoretical discussions on matters of peace machinery or peace strategy, it is obviously necessary to speak in abstract terms and to describe and analyze problems of a general nature, such as collective security, peaceful change, or disarmament, without reference to any particular political situation or to any specific countries. But it is quite another matter when statesmen are debating questions of practical application and actual policy. When they use the abstract approach, the chances are that it serves some political purpose. Thus when, during the period of sanctions against Italy, Eden declared that "these old phrases 'pro' this country or 'anti' that country belong to a past epoch," he was merely telling the Italians that British participation in League sanctions represented no British hostility toward Italy or no clash of national interests. The collectivists would have wished this phrase to mean that such conflicts between nations had ceased to exist altogether and had given way to conflicts between the law-abiding community and the lawbreaker. Abstract phraseology in the mouth of the collectivist was an attempt, therefore, to deny or minimize the particular national interests of individual countries and to speak as if they had been merged into the interests of the community.

Abstractness also served another purpose. Although it was hardly a secret which countries were regarded as being on the side of the police force and which were the potential aggressors, it was considered to be politically wise not to mention them by name and thus to avoid provocation and splitting up of the community. Abstractness, it should be noted, faded away as soon as sanctions against aggressors became a serious political issue—that is, after the Japanese attack on Manchuria and the development of Fascist power. Instead of speaking of a universal community of nations, the collectivists now came to use the term "community of the peace-loving nations." Its security was to be defended by common action against the "aggressor nations." Soon the differentiation became even more concrete; the Fascist nations were considered by their actions and principles to have identified themselves as the actual or potential aggressors. From that time on, Japan, Germany, and Italy were very regularly mentioned by name as the aggressor countries.

There was now no further objection to preparing police action clearly directed against this specific group of countries. Was not every country free to decide whether it wished to be on the peace-loving or on the aggressive side? Certain countries, it was assumed, had made their choice long ago and could be counted on the peace-loving side of the eventual police force. It always had been taken for granted that Great Britain, for instance, and also France and the United States would never be found in the camp of the aggressors; the citizens of a democracy would not accept a policy of aggression on the part of their government. This had made it possible from the beginning to be quite concrete about the kind of police action the League might undertake. Discussions centered upon economic sanctions; these sanctions could never be successful unless assured the support of the Anglo-Saxon naval powers and, on the other hand, they could never be effective against self-sufficient nations like the United States or against so dominant a naval power as Great Britain.

Winston Churchill, with a group of Conservative friends, took an attitude that differed from that of either the traditional or the collectivist school. He advocated a policy of the national interest, in the traditionalist sense of the term, but based wholeheartedly on a sanctionist League. When he first advanced his ideas, they seemed to indicate a complete break with traditionalist philosophy. Had he deserted to the collectivist camp and become just another passionate exponent of the idea of collective security? He did advocate collective security; but as he interpreted it, it was a very different thing from the ideal for which the collectivists were striving. Churchill was not concerned with any abstract community of nations, with the rule of law, or with the punishment of aggressors, although he did use these terms. His one and only concern, now as always, was Britain. He was seeking to defend the safety of the

British Isles and the British Empire against the threat of a German attack, which he believed was to be feared. Between him and the collectivists there was an identity of views, however, with regard to the means that Britain should employ. Both wanted a "League with teeth" and wholehearted British support for League sanctions.

This identity between collectivist internationalism and British nationalism existed, as Churchill explained, because Britain's national interest coincided with the interests of humanity and civilization. "The fortunes of the British Empire and its glory are inseparably interwoven with the fortunes of the world. We rise or we fall together," he exclaimed. The British had every reason to profit from this happy coincidence. They would gain the support of all peace-loving nations and of all classes of British society if, instead of taking a stand on the ground of British safety, they set out to fight for the great moral cause of collective security. Thus the one-time isolationist turned collectivist, not because he was converted from nationalism to internationalism, but because he had become convinced that Britain's safety no longer could be protected by the British navy alone or even by Britain and France together; what was needed was the support of a grand alliance. The League as a kind of superalliance presented itself as an ideal solution. A strong British navy and a strong League, Churchill said, were "allied insurances for our peace and safety," serving both the security of Great Britain and the moral cause of humanity. His was the same stand that France had taken all along, not merely because both regarded the function of the League to be that of a great coalition, but because both thought of it exclusively in terms of the "German menace."

INDEX

Accommodation: chances for, 141–142; limits of, 140; as a peace strategy, 138–142; unilateral, 140, 161

Acheson, Dean: 11, 14, 74n, 172, 174

Act of Chapultepec (1945) : 190

Acton, Lord: 121

Actors in international politics: 3–24, 90n; freedom of the, 37–38; individuals as, 3–19, 23–24, 86; international organizations as, 20, 22; nonstate corporate, 19–24; states as, 3–24, 82; subnational, 95, 148; transnational, 21–24

Adenauer, Konrad: 208

Adler, Mortimer: 59n

Afro-Asian bloc: as a transnational actor, 23

Aggression: collective security and, 119–120, 269–270; by communist countries, 173–175; definition of, 188–189; democracies and, 186, 188; idealist theory of, 96–97; indirect, 188–189, 197, 254; by non-communist countries, 176–178; punishment of, 170, 176, 178–180

Aggressor: identification of the, 168, 170, 188–189, 190–191, 202

Algeria: war in, 215

Alignment. See Alliances; Collaboration; Collective defense

Alliances: collaboration and, 182; collective security and, 184–185; conflict in, 208–209, 214; external threats and, 29; French commitment to, 44; as a means to security, 155; national power and, 105; the U.N. and, 175; wartime strains on, 207; world government and, 29. See also Alliance policy; Collective defense; United States: Alliance policy

Alliance policy: collective security and, 177; the League of Nations and, 258–262; French (1919–1939), 255–256; U.S., defined, 206–216; evolution of, 218–220; reasons for, 220–221. See also Alliances; Collective defense; United States: Alliance policy

Amity: 53, 56, 57; among allies, 29; collective security and, 194; diplomatic vs. emotional, 25–26, 32–35; intense, 27; nonalignment and, 27

Anti-colonialism: 216, 225–226

Anti-imperialism. See Anticolonialism

Appeasement: 140

Arab League: as a transnational actor, 23

Armaments: national power and, 105; as means to security, 155, 157

Arms control. See Disarmament

Attlee, Clement: 270

Bacon, Francis: 246–247

Baker, Ray S.: 86n

Balance of power: 112–113, 117–131, 218–219; alternatives to the, 130–131; bipolarity and the, 127; Britain and the, 120, 122–124; collective security and the, 119, 169, 176; in conservative thought, 121; defined, 118; vs. hegemony, 124–125; in historical perspective, 122–123; as an ideal, 118–122; ideological conflict and the, 128–129; independence of the new states and the, 224–225; the minds of men theory and the, 9; morality and the, 247; neutrality and the, 214; the new states and the, 128; the nuclear age and the, 129–130; peace strategy and the, 83, 118, 120,

275